Tolkien's Intellectual Landscape

ALSO BY E.L. RISDEN

Shakespeare and the Problem Play: Complex Forms, Crossed Genres and Moral Quandaries (McFarland, 2012)

Heroes, Gods and the Role of Epiphany in English Epic Poetry (McFarland, 2008)

ALSO EDITED BY E.L. RISDEN

Sir Gawain *and the Classical Tradition: Essays on the Ancient Antecedents* (McFarland, 2006)

Tolkien's Intellectual Landscape

E.L. Risden

McFarland & Company, Inc., Publishers
Jefferson, North Carolina

LIBRARY OF CONGRESS CATALOGUING-IN-PUBLICATION DATA

Risden, Edward L., 1957–
    Tolkien's Intellectual Landscape / E.L. Risden.
       p.   cm.
    Includes bibliographical references and index.

    ISBN 978-0-7864-9865-9 (softcover : acid free paper) ∞
    ISBN 978-1-4766-1998-9 (ebook)

    1. Tolkien, J. R. R. (John Ronald Reuel), 1892–1973—
Influence.   I. Title.
PR6039.O32Z8137 2015
823'.912—dc23   2015005555

BRITISH LIBRARY CATALOGUING DATA ARE AVAILABLE

© 2015 E.L. Risden. All rights reserved

No part of this book may be reproduced or transmitted in any form or by any means, electronic or mechanical, including photocopying or recording, or by any information storage and retrieval system, without permission in writing from the publisher.

Cover art: Ted Nasmith, detail from *Durin I Discovers the Three Peaks,* gouache on illustration board, 2011

Printed in the United States of America

McFarland & Company, Inc., Publishers
   Box 611, Jefferson, North Carolina 28640
      www.mcfarlandpub.com

To Tom Shippey and Verlyn Flieger
for heroic scholarship and friendly encouragement

Table of Contents

Introduction. The "Author of the Century" in His Century: Extending the Intellectual Landscape — 1

1. Tolkien as Scholar, Narrator, Stylist — 23
2. Heart of Darkness, Heart of Light: Externalizing the Internalized Quest — 67
3. The World of the Text and the Expanding Waste Land — 84
4. Tolkien on Heroism: Beorhtnoth, Aragorn, and Arthur — 97
5. Epic, Faërie, and Myth: The Mortal and the Monstrous Body — 124
6. Tolkien and Myth: Orientalism and Occidentalism — 147
7. Good and Evil, Choice and Control — 166
8. Teaching Tolkien and His World, and Why He Matters — 181

Afterword. Mechanized Landscape and Spiritual Landscape—In Retrospect — 200

Chapter Notes — 213
Bibliography — 222
Index — 227

Introduction

The "Author of the Century" in His Century: Extending the Intellectual Landscape

The growing body of scholarship on the life and works of J. R. R. Tolkien up to about the year 2000 had not necessarily placed him fully in the midst of the rapidly changing and vastly diversifying intellectual life of the twentieth century. Since then, Peter Jackson's films created, as Tom Shippey has called them, collectively, another road to Middle-earth, and so they have in another way "modernized" him and initiated another road to Tolkien scholarship as well. Shippey's sometimes controversial book (especially for those who didn't read it) *J. R. R. Tolkien: Author of the Century*—along with the movies—helped bring Tolkien from popularity among his readership and fandom to a focal point of social and cultural debates (again largely among those who didn't read Tolkien). How, Shippey's book asks, could a professor of medieval language and literature and author of fantasy fiction have continued to rise in popularity and admiration among both general readers and scholars in a century with an increasingly complicated and diverse intellectual landscape? Those willing to read Tolkien's work have long known the pleasure of his fictional world, but how could readers term a fantasy author "author of the century"? Shippey answered those questions profoundly—again, if critics bothered to read his book rather than simply to respond to its title. Yet we may say more about both author and century together: why has Tolkien remained for his readers so central to a time when so many readers have embraced him and some few critics have disparaged him? For one reason, while those who haven't read him often steadfastly keep

1

Introduction

their distance, those who do read him usually re-read him, periodically, and they want to talk about him, read what others say about him, and write about him themselves. We do so partly, I think, out of love for his fictional world, a place that we want to be real despite its origins in imagination, and partly because we find there and in Tolkien's nonfiction writing as well a landscape of ideas that we wish to consider further—and that stick with us whether we will or no. Tolkien's ideas connect as creeks do to rivers and rivers to seas, valleys to hills and hills to mountains: they map out the experience of a man and a century; they search for value amidst torrents of trouble dotted with occasional rays of hope.

The appeal of Tolkien's thought and world comes from many sources, one of which may seem odd to many readers in our time, though not those who have considered Tolkien as philologist: Tolkien the fiction writer succeeded *because of* Tolkien the scholar. He knew how to move from one frame of thought to another, to use what he learned about language and story to create a complex world full of language and story. Though he preferred fiction to criticism, his criticism tells us a good bit about how his ideas fueled his composition. In many ways he was an "ordinary" man—a family man, a Catholic, a lover of his country, someone who appreciated deep friendship, good talk, and good beer—with extraordinary gifts of language and imagination. He drew inspiration and got encouragement from his fellow Inklings, but didn't feel bound by their separate courses, nor did he get from them many ideas—though he did get significant response as he shared with them a great deal of his work.[1] His language study (from childhood on) and his sense that language held within it innumerable stories, his knowledge of many old and wonderful tales, his spiritual devotion and deep, abiding interest in moral problems (e.g., the genesis and practice of evil, and of good), his first-hand knowledge of war and yet his love of simple English country life obviously influenced his fiction. So did a childhood of loss and separation followed by an adulthood of family and male friendship; all contributed to the concentration of ideas that inhabit his work and that still find appeal for readers, even if all his ideas don't sit at the cutting edge of contemporary literary theory (though his practice sometimes does).

In Tolkien scholarship, what others have written about him, we have seen particular concentration on Tolkien as philologist, as Catholic,

Introduction. The "Author of the Century" in His Century

as war survivor, as beloved creator of the epic-fantasy trilogy and besieged author of "escapist fiction for boys"; scholars have seen those points (those right and wrong) as both positives and negatives, depending on their own preferences. While I think Tolkien's appeal comes mostly from the pleasures of the world he created, the realization of interesting beings with fascinating and terrifying problems to solve, I believe it comes also from his willingness to express the ideas that unfold in that world clearly and powerfully, whether he might have expected a broad audience to agree with his views on them or not. Those ideas come from his life and from the development of his world, and whether those persons in positions of intellectual power wanted (or want) to deal with them or not, they stand at the center of the great issues and great events of the twentieth century. My study here aims to expand on the context and ideas of Tolkien's work, to stretch the critical compass for additional examination of the landscape of his thought, and to extend the argument that Tolkien's writing fits rather better than one may guess amidst the intellectual movements of his lifetime. What we believe, how we understand meaning, how we live in a world afflicted with human-wrought horrors, how we deal with one another, how we forgive or at least go on, how we deal with death and our impulses toward destructiveness and self-obsession: everyone in the twentieth century who thought about anything thought about those issues. Tolkien's work, we shouldn't be surprised, creates a considerable, complex, and significant matrix of ideas that fill out the landscape of Middle-earth—and also that of academic and popular thought—with far more than a collection of mere fantasy stories. They touch heaven and earth and much of normal, daily life and of extreme circumstances in between.

Recent scholarly work has expanded into how Tolkien's work appears in music, its use in cinema, the larger-than-expected range of Tolkien's sources, and his influence on other areas both academic and popular, even LGBT studies, which might at first have seemed an unlikely connection, given the response of some critics who deem his work as exclusively heteronormative—and it has much more to say about Tolkien and the twentieth century.[2] These days much of the "central" response to Tolkien comes from areas of interest that would have been considered, at least in the academy, as "peripheral" a couple generations ago. But Tolkien's work has from the beginning defied limitations that

Introduction

critics—haters or lovers—would place on it; it has inspired continuing exploration and has stimulated new and varied creative response,[3] and it continues to provoke thought about the most important issues of our time. Brian Rosebury "places him in the same frame as other twentieth-century writers, explores his modernity, and evaluates ... individual works ... without special pleading or hyperbole" (6); Rosebury's point, coming well before Shippey's book, has significance as *defensio*, setting a course for the examination of Tolkien's ideas free of the prejudices and assumptions of critics of any stripe.[4] Chance and Siewers's collection *Tolkien's Modern Middle Ages* draws "connections between Tolkien's adaptation of medieval traditions and the influence of his work on modern audiences"; Tolkien's and others' medievalism "bears real social implications, primarily a looking to the past for a vision of more 'organic' alternatives to modern institutions" (2)—more even than he took material from sources, he provided source materials for writers, gamers, and filmmakers to come.[5]

My study looks also at what Tolkien wrote about his own ideas and how he used them in both fiction and scholarship; it considers some cultural loci amidst which he fit without particularly trying. We don't normally think of him for what in many ways he was, whether as fiction writer or scholar, a writer of ideas with great clarity and consistency. Reflecting on himself he didn't characterize himself so, but rather as a storyteller (and as a Catholic, philologist, and family man). Verlyn Flieger has even argued persuasively that we may see in Tolkien's work even elements of the *postmodern*: his eclectic use of sources and materials from many times and places, variations in style from "low" to "high," and variations in tone from the affirmative to the subversive (*Green Suns* 252ff.).[6] Certainly with the merest attention to his ideas we can see his work "grounded in the upheavals, the confusions, and the uncertainties of the twentieth century"; we can see how his "mythology for England" may have presented a "culture in decline, torn by dissension and split by factions" (238). We can see also, even in the decline in the century's interest in philology, how Tolkien fits in the rise of linguistics as a social and psychological discipline, such as Tolkien's belief (along with that of Owen Barfield, Edward Sapir, Benjamin Lee Whorf, and Ernst Cassirer) that our language gives shape to our thought (and our stories). Tyranny "characterized Tolkien's century," Bradley Birzer

Introduction. The "Author of the Century" in His Century

asserts, "and Tolkien passionately hated tyranny" (110)—few issues have had greater impact in the last hundred years than the horrors of fascism, mechanical war, and genocide. Tolkien may have believed that "communism represented a more dangerous form of tyranny [even] than did fascism" (116),[7] but he hated both, because both restrict physical, intellectual, and spiritual liberties: the keys to any kind of fulfilling life.

Shippey's work, beginning with *The Road to Middle-earth*, has done a great deal to assuage the problem of the lack of understanding of Tolkien as a writer of ideas; other scholars, too, have since extended that discussion. Flieger's *Splintered Light* examines the construction of character and event by the fragmentation of light and word—we must all live work from some point of shattering, short of the ideal or the original. Her *A Question of Time* deals with the tensions between past and present and the human and faerie worlds, and *Green Suns and Faërie* deals with world-creation and story-creation (especially as they derive from medieval traditions). Her *Interrupted Music* explores the design, voices, and music of myth and myth-making—among all Tolkien scholars who have dealt with Tolkien as a person of faith and ideas, Flieger's work has best kept their importance connected to his stories *as stories*. Patrick Curry's *Defending Middle-earth* approaches spirituality, ecology and ethics in Tolkien's work, and John Garth's *Tolkien and the Great War* deals expressly with how powerfully World War I affected Tolkien's thinking.[8] Jane Chance's *Tolkien's Art* digs out medieval sources of and influences on Tolkien's fiction, as do Jason Fisher's *Tolkien and the Study of His Sources* and George Clark and Daniel Timmons' *Tolkien and His Literary Resonances*, while Douglas Anderson's *Tales before Tolkien* collects stories that provided the "roots of modern fantasy." In addition to the biographies of Humphrey Carpenter, Michael White, Joseph Pearce, and the Charles River Editors group (as well as those written for children), many studies have linked the influences of Tolkien's life and times on his work. While I name just a few leaves of a growing tree here, scholarship on Tolkien continues, as I mentioned above, to diversify, and it gives no hint of slowing down any more than does the worldwide popularity of his fiction (and the films made from it). More readers from more cultures are finding that Tolkien speaks to them as well as to an English audience, because even in the medium of adventure fantasy he gives us truths about human experience. His work explores the qualities we all need to face the problems of our world, regardless of the differences in our daily lives, and he consistently gives encouragement to pursue the solace of spiritual and intellectual life. Everyone needs courage, compassion, imagination, community, friends, advisers, a livable earth, work to do, and occasional doses of good luck: Tolkien's major concerns apply to every reader equally.

My project here takes up where Prof. Shippey's and Prof. Flieger's arguments conclude and amidst those other works that aim to discern and elaborate on Tolkien's ideas, with the goal of filling out Tolkien's intellectual landscape, the growth and variety of ideas. Scholarship has more yet to show of the twentieth-century context of Tolkien's work and more of the range of his thought, not only in *The Lord of the Rings*, but across his scholarly as well as fictional and poetic works. Despite the assertions of many anti–Tolkien critics (many of whom Shippey discusses in *Author of the Century* and with whom most Tolkien critics feel some obligation to wrestle), Tolkien not only fits right in the midst of what was going on in the twentieth century's intellectual foment; his literary concerns also tie in with, grapple with, or even clarify new and old ideas that collided in a violent century that saw more change in the human condition than had any in our history. They continue to do so into our own century.

In their bibliographic essay in *Envoi* 9.2, Michael Drout and Hilary Wynne note the continuing and sometimes annoying tendency of scholarly responses to Tolkien to begin with (and sometimes proceed no further than) *apologia*. That critical trope remains understandable given the periodic reappearance of the "haters" who seem to want desperately for "lovers" and everyone else if not to hate, simply to ignore Tolkien, hoping that he will fade away from the literary landscape. Many readers and writers who have enjoyed, even loved Tolkien's work, when they gain a high-brow forum may leak into a tone of sly or even gently sarcastic ambivalence, as if they fear being identified with the lovers while in the (not so) polite company of current literati. In a recent editorial in the Sunday Review section of the *New York Times* (October 9, 2012, page 10) a reviewer recalls his own youthful dalliance with *The Lord of the Rings* before poking fun at the fact that many of Tolkien's papers ended up at Marquette University (egad, not in New York?) and decrying the continuing stream of works that the estate has issued from Tolkien's notes, drafts, and otherwise unfinished manuscripts, not to mention those that come from the cinematic response to the better known works. If even those readers who have responded favorably to the work feel a push to satirize it (even in the kindest Horatian way), no wonder scholars who care about the work and don't feel embarrassed to praise it feel an obligation to begin with defense. I will try to minimize any desire I feel to move in that direction so that I can concentrate here on what I find a more interesting question: to what human and contemporary issues does Tolkien return, and how does his work treat them? Fiction writers need not be philosophers to have much of worth to say, and they need not fall back on simple, standard, conservative answers to satisfy themselves or their readers. They may sometimes wrestle with the difficulties of living in a more thorough and interesting way even than philosophers, since storytelling allows for great complexity in character creation as well as narrative experimentation, which can enhance our capacity to show ideas more comprehensively. Tolkien's life and times led him to dwell on certain specific problems, and his work has nuanced and substantial "answers" to them. To set the stage for more focused discussions, the rest of this Introduction will consider first Tolkien in the "Modernist" world and then turn to the place of his thinking in a broader range of twentieth-century experience.

Tolkien's Modern Century

While some disciplines place its roots in the Age of Reason or even in the Renaissance, *Modernism* may well have begun with Realism and Naturalism as the nineteenth century drew to a close. Or, as William Everdell suggests,

> [t]he story of Modernism begins with German mathematicians and moves on to physicists in Vienna, Berlin, Bern, and Copenhagen; a French painter; French and American poets; a histologist and a politician from Spain; a Viennese psychologist; a Dutch biologist; English, German, and Italian logicians; a New York filmmaker; a Parisian painter from Spain; a Swedish playwright; musicians from Vienna, New Orleans, and St. Petersburg (Russia); a novelist from Dublin; and a Muscovite painter in Munich [12].

Everdell adds later his five basic "ingredients" of Modernism:

Introduction

> [F]irst ... there is embedded in every system for arriving at truth a recursiveness or self-reference that automatically undermines the consistency of the system. Second, that objectivity, the possibility of mutual agreement on "reality," gets no closer to truth than its contrary, a radical subjectivity bordering on solipsism. Third, that every truth implies the subjective perspective from which it was derived and that no one of those perspectives is privileged. Fourth, that any "objective" truths there are to be found are indicative in the extreme, seeming all to lie in statistical regularities... [And] fifth and last ... the assumption of ontological discontinuity [347].

While Everdell places the genesis of Modernism in mathematics, he shows how it quickly moved into many if not all the disciplines of its time. Though Modernism doesn't by itself define the twentieth century, it did set the tone for the changes that moved the intellectual life of the century from its beginning until its end, and the term has appeared pretty consistently in reference to the time from World War I to World War II. Parts of the second Everdell quotation above could as well describe Postmodernism, which had much in common with Modernism and in many cases simply extended what Modernism had already done: it cast further doubts on what we know or can know, brought up more questions about what we may reasonably believe, threw even more weight upon the importance (and limitations) of perspective, and deepened our sense that we humans don't have indefinite control over our earth. In the early part of the century we moved from the smooth continuities of the Victorian notion of the world and how it works to a sense of sometimes sharp, sometimes vague discontinuities and doubts: doubts that filled both the internal Heart of Darkness and the growing external Waste Land.[9] Asserting any knowledge of reality required either a great deal of courage, a great deal of arrogance, or a complete lack of attention to anything else that had happened for the duration of the century.

And yet amidst that sea of doubt Tolkien realized that we needed stories for the same reasons we always had: not just because we are by nature narrative creatures (we create stories for ourselves by narrating our lives' purposes and trajectories), but also because we continue to struggle with many of the same issues we always have. Our stories, both traditional (dealing with perennial problems) and contemporary (dealing with current problems), help us understand and deal with our doubts and fears and fill in some of our discontinuities. With the greater sense of an international community that the modern (or Modern) world brought, we needed even more stories, and more complex and diverse stories, for a more diverse world and worldview.[10] While Tolkien was no *Modernist* as such, nor would he have accepted radical subjectivism, his work emphasizes the differing points of view of all his various peoples, and it shows how none sees everything clearly or without prejudice. His stories show the conflict of viewpoints and perspectives, the position of uncertainty (and often error) in which we all stand—especially, from his understanding, in a pre- or non–Christian world.

The variety of story grew in the twentieth-century in the midst of competing notions of structure, style, and content: the realism and naturalism of the nineteenth century persisted, and the reach of the imagination and of experimentation expanded exponentially into new realms of fantasy and science fiction even as it delved more deeply into the curiosities and horrors of the individual mind. The intellectual climate in general changed in ways that would have been unfathomable in previous times. The growth in science, both theoretical and practical, and technology outpaced our learning in nearly every other discipline and our ability to deal with their growth morally and ethically. The beginnings of quantum physics in mathematical ideas stirred well before Albert Einstein's *annus mirabilis* of 1905, but afterward the theories of relativity and the doubt (for most scientists inspirational doubts) about the deep-down (and far-out) nature of the universe rocked traditional notions of our world and our place in it. Our thinking about nature and the universe changed even more as a result of those advances than from Copernicus and Galileo's rearrangement of our notions of the place of the human being and the earth in the cosmos. As physics and cosmology directed our thoughts outward to the structure and even origin of the universe, Freudian psychology directed them inward to deep and troubling desires; whether we actually had those desires didn't matter, since psychology implicated everyone and cast any notion of internal goodness into question.

Art, which often begins the tides of intellectual change, had already begun to pursue different ways of seeing in Impressionism, but quickly thereafter followed Post-impressionism, Fauvism, Cubism, Futurism, Dadaism, Surrealism, Abstract Expressionism, Pop Art, and Postmodernism, all within Tolkien's lifetime (though the latter appeared in art

Introduction

only near the end of his lifetime). Each term represents a movement toward a different way of seeing and a less tradition-bound way of creating—in many ways not so different than the movement in literature from realism to fantasy in fiction, from direct narrative to stream-of-consciousness in fictional stylistics.[11] With respect to art Tolkien would more likely have felt the influence of the Arts and Crafts Movement of the 1860s to 1930s, particularly in the work of William Morris. Contemporary architecture combined the medieval desire to build upward with the Renaissance desire to build outward and explored the tension between practicality and affordability with experimentation in style and material, while also indulging wealthy tastes for the extravagant and businesses' desire to reach for enormous wealth. The twentieth century saw movements through the influence of Art Nouveau, Expressionist Architecture in northern Europe, Bauhaus in Germany, Art Deco in the 1920s–'40s, Streamline Moderne (with its curves and nautical elements), and a general expansiveness internationally—I don't know how Tolkien felt about those movements, but he expressed clearly his fear that we had got too industrial and had failed to appreciate and preserve natural beauty as we ought.

Just as traditional religion fought a battle between a more conservative past and a desire for more openness, tolerance, and reform, so did nearly every field of human endeavor, artistic and otherwise—in some ways that tension between past and modern values defines "modern" better than does any other single concept. And though "the institutional influence of churches on states had declined dramatically" and "fewer people went to church" (Merriman 776), the effect of religion on individuals and the presence of religious institutions in all cultures remained significant and influential. If traditional religious practice receded as the center of civil life, consumerism grew enormously both as a financial presence and as regular part of at least civic experience. Those with money to spend became "consumers" and "shoppers" rather than citizens and parishioners, and whole industries grew spontaneously to draw and direct their spending, as if the entire purpose of having a society had changed—and perhaps it had. So did the influence of sport shake mass society (777–78), eventually internationally, from Olympic Games to "world championships"—the growth of sport has moved it from recreation into the more general "landscape" of our thought and

Introduction. The "Author of the Century" in His Century

study. The general availability of electricity and of public and private transportation changed daily living unprecedentedly (781–82). The movement from colonialism to imperialism had already begun to change the face of nationalism and international politics (820); nationalism became more aggressive, militant, and more specifically military as the century progressed (926). After the First World War the possibility of a League of Nations and corresponding retrenchment created tensions in national and international politics around the world (986): several Western countries were asking at once how we might have a positive effect on other countries and how we might exploit them financially, as well as whether we might not do better to keep to ourselves and firm up defenses at home. The forces of war and financial Depression (and even the flu epidemic) sent an unstable post–World War I peace spinning into oblivion (993 ff.), highlighting the question of how any country might expand its interests effectively and safely in a world where everyone was trying to build financial and military influence.

Just as the British Empire reached its height (and breadth), it began to decline; the Fascist desire for military empire brought the world to its knees, and the American desire for financial empire brought the world into depression, out of it again, then into an age of nearly continually expanding material wealth. All the social and ecological problems that accompany both worldwide heavy industry and the phantom idea of "financial products" followed, so that individuals and countries first gained wealth, then lost it and again faced material ruin. Methods of war-making grew from the last round of cavalry charges to mass manufacture of mechanized monstrosities, and war became ever more aerial and technological, a matrix of steel, stealth, and software. Tolkien briefly owned a car only to get rid of it and completely abjure use of one thereafter. He never had the opportunity to compose on a computer and apparently showed little interest in film, but for him art, cartography, music, and the sounds of language remained intimate parts of the fully sensual experience of literature and the world. While he kept his conservative views on many issues, the world changed fantastically (and to him horrifically) around him. His own work became, in ways he could hardly have guessed, a significant part of the change; in Tolkien's time, and perhaps partly from the international success of his work, *the book* became a commodity like any other, not the product of readers and publishers interested in books and authors, but another financial weapon in the arsenal of multi-product, multi-national corporations looking to make mega-profits with no particular regard for the type or quality of product.

Tolkien's own modern century, as it remains in tension with his writing, comes less from the growth of science and technology and the liberalizing of theology and learning than from a changing sense of place and peoples. The productive aspect of that tension created the mixture of old and new in his fictional world. His ideas come often from a desire to keep the good of the past in the face of a vastly changing world less willing to believe in *good* as an idea or practice. His life took shape from his being orphaned, from his religious faith, from his studies, and from his war experience, and in his ideas he struggled to hold some ground for old notions of goodness and traditional beliefs. Though he was hardly the sort to want to go to war, he wanted still to do his bit, even for the Second World War. In a 1941 letter to his son Michael he wrote,

> One war is enough for any man.... I suffered once what you are going through, if rather differently.... and we are alike in sharing a deep sympathy and feeling for the "tommy," especially the plain soldier from the agricultural counties.... To carry on the pre-war job—it is just poison. If only I could do something active! ... It is something to be the father of a good young soldier. The link between father and son is not only of the perishable flesh: it must have something of aeternitas about it. There is a place called "heaven" where the good here unfinished is completed: and where stories unwritten, and the hopes unfulfilled, are continued. We may laugh together yet [*Letters* 54–55].

He goes on to blast commercialism and sloth, to note that even enemies have virtues, thoroughly to denounce Hitler and Nazism, and to praise the true (medieval) Northern heroic spirit, especially as he believed it had at one time in England's past "sanctified and Christianized" (56). The sense of duty and faith, of love of family, of finding virtue in others, of appreciating the unappreciated, of hating oppression and valuing the courageous spirit that fights oppression informs most if not all of Tolkien's fiction. Those values inhabit that kind of work that drew his scholarly interest: *Beowulf*, *Sir Gawain and the Green Knight*, the Norse eddas and sagas. He expressed and recreated the ideas that allowed Europe to survive a disastrous century; his characters among the free peoples of Middle-earth fight the problems that nearly dissolved Europe in disaster.

Introduction. The "Author of the Century" in His Century

Tolkien in the 20th Century: The Center or the Margins?

In *Author of the Century* Shippey pursues the reasons why several British polls placed Tolkien or *The Lord of the Rings* at the top of their lists for most important, influential, and/or enjoyable writers or works of the twentieth century despite his preference for the Fantastic over Realism. Shippey suggests that not only Tolkien, but other significant and popular authors, including Lewis, Orwell, Golding, Vonnegut, and T. H. White, were "deeply involved in the most traumatically significant events of the century ... [and] had to find some way of communicating and commenting on them" (viii). They chose fantasy and science fiction as their means to objective correlatives, better means than realism to recreate the feelings and express the ideas that drove them, experiences not easy to relate to someone who hadn't gone through them. Tolkien stands out among those authors as master philologist, a subject on which he "had thought more deeply" and which he knew better "than anyone else in the world" (ix). Intense interest in and attention to language increase the potential of story.

Tolkien's success as fiction writer comes, Shippey asserts, not from "mere charm or strangeness"(ix)—though the completeness and depth of his world-creation stands out for its variety and detail in the entire history of Romance and of fiction generally—but also from his "deeply serious response to ... the major issues of his century: the origin and nature of evil," the plight of the human in Middle-earth ... cultural relativity ... and the corruptions and continuities of language" (ix). That last idea provoked interest not only for linguists and related academics, but also for those who want to know what drives style and exploration in fiction. As someone interested in "reconstructing ... his source texts," Tolkien aimed to reach back to a "collective imagination" and toward a fuller sense of national identity, as did the Grimms in Germany, Elias Lönnrot in the Finnish *Kalevala*, Friedrich Kreutzwald in the Estonian *Kalevipoeg*, and Nikolai Grundtvig through his revival of Danish sagic, epic, and balladic literature (xv). Tolkien built a fictional world on a foundation of philological scholarship and if not invented, then gave muscle, heart, and a healthy future to fantasy fiction which, as Shippey reports from a conversation with an editor at a major publishing house,

Introduction

is the only real genre that one can call "'mass market. Everything else is cult-fiction'" (xvii). The range of the audience Tolkien affected by what he had to say and how he said it—not only readers but also imitators, and not only in fiction but also in electronic games, film, and lifestyle—continues to grow considerably and unpredictably. How many medievalists (or linguists, or writers, or editors, or scholars in related disciplines) turned to their life's work through having first felt drawn to Middle-earth? How many environmentalists felt moved further by Tolkien's fervent love of the living earth? How many storytellers have turned to cosmopoiesis as a result of the cartographic depth of Tolkien's tales? How many persons having read *The Lord of the Rings* or *The Hobbit* or even *The Silmarillion* have felt moved to re-examine their spiritual roots and experiences?

Yet Tolkien never sought any such influence. Again as Shippey points out, "It is in fact hard to think of a work (except perhaps in their different ways *The Silmarillion* and *Finnegans Wake*) written with less concern for commercial considerations than *The Lord of the Rings*" (xxiv)—however hard that may be to believe in retrospect, given the industry that has sprung up around it. If we ask for reasons for *LotR*'s success despite its almost anti-commercial concerns in an increasingly commercial world, Tolkien might have answered, Shippey says, that he was "satisfying a taste—the taste for fairy-tale—which is natural to us, which goes back as far as written records ... to the Old Testament and Homer's *Odyssey*, and which is found in all human societies" (xxv). *Timeless* also implies *contemporary*, and nothing gets more contemporary amidst the "issues and the anxieties" (xxvii) of the twentieth century than concerns over world-affecting war, world-threatening dictatorial fascism under the guise of a call for order and obedience, the thoughtless or even brutal destruction of forests and the entire natural environment in the name of "sharing" wealth, the horrors of profiteering or collaboration with the Enemy by those who have power and education and should know better, the importance of individual resistance in the face of seemingly impossible odds, and the threat to the vestiges of ancient learning and individual integrity that we see even in our colleges and universities, let alone government and industry. No "mainstream" writing can claim a greater litany of essential concerns, though some can claim other issues that Tolkien doesn't raise—often essential issues as

Introduction. The "Author of the Century" in His Century

well, though perhaps drawn from a special political agenda rather than from an expansive look at the broadest range of human problems.

While academic critics or those groups who considered themselves *literati* have typically resisted or even rejected seeing value in Tolkien's work, aiming to push it to the intellectual periphery if not into oblivion, as a writer of fantasy who addresses many of the major concerns of the century he fits pretty squarely in the midst of a challenging literary environment. The twentieth century faced not only the most destructive and wide-sweeping wars and technological, social, and political change in human history, but also continuing squabbles over who owned and had the right to comment in intellectual space: whose ideas dominated public discourse, who published what and how, what *mainstream* came to mean. Tolkien explored, as did many more favored authors of his time, the tensions in fiction writing between tradition and experimentation and in intellectual life between "real world" concerns and the aesthetic power of imaginary or invented worlds, between what our cultures demand of artists and what artists actually deliver. *Tension* is a key word here: like irony, it sits at the center of the century's literary expectations, the essence perhaps of New Criticism. We expect "Modern" characters to struggle with the Heart of Darkness within and the Waste Land without; Tolkien's characters do that as well and as fully as any, despite his placing them in a created world—they just don't do so in subways, cafés, pubs, brothels, or dark urban alleys. We expect "Modern" authors to treat their subjects ironically, so as not to seem to take moral issues too seriously; Tolkien sometimes treated his characters' situations or reactions ironically, but he never treated his world or his themes so.[12] He never winks at his reader to say, "Now, we don't believe in that, do we?" His fictional creation would have fallen apart if he had.

Prof. Shippey makes brief mention of Tolkien's relation to some of his contemporary literary movements, such as the Bloomsbury Group and the Children of the Sun, to other writers of fantasy, and to rising environmentalist literature[13] amidst the century's increasing industrialism. We may add that Tolkien's work floats also amidst connections between medieval and Modern notions of artistic order, at the fringes of the struggle in the Catholic Church between traditionalist and modernist theology and religious practice, and in the midst of squabbles between popular culture and remnant or fleeting notions of high art—

Introduction

the former term often coming from those who practice it, the latter imposed ironically by them on those who choose not to. A look at the century's intellectual "schools" strengthens Shippey's position that, if we consider without political bias, Tolkien remains more than ever at the center of the last century's intellectual/literary landscape and of potentially equal importance to the twenty-first.[14] The fantasy trilogy hasn't disappeared; it has gained momentum and in some instances become a dodecalogy, and the material of modern fantasy has spread from print to subway graffiti, role-playing games, film, tv, and online culture. It would spread to the neighborhood games of small children if one could only get them off their video screens and out into the air to play.

Tolkien's work draws attack also, I suspect, because those who think themselves above it fear its lack of sexual-identity questions, existential angst, and self-obsession: Tolkien's work is less *about Tolkien* than nearly any fiction from any time or anywhere is about its author, despite the fact that it comes largely from his own imagination. It deals with his *world*, not with *him*. Some readers and writers today seem to want to believe that writers must show in literary characters greater disease and prurience than any of their readers can by themselves imagine. But Tolkien made a living dream with no interest in its own dreamer, so that the voices in the world can say nothing in favor of the valiant personal struggles of their creator. Perhaps in lack of self-referentiality alone it diverges from its twentieth-century environment, an age often governed by self-promotion and navel-gazing. Tolkien moves his readers by means of story, not by self-revelation, appeal to contemporary celebrities, or trendy tricks of presentation.

In *Defending Middle-earth: Tolkien, Myth and Modernity* (1997), Patrick Curry sets up some of Shippey's argument—and mine as well. He notes that *The Lord of the Rings* is "probably the biggest-selling single work of fiction this century"—up to that pre–Harry Potter time, of course—though "it is certainly not a modern novel" (2, 1). Curry echoes the argument Shippey has been making for years that "the single greatest obstacle to appreciating Tolkien's work is sheer literary snobbery" (9)— Joyce faced a similar difficulty from such contemporaries as Virginia Woolf, who called him "illiterate, underbred" (Shippey, *Author*, 311). Curry also anticipated Shippey's question and the Waterstone's polls: "how could such a remarkably unlikely book, written by someone so [apparently] removed from (and indeed hostile to) mainstream cultural and intellectual life, achieve such a huge and lasting popular success?" (5). Curry finds in Tolkien's work "anti-modernism"[15] and "emotionally empowering nostalgia" (15), but also "the resacralization (or re-enchantment) of experienced and living nature, including human nature" (19), though not modernity: "[m]odernity is ... characterized by the combination of modern science, a global capitalist economy, and the political power of the nation-state" (12)—the lack thereof may well define part of high culture's rejection of *The Lord of the Rings* and its siblings.

And yet Curry finds in it something even more than Tolkien, who wanted to build a mythology for England, sought: "Englishness is not inscribed in the text ... I finally realized after talking to Russian and Irish and Italian readers" (21); the work has definitely and distinctly crossed liminalities of age, gender, and nationality. It includes, Curry adds, "no big money or sex ... cannibalism, serial murder, sadomasochism or lawyers" (3)—the elements that have contributed to the popular success of other fiction of the time. It does, of course, hint at cannibalism, though so does Golding, and Sauron and his minions conduct mass if not serial murder—the grand-scale horror certainly brings the work back amidst a less savory but vastly popular fold of fiction writers. None of them, though, invented a language (though many experimented with what language can do); few if any got to *all* aspects of the real struggle within even the kindest of us, and all would flee from the merest hint of an Ent (a big draft of Treebeard's water would do them all some good). And *Modern* implies more than science, sex, and money: it means struggling with the heart of darkness and the waste land, and Tolkien does both as well as anyone. He doesn't work with science because of the time in which he set his stories, but he does deal with issues of political power, economy, and freedom—I find that pretty modern and not at all nostalgic.

The environmental movement probably had its origins in nineteenth and early twentieth centuries, certainly well before Tolkien's time. Thoreau published *Walden* in 1854, naturalist John Muir founded the Sierra Club in 1892, Teddy Roosevelt began the process of wilderness preservation by establishing the United States Forest Service in 1905, and Woodrow Wilson inaugurated the National Park Service in 1916. While the first Earth Day took place in 1970, it had its roots in Rachel

Introduction

Carson's 1962 book *Silent Spring* and in Cleveland's Cuyahoga River catching fire in 1969. Tolkien falls in the middle of those events, but popular sympathy grew particularly from Saruman and his orcs' destruction of the fringes of Fangorn in *The Two Towers* and for love of the Shire, which the returning hobbits must rehabilitate after the War of the Ring. Tolkien added memorability and imaginative power to the real struggle for environmental awareness.

I should say a word or two also about a couple of the rather fuzzy but important literary/intellectual movements that have not only tried to thrust themselves to the center of twentieth-century aesthetic life, but that also did their best to push aside Tolkien and others whose artistic or literary tastes differed from theirs. They succeeded for quite a time among academics while failing sometimes miserably among popular audiences: The Children of the Sun and the Bloomsbury Group. Martin Green identified The Children of the Sun as a loosely affiliated group of dandyish writers and thinkers notable for a love of beauty and luxury and "concerned primarily with the high culture of the country, and within that primarily with the intellectual and imaginative literature" (9). He concludes that they, since World War II, "have staffed the establishment," holding "key reviewing and editorial jobs" (465), so that they have been or at least felt themselves in a position to dictate literary tastes. Green sets out to "show that a certain type of experience, appropriate to a certain mode of being, was cultivated by the young men who felt they were *the* generation of English writers growing up after the War ... [and] who convinced most of their contemporaries who cared about books that they were right ... [and] who brought a new meaning to 'being English' in the world at large and in the privacy of individual minds" (9). This group, associated with the Bright Young Things of the '20s and who petered out with the rise of the Angry Young Men in the '50s, included, to a greater or lesser extent, the more successful writers Evelyn Waugh, Graham Greene, George Orwell, W. H. Auden, Ian Fleming, and John Betjeman and also Christopher Isherwood, Louis MacNeice, Stephen Spender, A. L. Rowse, Cecil Day-Lewis, John Strachey, Nancy Mitford, Brian Howard, and Harold Acton. They rejected what they saw as the staid, weak, overly serious and narrow humanism and manners of the late Victorians and Edwardians in favor of a preoccupation with style, "ornament, splendor, [and] high manners" (12). They maintained an interest in a kind of realism of the rich, traveled, and influential classes, their rises and falls, failings and vagaries, family histories, estates, and expectations—one can see why Tolkien would have felt nothing in common with them, and they would have taken no interest in him. He looked like a thoroughly conservative academic philologist with a devotion to Roman Catholicism and his own abiding narrative with deep grounding in the great, perennial, perplexing questions of human existence—and he was. Among them only Greene and Fleming (and occasionally Orwell and Waugh) have maintained a presence in popular culture, Fleming for his influence in the spy genre and Greene for his novels having frequently shown up on college syllabi and as films, though Greene and Waugh would have had a particular sympathy for Tolkien's Catholicism, and Auden had a great appreciation of Tolkien's writing. At the time the Children of the Sun had more to do with contemporary notions of Englishness than did Tolkien—Greene's approach in particular had perhaps won out in mid-century, though Fleming's thrillers may have won out by its end. In the twenty-first century Tolkien has overcome them both in popularity, and even his notions of Englishness may have won out.

The Bloomsbury Group, including such luminaries as Virginia Woolf, E. M. Forster, John Maynard Keynes, Lytton Strachey, and to some extent T. S. Eliot and Katherine Mansfield, not only promoted the arts and their own modernist aesthetic, but also had an influence on the prevalent notion of "Englishness" similar to that of the Children of the Sun: as sexually, politically, and stylistically open and experimental but more feminist and perhaps even more elitist. Their aesthetic, broader than that of their predecessors, did not though reach so far as fantasy and fairy-story, wrapped as it was in issues of class, the peculiarities of personal perception, and the crossing of sexual and social boundaries. Again one can see why they would have had little to say to Tolkien and he to them: their interests, while mutually experimental, clashed in terms of religious belief and a sense of the kind of issues, experiences, and pleasures that fiction and poetry can relate. Again, while they have until recently had greater representation in academic syllabi, they have faded culturally as Tolkien has risen: their concerns may seem more personal and less universal, more localized and less spiritual, their stories more circumspect and of lesser magnitude, and their language, while equally exploratory and allusive, less fully interwoven into any sense of an expansive world with endless possibilities. Their stories take place within the individual skull rather than amidst a panorama of peoples stretched over an atlas of potentialities. That range of cosmopoiesis is perhaps what they most missed in Tolkien and what has made him central to later storymaking; they have remained more influential in the growth of autobiographical writing, while he has led us back to mythmaking and adventure. They turned to the personal marginalia, while he tried to turn to the central problems of story and theme that cultures could no longer marginalize, because they threaten the destruction of our species and our world: the problems of evil—individual, environmental, and cultural—the problems of war both personal and mechanized, the problems of home and friends and family (joyful, sorrowful, and impermanent).

While Tolkien's thought drifted far from some of the influential and authoritative literary centerpieces of the early to mid-twentieth century, he fit directly in the center of others. As Shippey describes in "Tolkien as Post-War Writer," other novelists typically thoroughly approved by the literati took similar courses in their fiction. George Orwell, William Golding, T. H. White, and C. S. Lewis all wrote "non-realistic" works with strong elements of "fable or parable," all "marked by war" (218)—we may see them all, like Tolkien, as post–World War I writers deeply concerned with the nature of evil (220), but turning to fantasy, not out of "escapism," but because "they felt that the theme of human evil was not one which could be rendered adequately or confronted directly through the medium of realistic fiction alone" (221). While they came to rather different answers because of differences in their political and religious thinking, they struggled with many of the same problems for most of the same reasons.

We may also see Tolkien, though, once we have removed him from the effete inter-bellum influences, as post–World War II writer. Shippey argues that we find him among those who

> drew their subjects from their own life-experience, little affected or assisted by the views of official culture, whether literary or political; and who wrote in non-realistic modes essentially because they felt they were writing about subjects too great and too general to tie down to particular and recognizable settings [235].

Introduction. The "Author of the Century" in His Century

Not among those "characterised by intense post-war irony, cynicism, and rejection of authority," not among the "Naifs, Dandies, or Rogues" (233), Tolkien kept his religious faith and his belief in the value of tradition, lived after the wars (until fame caught up to him) a pretty typical middle-class family life, taught in a traditional institution, and fought to maintain his subjects (medieval language and literature) as essential elements in the academic syllabus. Those aspects of his life don't make him a literary outlier; given the number of the century's military veterans, college graduates, caring parents, and adherents to religious faith, they place him in the center of life (intellectual and otherwise) in the middle of the twentieth century. Humphrey Carpenter records in his book on the Inklings that Charles Williams, readings Tolkien's typescript, remarked that "its *centre* is not strife and war and heroism (though they are all understood and depicted) but in freedom, peace, ordinary life, and good living" (123)—not always in themselves subjects for exciting fiction, but the life many persons would feel pretty happy living. The hope for an ordinary life and good living may motivate characters (and humans) to brave and marvelous deeds.

If Tolkien has *post mortem* fallen out of step with elements of the twentieth century, we can hardly fault him, since he choreographed the dance that nearly every fantasist has followed for about fifty years, and only film technology and the failure of readers to be able to distinguish the difference between Frodo's world and Harry Potter's now stand between him and the heights of international popularity. In his lack of interest in battle he charted a course different from that of the video games that have also sprung from the well that he filled, but in anti-war sentiment he anticipated the landscape for many intellectuals except the right wing—and those he has to some extent captured by his interest in what certain folk like to call "traditional values": courage, fidelity, love of home and friends and family, devotion to duty, belief in the value of something transcendent and glorious.[16] Where the love of battle scenes (and sometimes of sexual love scenes) has taken over film presentation and so won other segments of viewers, love of peace has continued to win him devoted readers who want to change the world for the better. At the beginning, middle, and end of Tolkien's work we find a love of peaceful, daily life in a loved and cherished landscape that, if we could find a way to remind readers of it and spread it to non-readers, could continue to make him as central to the rest of the twenty-first century as he was to the twentieth. Some concerns, and some needs, never change.

Building from the scholarship I have mentioned, in subsequent chapters I will explore Tolkien as scholar, narrator, and stylist (to look at scholarly and artistic influences on his methods and ideas), pausing at the chiaroscuro that affects so much of both medieval and modern art, at Tolkien in relation to Eliot's Waste Land, at what Tolkien does with ideas of heroism and then with epic and myth and the idea of Faerie, at the perennial problem of good and evil and the importance of free will, and at the growing importance of Tolkien in the classroom—he is entering more and more syllabi at various levels of instruction. Those topics don't cover all the significant intellectual facets of the last century, but they cover quite a bit of Tolkien's intellectual landscape. The map of ideas to which he constantly returned and that he explored and spread touches many of the major movements of his time. My concluding remarks will address some of the tensions between the mechanistic and religious elements of our world, I hope not too polemically—difficult to avoid in what became an ever noisier and more dialectical, polarized, and quarrelsome century. We read because we enjoy stories, but also because we enjoy and need to engage in ideas, and Tolkien found the means to develop compelling stories and characters that carry his ideas beyond the text and into our daily lives.[17] And his landscape, from the fiery depths of Moria to the glimmering beauty of Lothlórien to the heights of cruel Caradhras, lives.

1

Tolkien as Scholar, Narrator, Stylist

Much of the best work on Tolkien treats him as philologist, "word-lover," the professor who teaches love and understanding of literature through learning languages ancient and modern. But more recently the critical net has spread to include not only more varied approaches, but the greater range of Tolkien's own ideas and experiences. In one of the episodes of *The Young Indiana Jones Chronicles*, the character Lowell Thomas, an actual journalist of the time, says that people aren't interested in ideas; they care about personalities instead. Something of a cult of personality has sprung up around Tolkien, as typically happens with successful persons in contemporary popular culture, but it has come with little actual knowledge of Tolkien's personality—and little interest in finding out about it. However, interest in his fiction and its offshoots continues to grow, and his ideas, both in his fiction and in his scholar work, have sufficient force and usefulness to bear continuing elucidation and study. This chapter will briefly consider the range and influence of Tolkien's work as teacher-scholar and some of the scholarship that brings philology to bear, and then it will turn to considerations of how Tolkien worked as a narrator of story and a stylist of English.

On Roots and Branches, *with Some Particular Attention to Roots*

The growth of literary scholarship also marks the twentieth-century intellectual landscape. In addition to his intense philology—now all but disappearing from the Academy—Tolkien's criticism teaches us about interpreting metaphors, understanding temptation, and appreciating what dialect teaches us about character. This section explores Tolkien's scholarship generally, then focuses especially on what Tolkien really said about two of his favorite poems, *Beowulf* and *Sir Gawain and the Green Knight*—and what makes those points essential critiques for his fiction, too. The material in this section also encapsulates and summarizes Tolkien's published scholarship: it shows someone who loved language, but also someone who thought long and deeply and carefully about how one creates narrative and successful fictional worlds.

Among the many fine scholarly works on J. R. R. Tolkien, scholars (including Drout and Wynne in their excellent bibliographical essay) have repeatedly pointed to two of Tom Shippey's books as still the most significant and influential: *The Road to Middle-earth* and *J. R. R. Tolkien: Author of the Century* (with a brief nod to the first as most important). Shippey has the advantage not only of having followed in Tolkien's footsteps academically and having known him personally and worked with him, but also of having in abundance similar skills as an extraordinary philologist—and he demonstrates repeatedly the necessity of understanding Tolkien from a philological perspective. The least known (and most difficult to find, at least in the United States) of Shippey's works on Tolkien, *Roots and Branches*, which I'll treat here, concisely addresses Tolkien's accomplishments as a scholar, estimating the influence of the scholarly works and providing us a means of connecting them to his fiction. *Roots and Branches* pursues two critical "themes": (1) that the roots of Romance grow not only in the Middle Ages, but also in subsequent *medievalism* also influenced by philology (an approach that still bears fruit not only for Tolkien scholars, but for anyone in literary studies who has the opportunity and energy to pursue it) and (2) that academic and critical elitism has often colored the reception and response of the literary establishment to Tolkien's work, its popularity, its impact, and its methods. In the second theme we find the ubiquitous *apologia* that has often inflected Tolkien criticism, but that also helps argue for Tolkien in his time as a thinker, and in the first theme we have the means by which readers may continue to find useful points to illuminate both how and why Tolkien's work *works*. The goals of literary criticism remain, of course, to make worthy work more understandable and more enjoyable, useful ends that may elude scholars bent on other purposes (e.g., promoting a particular school of criticism, theory, or practice, or finding new intellectual space in the academy). Shippey's arguments help show how Tolkien communicated his ideas both clearly and powerfully; the fiction, while stylistically and structurally experimental, avoids trendiness, and its language, while fitting the world of the text, avoids the jargony quality that can afflict the work of academics. Careful study of *Roots and Branches* uncovers a great swathe of the landscape of Tolkien's most prominent ideas, especially as they fit in the realm of scholarly ideas.

Roots and Branches includes four sections. The first, "The Roots: Tolkien and His Predecessors," comprises essays on Tolkien's study, understanding, and use of *Beowulf*, the *Eddas*, *Kalevala*, the works of the *Gawain*-poet and the language of the English medieval Northwest Midlands, the importance of the nationalism, philology, the mythology of Jacob Grimm and Nikolai Grundtvig, Wagner's influence on the perception of Northern myth, and nineteenth-century scholarship on early northern cultures. The second section, "Heartwood: Tolkien and Scholarship," discusses the importance of philology in Tolkien's life, academic work, and fiction, his *Exodus* and *Finn and Hengest* editions, the influence on his work of things Icelandic, and Tolkien's academic reputation now. The third section, "The Trunk: *The Lord of the Rings*, *The Silmarillion*," looks at elves, the inclusion of poetry in Tolkien's fiction, images of evil and of class, and Tolkien's use of proverbs. The fourth section, "Twigs and Branches: Minor Works by Tolkien," considers his play-sequel to *The Battle of Maldon*, Tolkien's poem "The Hoard," the question of allegory in Tolkien's work, *Mr. Bliss*, and Peter Jackson's cinematic version of *The Lord of the Rings*. The essays provide means of reading individual texts and of seeing them as outgrowths of thought in the midst of a scholarly life while also giving an overview of implications of the *œuvre*.

Just as we benefit from a sense (or even intimate knowledge) of an author's body of work as we read any particular example of it, a special advantage comes from following an unusually knowledgeable and enjoyable critic work on that author over time: the criticism becomes part of the friendly process of returning to the work for re-readings, for study, and for teaching. Literature, as Tolkien and his critics teach us, first and last is a human and humanist endeavor, and criticism from a supportive voice has a greater likelihood of success than that from a derogatory or egocentric one.[1] Shippey's approach has special value given the tendency of Tolkien criticism to fall into the lover or hater category: lovers will find pleasure in greater appreciation of Tolkien's range, and haters, if they give the book a taste, should enjoy at least improved understanding of Tolkien's ideas.

The essential observations of *Roots and Branches* come both in smaller points of philology and in large issues of themes, sources, and consequences; concerns of influence or accomplishment and of literary history punctuate all the essays, those on familiar topics and those that take different directions. In the conclusion of the first essay, on Tolkien and the *Beowulf*-poet, Shippey notes that Tolkien believed "the heroes of antiquity *had not gone away*," but "were still there, in landscape, in names, and probably in the gene-pool" (18). Getting caught up in the details of language for their own sake, we can sometimes forget their practical applications: the ancient culture remains round about us. In the second essay he notes that the "flavour" of Norse myth comes out in the observation that though the "world of Snorri's myth is the exact opposite of a *divina commedia* ... Snorri writes habitually as a comedian" (28): Snorri finds humor endemic in the episodes, as does Tolkien. Shippey suggests in the third essay that *Sir Gawain and the Green Knight* comes from Staffordshire (part of Tolkien's interest came from the location), and that Tolkien probably thought that Shakespeare "could have been *good*—if he had not made the mistake of going to London and going commercial" (50)! He adds at the end of this essay that a "major advantage of philology (unlike, as far as I can see, Jungian psychology) is that it takes you outside yourself, to look at things outside your own head" (58)—a message that many a fiction writer, poet, and critic could helpfully heed, and one that moves this essay from strictly historical article to another kind of apologetic essay. In the fifth essay, on Grimm, Svend Grundtvig, and nationalist mythologies, Shippey addresses the tensions between Tolkien's Catholicism and his love of story set in pre–Christian times: Tolkien "seems to me to have turned the problem of reconciliation from one of belief to one of literary temper: from considering the *Echtheit* or 'genuineness' of the faith of his heathen ancestors to considering its literary attraction" (94). By moving to fiction Tolkien is "transferring the whole activity from scholarship to narrative" (95). Christian readers particularly have often struggled with similar questions. In the sixth essay, on Tolkien, Wagner, and the ring motif, Shippey concludes that Tolkien may have been "prepared to accept that in a way the 'great tales' might speak through and even against their individual authors." He thought both Shakespeare and Milton were "seriously misguided artistically and politically, but they were great poets, and sometimes ... it seemed as if the language spoke through them, [that] their stories took over" (114). Such provocative observations about *making* and interpretations of literary history proliferate in *Roots and Branches*, filling the whole with matter for meditation and clarifying Tolkien's thinking about what he read and wrote.

One of the especially notable chapters for anyone interested in Tolkien's ideas or Tolkien as academic addresses Tolkien's place and accomplishments as a scholar. His own university colleagues may have expressed that they believed he did too little (he occasionally concurred), but for most academics, especially those with any serious teaching load (as Tolkien often had), they add up to a pretty decent career's-worth of research publication. Here is a brief consideration of Tolkien's achievements as a scholar, expanding on some points from the list provided by Shippey in the essay on "Tolkien's Academic Reputation Now" (203–212).

I. "Chaucer as Philologist: The Reeve's Tale" (1931) (available online, copyright West Virginia University Press)

Here Tolkien urges that, though we know his language only through the lens of the scribes, who weren't his contemporaries, Chaucer uses genuine dialect both correctly and consistently:

> He [Chaucer] showed considerable skill and judgment in what he did: skill in presenting the dialect with fair accuracy but without piling up oddities; judgment in choosing for his purpose northern clerks, at Cambridge, close to East Anglia (whence he brought his Reeve). Indeed, in an East Anglian reeve, regaling Southern (and largely London) folk, on the road in Kent, with imitations of northern talk, which was imported southward by the attraction of the Universities [quoted from online text].

While normally in Chaucer's time only "those who knew it natively" used dialect, we must note that Chaucer used it not *for* Notherners, but for his London audience. If he errs at all, he does so not in northernisms, but in retaining southernisms that would not appear in northern dialects. His northernisms include long ā (the *ah* sound) rather than the southern rounded sound as in *awe*, as in *swa* and *ga* for *so* and *go*, and in the use of *slyk* for "such," which appeared only in England north of the Tees (from Middlesbrough north toward Durham), directing us more particularly to the home of John and Allan. As Shippey remarks, the essay is "fascinating in detail, and still completely convincing in its demonstration that Chaucer was trying to make a joke by close, careful imitation of the dialect of Durham: but it's a joke about *language*" (207–8, my italics).

II. *The Monsters and the Critics and Other Essays* (ed. Christopher Tolkien [London: HarperCollins, 2006]) collects a number of Tolkien's most important essays; I'll include just brief remarks on their contents to show the range of ideas.

1. "*Beowulf*: The Monsters and the Critics" (1936; the article also appears elsewhere, for instance in Lewis Nicholson's volume of critical essays on *Beowulf*)

This famous essay requires little additional comment here other than the reminder that it both does and encourages a reading of the poem *as poem*, not just as a historical document to be picked over for allusions that lead elsewhere. It includes the image of the ruined tower: the poem broken apart by critics failing to see it and enjoy it for what it is, a great work of art enjoyable and rewarding for its story and its poetry. It also has the advantage of showing us that criticism can and perhaps often should, if we let it, be fun to read.

2. "On Translating *Beowulf*" (1940)

Tolkien begins by lamenting that "[t]oo many people are willing to form, and even to print, opinions of this greatest of surviving works of ancient English poetic art after reading only [a prose] translation, or indeed after reading only a bare 'argument'"(49). He notes the compactness and directness, the compression and riddling elements, and yet the difficulty of Old English verse, and he warns against "colloquialism and false modernity" in translations (54), and he reminds us of the deft structure and careful diction and rhythms of the original: *Beowulf* is a "tough builder's work of true stone" (71), echoing the famous tower image of "Monsters and the Critics."

3. "*Sir Gawain and the Green Knight*" (1953)

Tolkien sees behind the poem "the figures of elder myth and in it a focus on temptation" and how even a knight "involved out of humility

1. Tolkien as Scholar, Narrator, Stylist

... and duty to his king and kinsman" (104) will respond to them: it juxtaposes the medieval Romance narrative conventions of "Courtesy and Love with [secular or personal] morality and Christian morals and Eternal Law" (105). With respect to Gawain he believes that "nothing makes him 'come alive' as a real man so much as the depiction of his 'reactions' to the revelation" of the background of his adventure, and with respect to his character the poem ends with "a glimpse of that twofold scale with which all reasonably charitable people measure: the stricter for oneself, the more lenient for others" (97). Again we see Tolkien as philologist, but also, as in the *Beowulf* essay, as appreciative (and Christian) reader who urges reading (and enjoying) the poem as a work of art.

4. "On Fairy-Stories" (1939) (see also *The Tolkien Reader* [New York: Ballantine, 1966])

This essay, Tolkien's most important theoretically, introduces his idea of story-maker as sub-creator under God, one who "makes a Secondary World your mind can enter" (page 132). The writer can be both traditional "bard" and inspired Christian, using God-given gifts to extend the process of creation begun by God. The "Cauldron of story" (125), or process of making, means the place where "Faërie begins" (122), not Supernatural but super-natural (deeply a part of nature, not above it). Faërie refers to the "Perilous Realm" (113) of magic and adventure—but not of allegory or dream—where the unusual has its own existence apart from the limitations of our everyday world. Fantasy, Tolkien argues, has "arresting strangeness" (139), the potency of creating in the reader the desire to enter the created world, the "inner consistency of reality" and reason (139–44). It evokes wonder, has elements of "spell," and includes a sense of Recovery (or healthy renewal), Escape (not from reality, but as a means to better reality), and Consolation, of a brief "happy" turn, the Eucatastrophe, the "fleeting glimpse of joy" (153) both poignant and invigorating. The ideas in this essay have ever since inspired scholars and writers of fantasy alike, and they provide a pretty clear sense of why Tolkien's stories took the direction they did and why he liked what he did.

5. "English and Welsh" (1955)

While C. S. Lewis "asserted that the man who does not know Old English literature 'remains all his life a child among real students of

English,' I [Tolkien] would say to English philologists that those who have no first-hand acquaintance with Welsh and its philology lack an experience necessary to the business"; Tolkien added, then, and yet "it may well be true that its intimate heart cannot be reached by those who come to it as aliens, however sympathetic" (163). Tolkien questions, too, in a whiff of Heaneyish foreshadowing, if *Beowulf*, though in English, must ... [in its imagination] be far more Celtic—being full of dark and twilight and laden with sorrow and regret—than most things that I have met written in a Celtic language" (172). For many English, he wonders whether Welsh "stirs deep harp-strings in our linguistic nature," so that "for satisfaction and therefore for delight—and not for imperial policy—we are still 'British' at heart. It is the native language to which in unexplored desire we would still go home" (194). The imaginative connection reinforces his idea of the "Celtic" qualities in *The Lord of the Rings* as well as the surprising, joyful instants that dot the landscape of comparative language study.

6. "A Secret Vice" (1931)

Tolkien begins by asserting the value of an artificial language such as Esperanto as a means for "uniting Europe, before it is swallowed by non–Europe" (198) before announcing that "few philologists [including himself] ... are devoid of the making instinct" (200)—the drive to invent personal languages, that is. He mentions hearing a fellow soldier at a World War I camp lecture suddenly and unguardedly utter "Yes, I think I shall express the accusative with a prefix!" but he could get no more out of the man, who may have been engaging in his own language creation. Tolkien concludes that "[l]anguage has both strengthened imagination and been freed by it" (219)—he might have added that in his own case language drove his imagination to nearly unimaginable heights and depths of world-creation.

7. "Valedictory Address to the University of Oxford" (1959)

The purpose of this essay seems to me largely to apologize for his never having got around to giving the inaugural address required for the two research chairs he held at Oxford and to defend the Niggling of the "philologist and the orthographer" (226). He defends first the "desire for knowledge," which even in his time was fading before notions of the practical application of academic degrees, and then the value of "reading and learning"—he was still, even at the end of his career, digging at the problems of the Lang. and Lit. syllabus and urging that Lang remain at the foundation of Lit. He had, he said, alluding to Africa, "the hatred of *apartheid* in my bones," but the metaphor turns to what he saw as the ridiculous "separation of Language and Literature." "I do not care," he adds pointedly, "which of them you think White" (238). I find it sad that to this day would-be critics (in the pejorative sense) suggest that they find racism in Tolkien's fiction and that would-be literature faculty state proudly that they have never seen the need to study linguistics or Old English (or to read Milton or *Beowulf* or Chaucer or occasionally even Shakespeare). Sad for them, their colleagues, and their students...

III. The edition of *Sir Gawain and the Green Knight* (with E. V. Gordan, rev. Norman Davis), which remains the standard, and the one of *Ancrene Riwle* (or *Ancrene Wisse*) and *Hali Meiðhad* for the Early English Text Society (1962), plus the posthumously published editions of *Exodus* and *Finn and Hengest*, plus his "glossary" for Kenneth Sisam's *Fourteenth-Century Verse and Prose*, "Middle English Vocabulary" (1922), all show the pedagogical productivity of Tolkien's scholarship: many students and teachers have used them, are using them, and will use them. Additional works on philology include chapters in *The Year's Work in English Studies* (1923, 1924, and 1925), "Some Contributions to Middle English Lexicography" (1925), "The Devil's Coach Horses" (1925), the "Foreword" to Walter Haigh's *Huddersfield Glossary* (1928), his preface to Clark Hall and Wrenn's translation of *Beowulf*, two articles on *Sigelwara Land* (1932 and 1934), one on *Ancrene Wisse* and *Hali Meiðhad* (1929), a short piece on "The Name *Nodens*" (1932), an article on "Middle English *Losenger*" (1951), two essays to accompany *The Homecoming of Beorhtnoth Beorhthelm's Son* (1953), a prefatory note to the Old English *Apollonius of Tyre*, edited by Peter Gooden (1958), some translation and editorial contributions to *The Jerusalem Bible* (1966), a number of small bits (e.g., "The Oxford English School" (1930), and two articles in collaboration with Simone D'Ardenne—not including the "creative" work with strong philological elements, such as *Songs for the Philologists* and all his fiction). Those studies include no monographs, but they do entail a fair number and diverse array of philological queries.

Tolkien's Intellectual Landscape

Shippey's "verdict" on Tolkien's scholarship, at least as a modern inspector of university researcher might cast it, sums up so: "Primary Citations: low. Secondary Citations: amazingly high," especially for the essays on *Beowulf* and fairy stories (211). Tolkien might not get a particularly high rating for academic productivity, unless one were to consider the fiction as a product and demonstration of philological knowledge, understanding, and practical application—and as an exhibition of a fundamental technical skill, acquired from careful study, in story-telling. I suspect most academicians with any sort of difficult or time-consuming teaching schedule would feel quite happy with that scholarly output at career's end, especially if one may include the posthumous *The Monster and the Critics and Other Essays*: perhaps for our time publication of the *book* makes the difference. That book, assembled by his son Christopher Tolkien, may not have appeared in print had it come from someone who hadn't a fiction fandom, but it has great value nonetheless, and for far more than fans: it includes a great deal of useful thought all in one package, and it lays out the range of scholarly thought from which the fictional world evolved—a map, essentially, of Tolkien's teaching and scholarship.

I'd like to call attention also to a few points from some of the remaining essays from Shippey's book, as they also show directions that influenced Tolkien's fiction. The essay on "Heroes and Heroism" notes that Tolkien "was one of the world's most determined writers and rewriters, a man who spent enormous amounts of time on his fiction, both what he published and what he did not.... I ask readers once again to reflect on work: it is the Great Unsaid of fiction, and of criticism" (268): we may easily forget the trouble that Tolkien created for himself by repeatedly re-writing his stories and the magnitude of the work that went into writing and re-writing them, all occurring in the midst of academic duties. But we must not fail to remember that quality fiction (and scholarship) doesn't come, like the song of Shelley's skylark, in profuse strains of unpremeditated art. It comes through labor, sweat, and dedication. Myth and mythmaking may have served for Tolkien as means to "reconcile or mediate between irreconcilables" of culture (282)—a greater task than *mere* philological niggling, and one that requires melding the old, the new, and the timeless.

The conclusion of the essay on "The Hoard" iterates that Tolkien's

1. Tolkien as Scholar, Narrator, Stylist

literary imagination was often "triggered by a textual problem, or set of problems, already seen by many scholars, but treated by them as a textual problem alone, not one which also had both a mythical explanation (a man turning into a dragon) and a real-world meaning ('dragon-sickness' as a disease of ownership)" (349). He adds in a similar point in the book's final essay, one that Tolkien saw and that Jackson's films may have missed: the harrowing notion that "there is always a price to pay for weakness," however understandable and forgivable (385). But Jackson did succeed in showing "the difference between Prime and Subsidiary Action, the differing styles of heroism, the need for pity as well as courage, the vulnerability of the good, the true cost of evil" (386)—quite a lot indeed. Those concerns never become trivial because we need to remember them on a nearly daily basis. Neither does passionate and respectful criticism become trivial, because it returns us to the pleasure and power of great work past, and it also leads us—through roots and branches—into the dangerous but alluring streams of sub-creation that Tolkien would have encouraged us to swim for ourselves.

Of course, the essay on *Beowulf* has had the most influence, and the one on *Sir Gawain and the Green Knight* may have sat even nearer to Tolkien's heart, given his special interest in the Northwest Midlands—I therefore give them additional attention here. Clear statement of the essential motif or theme of *Beowulf*, the inevitability of death and the problem of how to meet it, appears throughout Tolkien's famous "*Beowulf*: The Monsters and the Critics" essay, just as it does in *LotR*. One of the problems with that theme, of course, is that among the most important facets of literature for modern readers and for culture in our time one stands out: getting our minds *off* death, at least actual dying in any realistic sense. The medievals accompanied shorter lifespans with their omnipresent *memento mori*; we sanitize death in melodrama or exaggerate it to something quasi-comical in horror genres. While *The Lord of the Rings* confronts death (as does *The Silmarillion*), it also provides resurrection (Gandalf's) or an alternative to death (the Grey Havens for Bilbo and Frodo). Death, both eminent and imminent, haunts most episodes of Tolkien's fiction, just as it moves out of the shadows and into the flesh in *Beowulf*. The particularly troubling deaths of Boromir, Denethor, and Saruman haunt readers' experience of *The Lord of the Rings*, and "Leaf by Niggle" deals allegorically and yet powerfully enough with the tension between one's own mortality or immortality and that of one's art.

Sir Gawain and the Green Knight, Tolkien says, is mostly about temptation and how to face one's giving in to it; in *LotR* the temptation to possess and use the precious Ring undermines (or nearly so) many of the important relationships, and Frodo's departure from the Shire at the end of *The Return of the King* suggests that redemption from failure in the face of temptation may lie beyond our scope, may constitute the ultimate tragedy of human (and hobbit) experience. Gawain succeeds in his mission about as well as any human could, but not sufficiently to assuage his own sense of guilt at small failings—not even confession and the praise of Arthur's court can cleanse his mind and heart of the feeling that he has failed. Four years after the War of the Ring, Frodo complains of the pain in his shoulder from the wraith-king's sword, but his spirit wastes away, I think, from his own failure at the endpoint of the quest: only Gollum, an enemy nearly as treacherous as Sauron himself, saves Frodo from ignominy and his world from slavery—a source, one might suspect, of shame or at least sorrow.

Tolkien's thoughts, the ideas essential not exclusively to his Catholicism but also to his work in both fiction and criticism, hardly simmer with earthly hope, but they do confront essential human limitations or weaknesses in understanding ways—as do both *Beowulf* and *SGGK*. Tolkien found necessary that, as Professor Eastwood might say, were he the sort to elaborate, we must know and confront our weaknesses, appreciate and circumvent them where we can't forgive them, press on despite them, and find ways to get past their inevitable consequences (shortly, *know our limitations*). Yet even the willingness (and ability) both to forgive and accept forgiveness may not cleanse the heart of the pain of failure in the face of temptation. Joseph Conrad's Marlow, as he prepares his wild tale of watching and listening to the enigmatic Kurtz in his last descent into the heart of darkness, claims to hate a lie because it bears the stench of death. Failure in the face of serious and unsought temptation carries a similar, lingering, noisome taint, more for the bearer than his fellows. Temptation, like death in *Beowulf,* occurs in the shadows: in bedrooms, in the clefts of fiery mountains, in our own umbrous, half-shaped thoughts. There comes our suffering for and with Frodo, whether or not such demons loom largest in his own conscious thoughts.

1. Tolkien as Scholar, Narrator, Stylist

To what degree Gawain suffers in later years from his own sense of failure we can only speculate—or write our own sequels. We suffer with Frodo, but we experience his *eucatastrophe* and his epiphany as well. They give us a means, as Joseph Campbell would say, to throw ourselves back into life again.

While critics have plenty to say about Tolkien as philologist, as Christian, as sub-creator mytho-poet, and as post-war writer, the impact of his fiction often so outweighs that of his scholarship that we fail to pay sufficient attention to exactly what he says about the works that influenced him most and perhaps most drove him to creative work of his own. His own particular way of parsing *Beowulf* and *SGGK* lead us directly to some of the most potent philosophical problems of *The Lord of the Rings*. While Tolkien had a fondness for saying his fiction wasn't really about anything, that he sought in it an integrity of plot, character, and world all its own, any writer who begins as a scholar inevitably brings a toolbox—I won't say *baggage*—from his or her scholarly world to the fictional construction project. He did so perhaps mostly as a protection against rude questions. The writer may of course mine his or her scholarship (or someone else's) selectively and polish the yield according to personal pleasure, but what pours from the vein must have its lively effect. I think Tolkien's criticism often bled blue-blood into his own fiction, though he felt no compunction about varying from what his sources said to avoid explicit didacticism and to let characters grow truly into themselves rather than to stagnate as allegorical notions. For a scholar, a creative work can serve just as fully as a critique, in many ways better, to dig after what analogues and influences accomplish. Fiction as criticism can show what earlier work doesn't do, but could have done.

Let's turn now to a few of Tolkien's specific comments on *Beowulf* and then a few on *Sir Gawain*, and I'd like to show how those ideas reappear productively but problematically in *LotR*. Traditional ideas of heroism and sin that inform the poems blend and reappear in both old and new forms in the fiction.

With Sir Gawain let's get immediately to one of the most important comments Tolkien makes on character. He argues that Gawain's "'perfection' is made more human and credible" by his acceptance of the sash from the lady and his failure to turn it over to the lord ("*Sir Gawain*"

97). We can't blame Gawain for wanting to save his life, he accepted the sash as part of a game, and though he accuses himself of cowardice and covetousness, his error constitutes a very small sin indeed. Perhaps worse: the bitterness that comes from his failure leads him to condemn women, and a tendency to "excess" in his character makes forgiveness or self-forgiveness difficult (98). "The sting of shame on morally less important or insignificant levels will bite still after long years as sharp as new," Tolkien profoundly observes, and warns (98); whether Gawain rightly or wrongly identifies his error we may well discuss, but for my purpose here, Tolkien's analysis of the scene cuts deeply and painfully into what I'd like to assert, following Shippey's argument in *J.R.R. Tolkien: Author of the Century*, as that moment of deepest and most dangerous evil in all of *LotR*, and which I have mentioned above: the point inside Mt. Doom when Frodo finds himself unwilling to destroy the Ring.

Frodo, of course, has a character quite different from Gawain's: he hasn't the baggage of *courtoisie*, of Arthurian knighthood, of Solomonian wisdom or Marian spirituality. He hasn't quite the same feeling of shame that Gawain experiences because he hasn't the level of pride that drives Gawain to adhere to his complex and often self-contradictory code of behavior. The emotional wound re-infects the physical wound: his failure in the crisis and yet astonishing luck along with the deeply mean and deeply diseased obsession that brings Gollum's teeth to his finger at the moment of truth could hardly fail to resonate for someone like Frodo in a kind of repetitive post-traumatic stress. Truth says, finally, that even the best of us—and Frodo is the best of us, the one least likely to fall to corruption because he has no ambition to rule any other—will fall at the moment of greatest temptation. Gawain, best of Arthur's knights in that Romance, and Frodo, best of hobbits and related creatures of Middle-earth, fall to temptation when it reaches its greatest test. The suggestion to Tolkien: so would he, so would we, so would anyone. We can call that understanding Tolkien's Christian sense of Original Sin, but I think Frodo's incident comes about as a specific revision of Gawain: what holds true for noble Gawain must hold true for anyone, however kind and unassuming, however unwilling to pass blame to the frailty of women or even to cowardice and covetousness—that is, even for someone *better* than Gawain. Frodo fails because the Ring has too much power for anyone to wear it; he need not feel any more shame than any sentient creature would, and yet he must feel shame, because any caring, sentient creature would.

If we follow Tolkien's argument, we find many points that he makes about *Sir Gawain* fit *LotR* as readily—or stand in explicit and telling contrast. Gawain takes up the Green Knight's challenge to protect Arthur (75); Frodo unwillingly takes up the quest of the Ring to save the free peoples of Middle-earth. Gawain represents unflinching courage and loyalty (76), and though he doesn't fully achieve them, he comes as close as anyone reasonably can. Frodo does the same. Tolkien asserts that Gawain "was led into a position from which he could not withdraw by the thought that it [the green girdle] might save his life" (93–94); not exactly so: he finds himself in an impossible situation because he must *both* keep the girdle and keep silent about it and also give it up to Bercilak. Similarly, but with an important difference, Frodo must first keep and preserve the Ring from others, then destroy it himself, even as it gains a greater and greater hold on him. Gawain both consummately wishes and fears its loss or destruction. The *Gawain*-poet dealt with the tensions between *courtoisie* and virtue (95); Tolkien took great pains in the selection of Bilbo and Frodo as his protagonists to show that courtliness and nominal nobility matter not a jot at the instant of moral (and mortal) conflict. Only courage, fortitude, commitment, and adaptability matter, and they can arise as readily in the small as the great—and even then they may not produce success. Frodo, like Gawain, expects to lose his life in the quest, but hopes not to; both emerge alive, but "tainted," and each will depart Middle-earth before his time. Doom, or the course of events, must cut its path, saving once, destroying next—a point that haunts *Beowulf* as well. Both knight and hobbit emerge from their tales as fully "human" creatures, given by nature to the vicissitudes of heroism and failure, more human because they can fail (97). In contrast Gawain tends toward excess in his reactions, and he gives in to bitterness at failure (99); Frodo, despite the natural hobbitish impulse for simple pleasures, maintains a guardedness, and when he fails, sorrow and pacifism, along with relief, whelm in him without overwhelming. Both characters give in to possessiveness and pride, but Frodo, without all the chivalric baggage, deals better with shame. "From the moment of absolution," Tolkien observes, the Girdle seems to have been of no comfort to

Gawain" (102); the Ring never offers Frodo comfort, though, as it did for Bilbo, it allows him an escape or two, but in the long run it puts him in the position to receive the wound from the Ringwraith's sword. The major motif in *Sir Gawain*, according to Tolkien, the temptation that the Girdle presents, magnifies a thousand times in *LotR*, because a world depends on it: Frodo feels the need both to use the Ring and not to use it—he *must* use it and not use it. Everyone must use it and not use it: therein lies Sauron's goal in creating the Ring, reducing all peoples to despair, utterly vanquished by the Ring and by his will. Anyone who gives in to temptation must fall to it, suffer from it, decay from it. Tolkien takes the theme and extends its power from the context of didactic game to deadly serious, even apocalyptic event: any submission may be the individual's and the world's last.[2]

Once he realizes his sin, Gawain loses his desire to fight the Green Knight; Frodo will not participate in the military necessities of the Scouring of the Shire. Failure enervates, because, having realized one's own fallibility, one then has a difficult time passing deadly judgment on another. As we know from later episodes in the Arthur story—at which the *Gawain*-poet only metaphorically hints with his Troy references—Gawain will later help bring about the fall of Arthur's court by insisting that the king besiege Lancelot. Frodo will do no violence, and he will lose the heart even for the Shire and the friends he so dearly loves: his experience of the Ring drains both his physical and moral strength, though he retains enough courage to limit the violence of others during the Scouring.

We can treat the *Beowulf* essay similarly and with similarly productive results. Tolkien observed that some *Beowulf* critics had faulted the poet for "placing the unimportant things at the centre and the important on the outer edge" (52). Regardless of whether we consider such a structure a flaw, we may observe what Tolkien placed at the beginning and end of *LotR*: the Shire. The book (or books) begins in Middle-earth's last peaceful moments before the War of the Ring, with Bilbo's birthday party and the passing of the Ring to Frodo, and it ends with the "Scouring of the Shire," Frodo's departure to the Grey Havens, and Sam's return to the Shire. While I certainly wouldn't say that anything unimportant occurs in the middle—I can think of nothing I'd want excised, though I've often wished for more—I believe I can argue that, even allowing for the destruction of the Ring, the most important parts of the book, those that contribute most to its most important ideas, appear at the narrative poles, beginning and end. The Shire metaphorizes English life before and after the First and Second World Wars, something with its own peculiar flaws, but also with its own particular beauty, and worth preserving. And after the War, the war hasn't really ended: the veterans must return home, and they must deal with whatever has happened in their absence, both to their homes and to themselves. The War lingers like shell-shock in their experience of daily living, and it lingers among the peoples and in the landscape, however much Galadriel's magic soil may help.

Tolkien notes also that *Beowulf* has suffered in some critical appraisals because of its "illusion of historical truth and perspective" (54), a trait that he very much aimed to employ in *LotR*. He built a whole fictional world with its own mythology, creatures, habits (and habitual hobbits), and languages to accomplish that sense of depth and completeness—apparently he didn't consider that a flaw in *Beowulf*, either. Myth works best, he writes, "when it is presented by a poet who feels rather than makes explicit what his theme portends" (63): Tolkien seldom allowed theme to subsume story: perhaps in "Leaf by Niggle," but never in *LotR*. But the themes that he uncovers in *Beowulf* Tolkien applied liberally in fiction: "man at war with the hostile world, and his inevitable overthrow in Time" (67), the "theory of courage" and "unyielding will" that characterize the stories of the ancient North (70), the "intense emotion of regret" that accompanies resolve in the face of transience and mortality (73), and perhaps most important, the motif of opposites, "martial heroism as its own end" and yet "the wages of heroism is death" (77), which highlights the "opposition of ends and beginnings ... the contrast between youth and age" (81)—youthful spirit, for all its beauty and vigor, must end in death. Those points create the poignancy of *LotR*: for all his heroism, Aragorn must pass away, and so must even the undying Arwen, once she chooses to join him. Frodo and Sam combine heroic resistance to evil and determination to complete their mission; Frodo will barely outlast it, and even Sam, who at least returns home at last to a loving family, must go the way of all flesh, bound by Time and Decay. A reader can hardly escape regret for the passing of the Shire, that gentle land, even in the imagination, of long ago and far away.

Tolkien notes the "high tone, the sense of dignity" (61) that characterizes *Beowulf*, and we note it as the major tonal change between *The Hobbit* and *LotR*. Some readers have found that change a critical failure in *LotR*, but Tolkien got the shift honestly from his sources and used it to show that the larger work had moved into a larger sphere of influence: today a dragon, tomorrow the world. Critics may also have difficulty with Tolkien's monsters, as some do with *Beowulf*'s. He suggests that "triumph over the lesser and more nearly human is cancelled by defeat before the older and more elemental" (86), referring to Grendel and the dragon. *LotR* reverses the order: Frodo's quest defeats the far older and more elemental Sauron, but he loses the Ring at last, in a *felix culpa*, to the lesser and more human Gollum. The greater fall at last comes from inside, not from an external enemy, and so the lesser monster may function quite as powerfully, nearer to ourselves and our sympathies, knowing better our weaknesses and failings. As in *Beowulf* the servants of good in *LotR* have no "immunity from temporal calamity" (103) and, while giving us a clear notion of what hell may mean, the story gives no certainty of "heaven as its opposite" (94). Tolkien's pre–Christian worlds, the semi-historical of his beloved *Beowulf* and the Middle-earth of *LotR*, offer no definitive reward for deeds well done—one must look to the hope amidst the horror of *The Silmarillion* for that. In my estimation no emotional difficulty more powerfully—or more realistically—encumbers Middle-earth than that one: the greatest creatures, the greatest deeds, the best of friends all crumble at the feet of Time. That's also why the departure of the elves from Middle-earth presents such a great tragedy—and yes, I must call it tragedy in the Aristotelian sense. With their loss, we lose the world's connection to immortality. Beauty inspires regret because it hints at possible perfection in the face of awe-inspiring brevity.

No better criticism exists, I think, than the creation of one's own art in response to that of another: it both responds to and remakes, extends a former dialogue or tradition and begins a new one; it derives from emotional as well as intellectual closeness to the original and expands the critical audience by tying the newer work to the older. Making art as a response to a work of art connects audience to both works by a means more direct and visceral than theory, which may present it with too esoteric a façade and too much emotional distance. As T. S.

1. Tolkien as Scholar, Narrator, Stylist

Eliot wrote in "Tradition and the Individual Talent," every poem I read or write remakes the whole history of poetry: I (or anyone who comes into contact with a text) reshape everything I have read or will read, have written or will write, as a consequence of the new intellectual and aesthetic experience—I understand better and feel more fully what I've read and how to make new work. Tolkien's particular critical slant on *Beowulf* (he first delivered that paper in 1936, right before the appearance of *The Hobbit*) and on *SGGK* (1953, right before the appearance of *The Lord of the Rings*) shows concerns that came to shape his evolving fictional world. Those concerns direct our attention to the sorrows and failures from which we often most want fiction to relieve us. They may create problems for us as readers or simply as human beings, but they powerfully illuminate something that, for good reasons, Tolkien felt loath to explicate: war, loss, mortality, love that time must erase, keeping good spirits in the midst of all—what his fiction was really *about*. Fiction works better, but criticism too can provide us escape and consolation. We must find that consolation.

Narrative Experiments: The Linear versus the Gothic

Tolkien's fiction resists linear narrative and builds a world by incremental addition after the fashion of ballads (leaping and lingering) and in a way metaphorically similar to Chaos Theory which, though it came after his time, Tolkien's world-building anticipates. His narrative moves through asides, periods of rest and waiting, quick pacing through major points of action, and, in the later parts of *The Lord of the Rings*, by parallel plots.[3] The narrative also shows elements of the Gothic, of the patterns generated in Gothic churches particularly, to move the plot toward liminal boundaries where major narrative nodes appear. Tolkien managed to capture something of the scientific zeitgeist while remaining in touch with the aesthetic of his historical period of scholarship, and narrative experimentation comprised an important part of the twentieth-century literary landscape.

In interviews from around the time of the release of the film version of *The Fellowship of the Ring* (2001), Peter Jackson remarked that he found the first film of the *LotR* series easiest to plot because the story in the first segment of the trilogy exhibits a greater inherent linearity. But even *FotR* presented interesting problems not merely with respect to cinematic method and expediency, but also given the necessary consideration of the expectations (and demands?) of Tolkien fans. The essential story, Jackson observed, involves Frodo carrying the ring to Mordor. Though we enjoy them in the book, Old Man Willow and Tom Bombadil don't advance that story or provide information that we "need to know" with respect to the history of the Ring (see "From Book to Script," accompanying the extended version of the DVD; actor Christopher Lee makes the same point there). In Jackson's cutting the material of Tolkien's plot (and occasionally adding to it, usually action sequences) to suit the medium of film, he aimed to produce as nearly as he could a linear narrative throughout. Even where linearity becomes impossible— when Gandalf seeks Saruman's advice, or when the plot must follow parallel courses (i.e., with the splitting of the Fellowship)—Jackson sought to maintain compelling progress toward the destruction of the Ring with as few asides as possible while remaining true to as much of *Tolkien's story* as he could. With some exceptions, such as the expanded role of Arwen, he avoided introducing plot elements or tangential characters that would slow the film or confuse the viewer (in contrast with the new *Hobbit* films, where he adds characters to increase dramatic tensions and fill out the world). He omitted (where he thought he could) those elements (however appealing, such as Tom and Goldberry) that drove the narrative progress from its central movement, the disposition of the Ring, but further into the powers of Middle-earth (e.g., Tom and the Barrow Wight).

The Two Towers (2002), Jackson added later, conformed less easily to a linear pattern, exhibiting essential parallel stories: Frodo and Sam travel toward Mordor; Merry and Pippin get taken by Saruman's Uruk-Hai, and the others (minus Boromir, who has before his death contributed to breakup of the linear narrative) follow them, meeting the Rohirrim; offscreen (until later) Gandalf is "reborn" following his battle with the Balrog. *The Return of the King* (2003) again necessarily follows parallel plots that ultimately dovetail in the destruction of the Ring: Frodo and Sam progress to Mount Doom as the battle at Gondor concludes and the small army, led by Aragorn and Gandalf, waits outside

1. Tolkien as Scholar, Narrator, Stylist

the gates of Mordor to distract Sauron from the Ring's actual position. The aftermath of that apocalyptic destruction of the Ring returns to linear narrative both in the book and in the film, though again Jackson leaves out what he must have considered inessential material (the "Scouring of the Shire" and the death of Saruman—the latter appearing in a different way in the extended version of *RotK*) to move a long and expensive trilogy toward an ending satisfying for film audiences.

While few viewers would dispute the artistic success of *The Lord of the Rings* as film (I certainly do not), Jackson's choices—at least for fans of the *text*—to some degree undermine Tolkien's clear resistance to narrative linearity. *LotR* itself (both text and film versions) takes the form of a ring, ending (like *The Hobbit*) where it begins: in the Shire. But from its seed in *The Silmarillion* to its root in *The Hobbit* to its completion in *The Return of the King*, the development of the narrative takes a form one may more accurately describe with other metaphors; for instance as a series of *fractals* the plot moves episodically or incrementally, guided by one or more "strange attractors," unfolding, varying, gaining complexity; as *Gothic* it explores, cathedral-like, pacing, *chiaroscuro* (major plot segments occur in the dark or semi-dark), and artifice that expands and completes the world of the text. In the perspective suggested by either metaphor, Tolkien's narrative constantly resists simple linearity, moving toward curve and filigree, leaving Jackson as film maker with an essentially impossible task had he stayed strictly with the original. By comparing the pattern of book-narrative to that of film-narrative, we uncover essential differences in media and throw particular relief on the exigencies of adaptation. We can also get a strong sense of what Tolkien accomplished by means of the more complex narrative pattern; a film maker could accomplish something similar only with multiple extended versions, each incrementally building the world and the whole remaining thematically tighter.

In this section I'll discuss some instances where and why Tolkien strays from linearity to suggest that though linear as well as incremental narrative could have supported his *themes*, a reliance on linearity would have neglected one of the great pleasures of reading *The Lord of the Rings*: the complexity and welcome redundancy of Tolkien's Middle-earth as fictional world. Narrative asides, for instance, also allow opportunities for the exploration of good and evil, joy and suffering, sense of character and place. I'll also briefly examine Peter Jackson's film versions, working mostly from the cinematic releases rather than extended versions, for narrative structure to determine where he pursues and where he strays from linear progression so that I may reflect on those choices and how they affect the translation of Tolkien's ideas to a different medium and a different time. Changes in medium will shift idea matrices as well.

Traditional scholarship provides us a number of ways of schematizing narrative. Episodic plots, for instance, such as those in Homer's *Iliad* or *The Odyssey* or Vergil's *Aeneid*, appear commonly enough. *The Odyssey* and *The Quest of the Holy Grail*, while nominally linear—they pursue, as does *The Lord of the Rings*, a plot with a fixed goal—also have episodic elements much like Tolkien's. *The Odyssey* alone (unless one adds to the narrative the full background of Odysseus and his departure from Ithaka for Troy) lacks his ultimate circularity, ending far from where it begins. The *Quest*, more circular like *The Lord of the Rings*, ends back in Arthur's court; the hero has not undergone a change of character, but has apotheosized (Galahad literally—compare Frodo's departure from the Grey Havens?). The bigger story of which the *Quest of the Holy Grail* forms a part, the adventures associated with Lancelot, moves inexorably toward an end in which the world of the story is worse, not better than it was. The death of Arthur and the fall of Camelot and its ideals (the fall of the elves and the rise of humans in Tolkien?) and particularly the loss of Galahad, the perfect Christian knight, Christ as Knight, leave the world lacking the greatness that had for a brief time defined its possibilities. Their loss seems almost to diminish human potential rather than to encourage one to seek an ideal: neither the Grail nor any character worthy and able to attain it shall ever appear again. Middle-earth, similarly, is not better for the loss of the elves and the dominion of humans. Wizards, too, have gone, leaving the now dominant people without their chief sources of magic, goodness, and guidance. Tolkien's "episodes" and narrative asides allow for the expansion of character and for the exploration of alternative sources of power and goodness in the world.

Like those of their Classical and medieval counterparts, they also deepen our sense of the romance of a world at the edge of our imagination but out of tangible reach, distanced from us by time and the

1. Tolkien as Scholar, Narrator, Stylist

inevitable changes of Nature. In eliminating Sauron, the Ring, the Wraiths, Saruman, and Gollum, they also remove the greatest sources of evil; Tom Bombadil and Old Man Willow remain as contrasting elements of good and evil, but they too will now fade into quiet. The remaining world, blander, has more narrowly circumscribed limits, and heroism becomes a more pedestrian (but no less necessary) experience: resisting no dragon, but the dragon-sickness within ourselves, no Dark Lord, but any evil person who seeks lordship over our lands and purse strings—hardly insignificant, but less grandly inspiring. Episodic structure provides clear items for narrative and thematic comparison: Hektor fighting Patroklos, Hektor fighting Achilles; Bilbo's birthday party in the Shire, the returning Hobbits' scouring of the Shire.

Geometric progressions also occur in narrative, such as in *Beowulf*, where the hero undergoes three increasingly difficult monster fights, though *Beowulf* also circles imagistically, beginning and ending with a funeral. *Sir Gawain and the Green Knight* we may also call circular: the hero begins and ends the story at Arthur's court; Gawain returns chastened, regardless of what Arthur's court learns or fails to learn; the poet begins with and returns to the fall of Troy. But *Sir Gawain* also uses geometric progression: the deer hunt, the boar hunt, and the fox hunt, and increasingly difficult temptations. The animals represent the increasing cunning Morgan applies to ensnare Gawain in error and that he must employ to avoid failure in a world tainted by Original Sin. Anyone who uses allegory—nearly all the writers of the Middle Ages and probably the majority during the Renaissance—employs embedding or layering, what the medievals called the fourfold exegetical method. One reads on four levels at once—literal, historical, moral, and anagogical (cosmological or eschatological)—but those layers don't represent simple parallels. For the Christian reader they increase in importance, ending with questions of Salvation. Gawain seeks to attain a perfection he can never reach, but he fails in the sole virtue that from the Christian point of view can get him nearest to it: faith. Faith can prepare him to accept God's mercy, but he turns from faith to a belief in the efficacy of a material object, the green sash; *trawþe* can establish him as the best of knights, but he fails to keep complete honesty with his host. For additional examples we need look no further than Dante's *Commedia* or Spenser's *Faerie Queene* to see an "everyman" learning the implications of a plenipotentiary cosmology or a field of virtuous knights who provide a young male reader with models of the quest for life's virtues. A multiplicity of episodes in Spenser gradually unfolds the development and display of all the facets of virtuous gentility, whereas Dante moves from the *contrapasso* of damnation to that of purgation to that of salvation—episodes unveil the choice of evil, the desire for penance, the acceptance of mercy. For Tolkien the medievalist (and the Catholic) those texts and ideas would have as much presence and power as any from his contemporary world.

Parallel structures such as arise in both *The Two Towers* and *The Return of the King* also have medieval forebears (or siblings) that Tolkien knew thoroughly, such as "Pwyll, Prince of Dyfed" in the Cymric *Mabinogi*, where part of the plot takes place in the human world and part occurs alongside it in the realm of the Otherworld. *The Quest of the Holy Grail* also uses parallel plot—the early movements of the three Grail Knights who succeed and of many, such as Gawain and Lancelot, who fail—that then meld into one for the achievement of the Grail. With all those examples Tolkien would of course have had perfect familiarity; in fact, the early literatures he knew so thoroughly seldom exhibit simple linear plots. Even such a brief work as the Old English *Battle of Maldon* employs what we may term a wave-style plot, with rising and falling action punctuated by speeches leading to a crest and a catastrophe, but with the story never moving physically from a single spot. *Sir Gawain and the Green Knight* has perhaps the most linear plot of all, but even it briefly employs a parallel structure, as Gawain resists the Lady's advances and Bercilak hunts for game: the pairing in the structure urges the reader to compare the events directly for emotion and meaning. *SGGK* also uses a kind of leaping and lingering to stress its major plot points: the appearance of the Green Knight, the temptations at Bercilak's castle, and the closing encounter with the Knight/host.

So while contemporary literary theory gives us some new language with which to approach narratology, we need not look only to contemporary literature for narrative complexity or innovation: the Old World offers many options. To consider Tolkien's method of plotting, we may apply the two models, one from contemporary science, then the other from medieval architecture. While he wouldn't have known the first and would have known the second intimately, both can help us understand his plot structure and show how he used it to build his world and reinforce his ideas, and both influenced his intellectual landscape. These models also highlight—usefully but not exclusively—some of the particular difficulties in transferring Tolkien's narrative from fiction to film, which requires a re-mapping from literary to cinematic time and from imaginative to two-dimensionally visualized space.

In *The Road to Middle-Earth* Shippey has called Tolkien's plotting *cartographic*; that is, it not only exposes but also is guided by the geography, topography, and *feel* of Middle-earth, with a built-in redundancy but with incremental variations that deepen our sensory experience of the world. "Frodo," Shippey observes, "has to be dug out of no less than *five* 'Homely Houses': Bag End, Crickhollow, the house of Tom Bombadil, the Prancing Pony, and Rivendell" (79)—we may add the home of Farmer Maggot as well. The pleasant pauses give opportunity for reflection and sensory experience beyond the flight in fear of the Ringwraiths. In *Author of the Century* Shippey lauds the neat complexity of *LotR*'s symmetrical design: three volumes divided into two books each, with the structure of each book paralleling that of the others as the journey begins, as the companions join forces, break up, pursue their separate adventures, then meet again in the end. Even the individual adventures have parallel sub-adventures, such as the "meeting with the helpful stranger": Aragorn, Legolas, and Gimli meet Éomer and the Riders of Rohan, Merry and Pippin meet Treebeard, and Frodo and Sam meet Faramir (50 ff.). In "On Faery-Stories" Tolkien says that Fairy Stories serve three functions: recovery (meaning regaining a clear view of the world), escape (not in a puerile way, but removal from ill fortune to something better), consolation. We may say that the "map" of *LotR* follows a pattern derived from those functions: each member of the fellowship must (and does, even Boromir) locate a sense of what's going on in the world, find a way to escape or, ideally, eliminate its horrors, and then seek consolation, a return to some sort of desirable life for oneself or others. Tolkien's book maps, through a variety of creatures, places, and encounters, the full range of fairy stories, providing all the boons that fairy-story can offer.

Derek Brewer has argued that *LotR* isn't really a novel, but a Romance (Tolkien himself called it so) in the medieval sense of the word. Romances typically pursue one of two plots, each of which follows a character as he or she grows toward and crosses some important barrier; one takes the protagonist from childhood to adulthood, the other from life to death, both by means of heroism and often through love. As Brewer observes, "[i]n one sense the *whole* story is Frodo's dream of growing-up and dying" (262), and "we do not live our lives in a single linear sequence" (263). The "map" in this approach derives not from cartography, but from the natural order of events in life. Such Romances tend to follow either a linear pattern, from birth to death (as in *Le Morte Darthur*), or a circular one, journey and return (as in *SGGK* or *The Hobbit*). Joseph Campbell's *monomyth*, another well-trodden model, has both linear and circular aspects: it moves toward a particular end, the completion of a quest, but as a journey it involves both movement away from home to search and a return home with a boon.

An alternative way to envision the circular tendency of the narrative suggests that we consider "loops," a useful term that Nick Otty uses in an otherwise often derogatory and deconstructive essay. Increments of the *LotR* story proceed as the separate groups pursue their tasks—Frodo and Sam on the way to Mordor, Aragorn and the others ultimately toward Gondor—then we loop back to pick up the parallel plot lines and weave them back into the whole. Though the loop is a potentially helpful structural metaphor, I think we can find a better descriptor yet.

A more comprehensive model appears, as I have mentioned above, in Chaos Theory in the geometry of fractals, the building of a pattern or a structure by small increments that may in themselves seem random, but that join together in a complex but discernible (even sometimes in its larger perspective predictable) movement. Though Tolkien wouldn't have known of Chaos Theory, the formalization of which came after his time, the idea of fractal movements—seemingly occurring by chance but directed by some potentially locatable factor—provides an apt means of following plot development for someone who worked on long narratives in small increments often over many years. We may see almost a precursor of it in the Baroque and Rococo, division of curvilinear elements into more and more intricate ornamental details. By definition a fractal is an open-ended geometric pattern with repeated divisions descending to smaller and smaller scales into greater and greater detail, directed by an initial force upon a medium with sufficient chaotic properties to produce a unique, growing, not entirely predictable shape.

1. Tolkien as Scholar, Narrator, Stylist

Example: if when I cook pasta I add some olive oil to the water before it boils, the oil will spread out over the surface in a way difficult if not impossible to predict at the beginning, but governed by the laws of physico-chemical interaction and determined by the amounts, forces, and surface qualities present for the interaction as the water heats. The splashing of the oil on the water creates a dynamic, chaotic system, and the oil moves and spreads fractally, though the final result, because of the tendency of oil to bead, doesn't take a fractal shape. An example of a fractal shape is a snowflake: we know on a large scale the forces that create it, but the shape of each individual flake evolves fractally according to ambient conditions too variable on a small scale for one to predict the exact result, at least until a good deal of it has formed. In either example, the system does its job: the oil (some, but by no means all cooks believe) helps create a better cooking environment for the pasta, and the shape of the snowflake gives it temporary stability as it falls. In *Author of the Century* Shippey notes the "inching, small-scale progress of Frodo, Sam, and Gollum," with respect to the day-to-day chronologies of the movements of different groups, and he adds "that the effects created of variety, contrast, and irony are in major part responsible for the book's phenomenal ... success" (52). Fractal variations, the inching progress of characters' movements toward an end, allow the author to throw especial light on the contrasts between one group and another, each group fragmented from an original fellowship with a mutual goal, but moving toward uncertain or variable ends. Shippey observes that even in *The Hobbit* the maps and the wide range of names "do their work by suggesting that there is a world outside the story, that the story is only a selection" (68): we attend to only a small swirl amidst the rapidly boiling whole.[4] No surprise that such a narrative as *The Lord of the Rings* would develop fractally: in his letters Tolkien describes developing the plot and characters sporadically over years, reading parts as he completed them, and rewriting often after long periods of quiescence. Stop-and-start plotting means that incidents will arise that one must, for the sake of unity, cut, while others that one *may* cut one will choose to keep: despite their turning from linearity, they add enough coloring or depth to the world that the author will keep them for aesthetic (or philological) if not philosophical reasons—to which they may contribute as well (as Tom Bombadil and Goldberry do to the environmentalism at which *LotR* hints).

Now to textual examples: in the first book of the trilogy alone, Bag End, Maggot's farm, Crickhollow, the House of Tom Bombadil, Rivendell, and Lothlórien represent encircled, fractal microcosms that resist danger or change, deepen the variety of creative space, exemplify the sustaining and redemptive powers of Middle-Earth, and offer necessary respite. The truth and power of *LotR* lies as much in those moments of respite as in the narrative climaxes, and they, as much as the pursuit and fulfillment of the great quest, attract readers to the text, giving it shape, verisimilitude, completeness, clarity, a sense of "reality" because it doesn't rely wholly on breakneck adventure. The theoretical and aesthetic implications of those fractal narrative "asides" may establish Tolkien's greatest accomplishment as a storyteller because each represents, in its straying from the linear path, a setting into which the reader may expand his or her own imagination for additional and equally appealing storyline—what in the study of Shakespeare we might call offstage action. We could eliminate any one of those locations from the plot and still have an effective, moving story, but the loss of any one diminishes the *affective* quality of the text as a whole: repeating a motif with variation reinforces the feelings and themes associated with the motif. That capability accrues particularly to the best-written fiction; films, even the best films ever made, have yet to exhibit that power, not because of bad filmmaking, but because of the inherent limitations of the medium. Just as written fiction lacks the incarnated physical, sensory properties of film, film hasn't the same capability as written fiction to stray in plot without losing its audience (note, for instance, the informational chapters in *Les Miserables* or *Moby-Dick*). Television series can come closer to the same effect, especially those with consistent settings and ensemble casts. One may say that for physical immediacy, a stageplay surpasses film or television, not making it a better medium, but allowing it a different range of motion because of its physical and mobile presence—the roar of the greasepaint and the smell of the crowd. What a book lacks in sensory immediacy, it gains in imaginative potential—especially in the hands of a writer so expert in world-building as Tolkien.

We begin *LotR* as we do *The Hobbit*, at Bag End, from the viewpoint of any hobbit the ideal homely house, because it is the ideal house and home: well-situated, well-protected (except perhaps for the likes of Lobelia Sackville-Baggins), and well-pantried, it evolves fractally in *LotR*

1. Tolkien as Scholar, Narrator, Stylist

from Bilbo's perfect home to Frodo's perfect home. As was Bilbo, Frodo is rousted from its warmth and nominal safety by visitors so that he may undertake a quest, but a quest that has also evolved considerably, though it retains important connections to its narrative parent. With fractals one knows that new wrinkles will appear and that they will have connections to the old, but one can't know the exact direction any wrinkle will go or what magnitude it will reach.

The house at Crickhollow of course represents little change from Bag End in terms of hobbit comfort, though in its stand-apart, aboveground structure it more particularly resembles human comfort—Frodo is migrating toward the bigger world with a greater variety of preferred accommodations—and it resituates him at the border of wilder lands, another significant wrinkle in his experience. It shows Frodo's remnant unwillingness to abandon the Shire and the life he has loved. Even the best of hobbits changes slowly, and even for him the burden of heroic action to come weighs heavily. Frodo's journey has astonishingly more significance than had Bilbo's, and he and we would readily suspend it for a short holiday at Crickhollow or Bree. Occurring too soon for a furlough, the Crickhollow episode gives one more (very brief) free breath of Shire-air before the inevitable rush of the narrative events to come.

As we pass into the Old Forest and find trouble with Old Man Willow and other evil trees, we have moved, apparently, thoroughly beyond the world of hobbit-comfort until we meet Tom Bombadil as rescuer and protector. As the hobbits will further learn at Bree, they have actually had such protection at their borders all along, though they didn't know it. But Tom's help demonstrates that point and returns them briefly to comforts of "home," though they arise in someone else's home. There we see a continuation of the fractal pattern of homely houses, but a much different incarnation in the individual branch of the larger fractal arch-patterned tree. Tom's home has food, comfort, safety, humor, and fun, but it also leads to the stray adventure of the Barrow-downs. That wrinkle serves, perhaps, like Eve's dream in *Paradise Lost*, as instruction against the horrors to come.

The Prancing Pony at Bree provides another homely respite for hobbits with its familiar food and beer and comfortable rooms, but it adds additional twists and variations: a dispossessed warrior-king, different sorts of men with less than kind intentions toward the hobbits, and probably even mixed-breeds with the blood of orcs in them. The dangers that the hobbits risked in leaving the Shire have worsened, and Frodo sees a new, larger pattern emerging—and a much more dangerous world opening before his feet. Through subsequent iterations of this aspect of his adventure he gains a growing sense of the absolute seriousness and inevitable horror of his quest—while Bilbo had to survive trolls, a dragon, and a great war, the fate of the world lay not yet in the balance, as it does with Frodo's quest. And of course the Black Riders catch up to the hobbits at Bree. We may suspect on first reading that no more homely houses remain available to shield them from the Wraiths, who have by the plot point of Weathertop (an otherwise potential homely house, though one less homey) got to Frodo physically.

Yet with Aragorn's help, they reach Rivendell, the greatest and Last Homely House of all, with the possible exception of Lothlórien later (it serves the same function without taking the form of a house *per se*). Weathertop suggests a parody or antithesis or mirror image of the pattern, something that was once to some a safe fortress but has become a ruin and the site of a desperate and nearly disastrous battle (as, soon ahead, Moria has become a dwelling for monstrosity rather than the home of welcoming dwarves). But the hobbits survive their less homely stops, again with the intervention of yet unknown friends, to reach the safety and healing of Elrond's home, the antitype of the homely house and the antithesis of fallen Weathertop, a retreat that has retained its power. Rivendell provides rest, safety, advice, fellowship, and—for a short time—safety. We follow in the narrative possible directions that evolve into actual events, likely destinations that appear then as actual places, places that have differences but that conform to a pattern, that of the homely house, safe, if only for a time, from the dangers of the greater world: fractal variants.

What then does the fractal development of the homely house do for *LotR*? First, by repetition of the motif we find the range of possible havens, greater than even the hobbits suspect as their quest introduces them to evils beyond their imaginings. Friends, like enemies, come in many shapes and sizes, and their presence in the world holds at bay what might otherwise have already become deadly despair (or simply death)—we may even call them mini-eucatastrophes. And along with the journeying hobbits we meet the charming and marvelous array of folk who dwell in the world of Middle-earth. Aren't we willing to risk meeting orcs if we may also find a Bombadil? Who doesn't enjoy a basket of steaming mushrooms and a hot bath and a quaint inn with good beer, and who, as Sam says, would miss a chance to see and hear real elves singing under the stars? The varied repetition expands the potentials of the world of Middle-earth; though it has great and horrible evils, perhaps worse than ours, it has great good and beauty, perhaps also greater than ours. The world of our Romantic longing—in the medieval sense of Romance—unfolds to our ever-increasing awe. That awe contributes to the grandeur of the world, to the "spiritual" feel of Middle-earth, so that despite a dearth of what we may call religion, the book leaves us with a strong sense that our actions and our stories *matter* on a stage grander than our daily quibbles and squabbles. The various havens also allow the hobbits incremental steps toward their goal at a stage of the journey when they would not likely have had the wherewithal to manage the full import and horror of their undertaking without them.

Second, a linear plot would limit if not disallow the repetitive retreat to the homely house: a linear plot does not need a Bombadil. But Middle-earth needs a Bombadil, a protector and an eldest, and thematically the character serves as an embodiment of love of woods and trees. And we readers need a Bombadil: a representative of the Old Forest so that the environment may speak for itself (even as we, in our own lives, destroy it). Tolkien persists in the pattern to ferret out as many as he can of the variable incarnations of a motif that appeals to our senses and also to our desire to believe that good may prosper in the world and that we may find and share in it, and that we may enjoy the daily pleasures of life—food, drink, companionship, sight-seeing, restful sleep—without guilt, free, at least for a time, from the clutches of evil.

Aside: as an American reader, and given the timing of the appearance of the first film, I can hardly help comparing the arrival of the Ringwraiths to the September 11, 2001, disaster—I think Tolkien's notion of "applicability" allows for such a reading, non-allegorical and non-intrusive, not imposing anything on the text itself, but useful as an analogue for a reader looking for a means to make sense of disaster. To the hobbits the wars of the past lay as distant as Pearl Harbor had to us, and we may have thought or wished Sauron dead with the end of the Cold

War (if it has entirely ended). We dwelt comfortably in our homely houses only to be roused again; we have yet to find whether we may form a laudable fellowship or whether we have in the meantime become Sarumans and Wormtongues.

One can trace fractal variations throughout *LotR*, even to open-ended allusions such as Aragorn's references to Queen Beruthiel's cats and the Forsaken Inn east of Bree, but I have another metaphor to apply as well, one unlike the fractal in that it would have had immediacy and significance to Tolkien himself, but like it in its serial variance: the architectural pattern of the Gothic cathedral. In his preface to Max Dvořák's *Idealism and Naturalism in Gothic Art*, Karl Maria Swoboda succinctly defines "the basic problem of Gothic art as the relationship between transcendental ideas and the finite world" (xxvii)—a good description also of Tolkien's development of Middle-earth. Both Romanesque and Gothic art would have influenced Tolkien's religious experience as well as his imagination, because he would have had them around him regularly.[5] Henri Focillon observes that

> Romanesque sculpture was the expression of faith ... [and] Gothic sculpture was the expression of piety.... Romanesque faith, shot through with visions and prodigies, accepted and cherished the mysterious; it moved among superhuman things; it trembled in anticipation of rewards and punishments ... [while] thirteenth century [Gothic art] brings us back to the paths of the Gospel; in God-made-man, it cherished humanity; it loved and respected God's creatures as He loved them [71].

While Tolkien expressed his faith in his daily devotion to Catholicism, and would have experienced in part in the Gothic aesthetic, he also expressed his piety in the creation of Middle-earth, in the quest to be good amidst the temptation to do evil, to find light in periods of darkness.

Please consider for a moment the environment surrounding and also inside a Gothic cathedral: entering the cathedral is like moving into a separate, discrete, sacred world, much like opening a book for which one has especial reverence and engaging the world of a text. The cathedral structure (from an internal or external perspective) takes the shape of a Latin Cross, indicating its purpose clearly, were anyone in doubt. If one is nominally a Christian and absolved of sin or seeking sanctuary, one finds there a safe haven, dry, open to the light, forbidding

1. Tolkien as Scholar, Narrator, Stylist

violence. The medieval visitor met there the glory and the danger of a hierophany, of an encounter with God or Church hierarchy that would require a reckoning, perhaps atonement or sacrifice or even conversion or judgment. Thus the sanctuary presents, like the Fairy Story, potential consolation, escape, or recovery or, if the protagonist fails, death and suffering.

The Gothic cathedral, though, unfolds not merely a single experience, but a huge and varied world. Through the massive, often elaborately decorated front door the Gothic world may open into a lobby or *narthex* or directly into the cavernous nave or body of the church, a long, open passage through which one moves forward underneath the great sky-like arch. Toward the far end appears the *transept*, the cross-arms that cut across the nave at right angles. The hemispherical dome sometimes arises above the point where *nave* and transept cross and sometimes above the *apse* or choir, the enclosure opposite the entrance and usually at the east end of the building, which houses the altar, the point at which the ritual "sacrifice" takes place and around which curls an *ambulatory* for access or egress. The variable movement of light through many high windows inflects one's experience of the cathedral according to the time of year or of day or in response to weather: a break in cloud cover can send a ray of light beaming through a tall window directly onto an unsuspecting worshipper.

But the cathedral has many other architecturally "episodic" facets. It has more than one aisle by which one may approach the altar. It has high walls and galleries above and stained-glass windows, often decorated with biblical, historical, or natural scenes, each fractally illuminating a story and individually or together aiming to evoke a theme or mood. It may house tombs or treasures. And along the outside isles the visitor may filter off into any number of small specialty chapels with representations of saints, designed for small services or private prayer, but aiming in the short or long run to accomplish the same goal—though with a different emotional path—as a visit to the altar. Depending on when or where one visits, the cathedral may offer silence, music, public or private services, or it may be closed entirely. It may serve as a seat for judgment or inquiry, but historically almost without exception it represented the centerpiece, both physically and psychically, of a city.

The astute reader will already have noticed metaphorical similarities between the cathedral and the world of Tolkien's Romance: the discrete world waiting for one to enter, the decorative door (cover), the passageway with events and items of interest (opening the book and beginning the plot), the play of *chiaroscuro* and its influence on one's course—like the Gothic cathedral *LotR* visually exploits movements between light and dark (see particularly Verlyn Flieger's *Splintered Light* on this point). I think the metaphor applies especially well structurally to *LotR*, particlarly in its similar resistance to simple linearity; a significant turn occurs, of course, in *LotR*'s climactic liminality: the destruction of the Ring occurs at the Crack of Doom, whereas the epiphany of the Eucharist occurs at the cathedral altar—infernal rather than celestial, yet eucatastrophic both.

A walk through cathedral and plot shows many other connections. Frodo and Sam follow an aisle as directly as they can, yet filled with altneratives, to Mordor: the place of their sacrifice, the altar in the apse. Along the way good fortune allows them respite at the "homely houses" we've discussed, which we may fashion here as side-chapels of spiritual rest, prayer, and preparation for the greater service at the head of the church. They also experience suffering, which we may parallel to Stations of the Cross, tombs (barrows!), representations of martyrs (the giant stone pillars of the Argonath). They enter Mordor through an "ambulatory" and achieve their quest at the brink of death—accepting the Eucharist represents the movement through death to life again with concurrent cleansing of—but not yet final escape from—sin.

The other characters take different paths, but they also seek or even find epiphanal ends. Merry and Pippin visit the sexton or caretaker (Treebeard), while Aragorn and the others visit the underground crypt (Helm's deep) and, through a side aisle, the attached chapter house (Gondor). Gandalf has entered a tomb and Galahad-like fought and exorcised a demon; by Grace he has returned, resurrected, to join with the others for the final ritual: in this case "good" battles to survive, to return from darkness to light, the experience that typifies the visual/tactile spirituality of the cathedral experience. The remaining members of the Fellowship face an infernal Dark Night, another "descent," at the battle before the gate of Mordor, but they also have ahead of them a return to the "altar" in the crowning of the king at Gondor.

When Frodo and Sam's ritual rebirth occurs, they are carried by a symbol of the spirit, the eagle (John the Evangelist!) out again, and their service has ended—they join the others for its culmination (or its recapitulation as holiday) at Aragorn's official ascent to kingship. Then they must leave the cathedral to return to their daily lives. All may meet afterwards for tea and cakes, but the spiritual struggle continues, not only in the Scouring of the Shire, but in its aftermath and in their suffering the effects of their adventures. One may find family, the Grey Havens, further troubles, or death at the end of the journey: an image for life as a whole (or for war) as well as for an adventure.

I don't propose that Tolkien had specifically in mind such a Gothic structure as he composed *LotR,* any more than he would have been thinking of fractals as such; I suggest only that the Gothic cathedral may have influenced his imagination in a productive way, as it must affect anyone who visits one and pays it the least attention. The structure provides a useful metaphorical means of envisioning his plot patterns; whether we call a plot linear, circular, or episodic, we are seeking a way of reading, a structural metaphor that may better help us grasp its movement. In visualizing its structure as we read, we may find another productive way to enjoy and appreciate Tolkien's work, its variety, artistic depth, and spirituality. The concept of fractals has entered the larger community of intellectual life, and our familiarity with it may increase our appreciation for the value of the apparent redundancies of the text: while fractals may not fit in the traditional aesthetic of the cinematic medium (though they may more recently in the idea of *pixels*), they beautifully enrich the fictional one.[6] And that is the critic's job: as the Roman poet Horace would have said, to make our reading more sweetly useful. Linearity may limit a reader's pleasure, and complexity may increase it; Tolkien sought to make his work more complex and thus more satisfying and illuminating.

The difficulties of his own medium led Peter Jackson to attempt to linearize the plot, but given the structure of especially the final two volumes, he had no chance of avoiding parallel plots and frightening complications (Shelob!) in the second and third films if he was to stay at all true to the original. Scriptwriting wisdom has for more than a generation followed Syd Field's 1979 book *Screenplay* almost biblically: the idea of the three-act structure divided ¼, ½, ¼ deeply embedded both in lore and in practice. Kristin Thompson's clear and insightful *Storytelling in the New Hollywood* revises some old notions, reinforces others, and introduces some new ideas about cinematic narrative structure. She elucidates both theoretically and practically (with detailed discussion of ten successful films from the 1980s and '90s) a four-part structure of often roughly equal-length sections comprising setup, complicating action, development, climax and epilogue. She begins with basic principles of filmmaking that apply, she argues, to both classic and recent Hollywood films: a preference for clear and unified narratives assembled through a "conglomeration of blocks" (shots and scenes), clearly to relate causes and effects, to assign characters a clear set of traits, to relate protagonists' goals or desires to the main lines of action (often two in number), to move forward with temporal and narrative clarity, to include romance, and to centralize a turning point (10–31).

Jackson sought and in fact produced that clear and unified narrative not only in each film individually, but for the three as a whole—an incredible achievement given the inherent resistance of his source to that process, the financial demands of film production, and the knowledge and expectations of a multi-generational fan-base. The three *LotR* films, that other road to Middle-earth, neatly adhere to the four-part structure, with only a slightly truncation in the epilogue—no surprise given the length of the series up to that point.[7] I have wondered if including the Scouring of the Shire, as an extension of the epilogue, may not have provided both fuller balance to the plot and fuller expression of Tolkien's theme of the persistent evil effects of war, of the fact that war has not "ended" just because one has got home—for Tolkien's fans it would have added more than the additional battle scenes. We have, of course, dispatched the Ring as physical object, and maybe even the most devoted fan would have grown weary with the additional of another fifteen-minute battle sequence well after the climactic war has ended. Yet Tolkien was a writer of ideas as well as Romance plots. Fractals persist, and one may always take another turn around the ambulatory or pause over another tomb or artifact, particularly in the medium of print. Film scripts, though, must attract producers who see them as makeable and marketable, and they must finally end, allowing even the most stalwart of hobbits a drink and a well-earned rest.

Romance plots, though, may take bolder courses, especially given the turn toward experimentation of Modernism. Tolkien's fiction par-

1. Tolkien as Scholar, Narrator, Stylist

allels series of events, backtracks, turns to occasional cubbies, and makes bold leaps after gentle or violent lingerings. And perhaps most important they aim at depth, *copia*, one might say, amidst the *plenitude* of plot points and devices. The deepening of the world builds history and geography necessary for characters and events that seem fully marvelous and complex and at the same time fully real: the elements of serious and successful fantasy fiction.

The Linguistic Landscape: Mapping with Style

As I have mentioned above, in *The Road to Middle-earth* Shippey calls Tolkien's method of plotting *cartographic*. The maps do play a significant part in how we understand and visualize Middle-earth, and the peoples do in some ways define themselves by their landscapes—the maps of Middle-earth, such as the one the dwarves and Bilbo use to get to and into Erebor, are almost characters themselves, drawing reader interest for their own sake as well as for how they help us sort out plot movements. But Shippey is referring more to a linguistic map, based on the interactions of different people and languages in varying landscapes, and maps also emerge from narrative patterns and matrices of ideas. So much of Tolkien's storytelling comes from places and names: elves and ents are sylvan folk, hobbits hole-dwellers, dwarves (and orcs and trolls) are delvers and so cave-dwellers, humans build on plains or at the feet of mountains. Through traditions of philology and fairy tale, Middle-earth often draws return readers because of the appeal (or horror) of its various habitations and through its range of linguistic experiment. Tolkien reminds us repeatedly that his work was *fundamentally linguistic in inspiration*: that implies not only morphology, but also syntax. He had an abiding interest in words, particularly as names of persons or places, but also in how combinations of words combine to create effects and stories—that is, *style*.

Yet Tolkien also uses what we may call a *map of style*: he chooses prose and poetic styles to map his characters and his plot movement. Not only do languages change, but so do registers: characters, without switching languages, can change registers in different circumstances or for specific purposes. Frodo, for instance, does so fairly frequently, though Sam does so only once. Drout and Wynne called for more scholarly attention to Tolkien and stylistics, and since then Drout has himself responded to that call, as has Robin Reid, both quite productively in terms of approach and content. We may say much more yet about style, because it defies easy description both for what it is and how it works on us affectively.

Elizabeth Kirk, an early respondent to those critics who argued that Tolkien was a poor stylist, argued in a 1971 essay that Tolkien aimed at a "communal consciousness" by differentiating styles and linguistic registers through counterpointing, contrasting accounts of the same events told by different characters in different styles. She suggests that negative responses to Tolkien's style come from the "modern assumption that the function of language in any work of art is to force the reader out of the reaction, awarenesses, associations of ideas and value judgments which he shares with others and to substitute ... more individual and original modes of awareness" (10). Of course, Tolkien's style accomplishes exactly that kind of shift, but with the purpose of directing the reader to traditional questions of human experience and morality. The dynamism of Middle-earth's nature may have more in common with ancient myths than with contemporary environmentalism, but it can urge readers to get to the same issues through either means: issues of the human's place and responsibilities with respect to the natural world.

Reid's essay from *Style* (2009) uses M. A. K. Halliday's work on functional grammar to review passages from *The Lord of the Rings*, including one from the "Council of Elrond," one when Sam And Frodo join Gimli to view the Mirrormere after the Moria episode, and one from "The Ride of the Rohirrim" that directs attention to Théoden and Merry at the Battle of the Pelennor Fields. Reid's analysis shows "how the discourse of mythology and history are blended in Middle-earth" (519). Reid connects theme and subject to verb usage ("processes"), whether they follow or diverge from standard English syntactical practices, to show how discourse differences illuminate differences in characters' perspectives, giving a more complete view of events and their consequences. Drout's essay approaches some passages that look "most obviously unlike traditional Modernist literature: the battle of Éowyn against the Lorf of the Nazgûl and Denethor's self-immolation" (137). Drout finds the prose "not ... over-wrought or archaic" but with a "tight

1. Tolkien as Scholar, Narrator, Stylist

interweaving of literary references [particularly connecting with King Lear] ... with grammatical, syntactic, lexical, and even aural effects" to achieve a "stylistic consistency and communicative economy that rivals his Modernist contemporaries" (137). Through close syntactic analysis Drout shows (echoing Kirk) how the style adjusts with points of view to produce multi-level aesthetic affects, a major point that readers experience but that Tolkien criticism (by both haters and lovers) has often missed. More recently Steve Walker in *The Power of Tolkien's Prose* dramatically asserts that

> Tolkien maintains compelling artistic balance on a tightrope of ambiguity where fantasy verges on deepest reality, tall tale approaches archetype, and magic merges with the mundane, where metaphor assumes actuality and flexibility finds lasting form, where semantic magic comes perilously and provocatively close to life [5].

While our passion may lead us to overstate a point, Walker's text, inspired by a litany of off-hand comments (some perceptive, some silly, some learned, some nearly ignorant) by critics writing on Tolkien's prose, has yet more extensive and useful analysis of what comprises Tolkien's style. He focuses on how the magical or the unusual or even the ambiguous connects with the ordinary or commonplace, allowing the reader to join the author's process of sub-creation.

Brian Rosebury's *Tolkien: A Critical Assessment* (1992) has some of the most compelling arguments about Tolkien as stylist. He dismantles assertions that Tolkien's narrations or descriptions fall into archaism or either lexical or syntactic peculiarity or inexactness, arguing instead that Tolkien's style (not only his variations from modern patterns or choices), compared to that of other writers, "achieves greater clarity and fluency as well as an appropriately grave tone" (67): flexible word and phrase order, for instance, allows for more effective juxtapositions of images, more productive resonances, and more intense sensory experience. Tolkien's stories required an unusual variation from "episodes of grandeur or solemnity or violence" to those of quotidian life, maintaining a concreteness and a feel of authentic "history" within the world of the text (67–68). His narration allows for "gradual modulations between the exalted style and the plain," the dignified, the elegant and musical, the horrifying, and the humanely sad (68–70). He had to differentiate not only the speech of those characters with different primary languages, but also dialects, as well as how speakers of different dialects and languages would converse when they met together in the "Common Speech": from our own experiences with speakers of dialects divergent from our own, we may expect that sometimes they would sound to one another odd, inappropriate, or even hardly comprehensible. Yet Tolkien, using that flexible style, showed a remarkable gift for a "transparent view of landscape" (83), and he did, despite his critics, consistently show, even within the realm of fantasy, "marked elements of realism" and a "predominantly non-archaic diction and syntax" (133) while, after the fashion of many "modernist" texts, making "creative and adaptive use of myth" (136). Tolkien's works, Rosebury asserts, both "reflect and transcend" the "literary-historical phenomena" of his time (152), making him in many ways the stylistic exemplar rather than the outlier. As with Harold Bloom's idea of the anxiety of influence, the works most truly of their time grapple with the influences from their past as well as with the competitors of their own time, and in some way they emerge to define their time, either as exemplars or as their time's most notable, outstanding, or creative achievements. As with Eliot's idea of tradition and the individual talent, that each work changes how we read and write literary history, so Tolkien as narrator and as stylist changes how we read his time and, because of his continuing popularity, how we read ours as well. He draws dedicated hatred and even more dedicated imitators, neither very often understanding how he did what he did but both often responding to the same linguistic phenomena.

 A close analysis of the details of Tolkien's style would take a book in itself to cover all the variations, so I will consider only a few passages here from *The Lord of the Rings* to exemplify how he worked and to what purposes. *The Silmarillion* takes throughout a tone appropriate to serious myth: it doesn't deal in comedy, but in how the world has taken shape from the glories of creation to the horrors of the humans' and elves' falls. In its simplicity, formality, and parataxis one may even call it biblical: "There was Eru, the One, who in Arda is called Ilúvatar; and he made first the Ainur, the Holy Ones" (3). So the "high" or mythic style matches the genre and subject matter. *Farmer Giles of Ham* takes a very different tone and so uses a different style throughout: it exploits mock-heroic and uses clear, common patterns both of short narration and Standard English grammar toward a comic purpose. While similar

1. Tolkien as Scholar, Narrator, Stylist

in its use of fairy tale, *Smith of Wooten Major* mixes common speech with a little more formal style to fit Smith's crossing from his usual world into Faerie. But *The Lord of the Rings* mixes styles repeatedly and informedly to create greater variation and range of emotional effects.

A simple example with which to begin comes in *The Return of the King* after the destruction of the Ring and Frodo and Sam's return to Gondor. After plenty of story-telling to catch up everyone on the events they have missed, Sam observes as the "The Field of Cormallen" nearly concludes, "Well, one can't be everywhere at once, I suppose.... But I missed a lot, seemingly" (290). The line has only the one "formality," the use of *one* rather than something more common in our time, where a casual speaker would probably say *you* instead. But that is more a prejudice or preference of our time than Tolkien's. The remainder of the line sounds much as Sam has sounded throughout: like a common Englishman of Tolkien's time, with a colloquial touch, "seemingly." It also has a particular unassuming charm: of course Sam has missed a lot. But he doesn't feel a need to redirect attention to himself and Frodo, even after what they've accomplished. He enjoys and appreciates the stories he's heard for the marvels and horrors they relate. He expresses only the slightest sorrow at missing them—right after thinking that he wishes he could have seen an Oliphaunt once more. Sam has kept the humble appreciation of his world and his experience that have made him and kept him Sam all along, what in fact he must keep to recover from his experience and re-assume a place in the post-war world. Tolkien makes the point with merely the briefest quotation in Sam's summary of his experience.

During the Council of Elrond we find a variation of style depending on who speaks and to whom. The following passages show fairly abrupt changes and variants:

> "And in the house of Elrond more shall be made clear to you," said Aragorn, standing up.... "Here is the Sword that was broken!"
> "And who are you, and what have you to do with Minas Tirith?" asked Boromir....
> "He is Aragorn son of Arathorn," said Elrond; "and he is descended through many fathers from Isuldur Elendil's son of Minas Ithil...."
> "Then it belongs to you, and not to me at all!" cried Frodo in amazement, springing to his feet....
> "It does not belong to either of us," said Aragorn, "but it has been ordained that you should hold it for a while."

> "Bring out the Ring, Frodo!" said Gandalf solemnly. "The time has come. Hold it up, and then Boromir will understand the remainder of the riddle" [240].

We should remember first that we're reading Tolkien and not one of his imitators who didn't fully understand why he chose the stylistic facets he did. We must also remember that the speakers assembled at the Council are using the Common Language, which is not in each case his first language, and that dialects would have differences and would have undergone semantic and syntactical drift—part of what Tolkien is showing. Aragon comes from a very old race of humans, and because of his history, rank, and relationship with the elves, his dialect would likely sound more formal (even occasionally archaic) to speakers of more recently emerging dialects (e.g., to hobbits). Elrond's would sound more like Aragorn's than would most others'; however, he is speaking not his first or even second language, but a dialect of one that came much later and would again in his experience have had different influences. Boromir comes from Gondor, so he would speak again a rather more formal dialect with its own particular drift, related to Aragorn's but without many of the other influences on Aragorn's speech. Frodo's would sound most common to Tolkien's audience and to ours, because he speaks a more recent dialect that would remain closer to what we would understand as the "Common." Gandalf can sound thoroughly formal and grand at times, but when he speaks with or to the hobbits, he often sounds more like them, except with some slight differences in tone one might expect from someone of his rank, power, burdens, and age.

The above passage exploits little more than an occasional grandness of tone suitable to the seriousness of the matter at hand, which Tolkien shows with a few simple syntactical inversions, the lack of contractions and homey idioms, and the tendency that he uses throughout the book in formal situations to give a character's lineage or at least the name of his father. Thereby he may show the importance the characters place on who they are and where they come from and why they have or accept certain responsibilities or why they expect certain kinds of courtesies.[8] Early in *The Fellowship of the Rings* the hobbits' speech is about as direct and "realistic" as one could find anywhere, showing as at the Council differences in class (who could mistake Sam's speech even for that of another hobbit's?), but the spoken language changes through the whole

1. Tolkien as Scholar, Narrator, Stylist

of *The Lord of the Rings* to indicate differences between the various peoples and races (Treebeard's speech has its own patterns, as has Ghan-buri-Ghan's pidgin, as have the orcs' variants, with their tendency toward brevity, exclamations, and threats).

In addition to Tolkien's unusual inclusion of poetry that can also move from high to very common styles, he used when he wanted it elaborate and poetic description, as in this passage from *The Two Towers* where Gimli describes to Legolas the beauty of the caverns of Helm's Deep:

> When the torches are kindled and men walk on the sandy floors under the echoing domes, ah! then, Legolas, gems and crystals and veins of precious ore glint in the polished walls; and the light glows through folded marbles, shell-like, translucent as the living hands of Queen Galadriel. There are columns of white and saffron and dawn-rose, Legolas, fluted and twisted into dreamlike forms; they spring up from many-coloured floors to meet the glistening pendants of the roof [534].

The repetition of the auditor's name and the exclamation show the speaker's emotional absorption in the experience and his desire to hold the attention of the auditor, and the appeal to so many senses brings the reader fully into the imagination of the place. Shimmering visuals and translucency contrast the stark solidity of the idea of caverns made of rock, the tactile "sandy floors" contrasts with the dreamy forms, saffron gives not only color but a hint of odor and taste, "fluted" suggests sound as well as shape, and the whole visual gives a sense of lifelike mobility to static shapes—surely a remarkable passage as fully realized as nearly anything one can point to in imaginative literature.

Descriptions can be fully as evocative with less heightened emotion, as in "The Great River" chapter in *The Fellowship of the Ring*:

> The rain, however, did not last long. Slowly the sky above grew lighter, and then suddenly the clouds broke, and their draggled fringes trailed away northward up the River. The fogs and mists were gone. Before the travellers lay a wide ravine, with great rocky sides to which clung, upon shelves and in narrow crevices, a few thrawn trees [383].

Both syntax and diction remain simple and direct, with the exception of the word *thrawn*, a Scottish dialect word that here probably means "crooked." The scene is common enough, yet Tolkien doesn't let it fall into cliché, but instead gives it immediacy, feel, and a hint of sound to accompany the panoramic visual. One may even fail to remark on the passage simply because Tolkien did it so well, without drawing undue attention to it while yet bringing it fully to physicality.

Tolkien uses maxims throughout *LotR* ("the burned hand teaches best," *TT* 584, and "night often brings news to near kindred," *TT* 650)—many characters say and recognize them, just as Bilbo and Gollum knew the same riddles—and characters readily change their styles when they need to or when they themselves change. During "The Taming of Sméagol" in *The Two Towers*, Gollum "spoke with less hissing and whining, and he spoke to his companions direct, not to his precious self" (604)—Tolkien always fit style to character.[9] Orcs from different tribes have discrete languages, so they too must use the Common Tongue when they speak among themselves, and they do so with perfect grammaticality and with a preference for such terms as "filthy" or "foul" for their enemies, just such as the other peoples would use to describe them. Perhaps one of the most interesting stylistic flourishes comes in "The Voice of Saruman" in *The Two Towers*. The voice of the defeated wizard, his greatest remaining power, begins, as it comes out of Orthanc, almost to woo his audience, seeming wise, kind, melodious, and weary. It changes to harsh and rude as each of the listeners defies him, it falls into silence as Gandalf breaks his staff and dismisses him, and it turns finally into a horrified and angry shriek as Saruman finds that Wormtongue has thrown the palantír from the tower. The stylistic range mirrors the character's change.

Tolkien's style, in prose or in verse, shifts from humorous to grim, high to low, elaborate to simple. Most exactly we can say that he works it to fit its use, to create language for a world both far away from our time and place and near in its ability to express timeless human experience and emotion. In Tolkien's fiction style is part of the *idea*, even an idea in itself, part of what he wants to communicate, an essential element of language. It always contributes to the feel, breadth, and depth of Middle-earth. While Tolkien may later have felt that he made some incorrect stylistic choices in *The Hobbit* (or even early in *The Lord of the Rings*, when he thought of the stories as aiming at a younger audience), he carefully selected a range of styles to fit the movement of the narrative and the development of the characters and found various linguistic means to distinguish them—all one can ask of any author as stylist and an important part of the intellectual landscape of Middle-earth.[10]

2

Heart of Darkness, Heart of Light
Externalizing the Internalized Quest

The tropes of the medieval Holy Grail quest and of Freud's and Conrad's respective quests for our internal, psychological darkness mix and meld in Frodo's journey; the tension between the two, the internal quest to resist the Ring and the external quest to destroy it by a journey through an enemy-infested waste land, places Tolkien's work directly in the midst of Modern thought. While Tolkien may never have explicitly used Freud or Conrad or Eliot, or even alluded to them (only brief mentions of Eliot appear in his letters), their work formed part of the consciousness of the time, and anyone writing in the intellectual milieu could hardly have avoided their work and thought. Tolkien did employ the old notion of microcosm/macrocosm in the dual nature of his quests: they have both small and large as well as internal and external implications, all filled with horror and heroism. And as we see in art and film, Tolkien exploited chiaroscuro, the contrast and even mixing of light and dark, to give plot and character psychological as well as narrative complexity. This chapter will consider some theoretical implications of this essential impact of dueling metaphors of the heart of darkness and the heart of light in film and literature, with comments on how they appear in Tolkien's work to powerful effect. Frodo's quest, for instance, has very different implications than Bilbo's, and the whole of *LotR* has a good deal in common with many Arthurian stories in their thematic aim to preserve something good, and grand, and green.

Tolkien, Excalibur, the Grail Quest, and the Moderns

The essential difference between the "feel" of medieval literature and modern literature lies, I would like to propose, not in an interest in symbolism vs. realism, spirituality vs. commerce, or patronage vs. politicality, individual psychology vs. public didacticism, or even in the seeming gulf of centuries that separates them, but in what quest they privilege, what they most commonly seek. The medieval world, exemplified by Dante, or more allegorically yet by *Piers Plowman*, or perhaps by *The Cloud of Unknowing*, or best of all by the various versions of the quest of the Holy Grail, seeks in its quests what I would like to call here the "Heart of Light." The twentieth century, in the process of producing its "war to end all wars" then pursuing additional horrors out of a fascination with the grimmer aspects of our psychology, sadism, and the technology of mass destruction, troped its "literary" art toward such ghastly business as *The Birth of a Nation*, *In Cold Blood*, *The Exorcist*, and even the first twenty minutes of *Saving Private Ryan*, all foreshadowed by Joseph Conrad's aptly named *Heart of Darkness* and reshadowed by T. S. Eliot's *The Waste Land*. From the aesthetic ambivalence in the pull between the heart of darkness and the heart of light comes, among other works, John Boorman's classic Arthurian film *Excalibur* (1981), which has much in common with *LotR* thematically and imagistically.

Quest literature persists, but in the last eight hundred years, our general human quest has, for the most part, reversed itself; when the two traditions, medieval and modern, meet in medievalism, they often result in something at once interesting, appalling, ambiguous, and curiously achronic, such as *Excalibur*, which moves from darkness to darkness, never staying its narrative movement, but inflected by an occasional moment of light and a touch of color.[1] I don't think that in the modern age the direction of the quest has changed exclusively from external to internal, though that is partly true: to some degree the quest for the Grail or the Heart of Light aims internally as well as externally. However, in the twentieth century particularly we replaced the urge to seek the Heart of Light with a (perhaps Freudian) fascination with the Heart of Darkness, perhaps because we no longer trusted the Heart of Light or because we believed more power or more wisdom or our true nature or

2. Heart of Darkness, Heart of Light

"reality" lives not in the Light, but in the Darkness. Perhaps we came to believe that more power lies in the "dark side of the Force" or that our best hope for survival lies in exorcising or at least purging the Heart of Darkness.[2] Eliot's dark Waste Land taunts us with a notion of peace that he dared not deliver with any hint of belief, let alone finality, and Conrad's Marlow closes his *mise en abyme* novel far from the Congo, yet just as surely looking into "the heart of an immense darkness." As the twentieth century ended and the twenty-first began, international politics remained at the brink of renewed conflict, everyone claiming righteousness but all uneasy turning toward anything like a Heart of Light, which would require honesty, generosity, and humility rather than desire for even more money and power.

Excalibur, appearing in the medium that touches more people than literature can beg to do in our age, concludes with the visual expression of an unbelievable shred of hope that a just power from long ago may one day return to lead us, if we are willing to allow the dubious assumption that we have known a just power already. In *Excalibur* the Heart of Light, the Grail, becomes equivalent to the king and the land, detached from notions of salvation or even virtuous behavior. Lancelot, the world's greatest knight, has found Arthur, the world's greatest king, and intends to serve him. Though he helps promote the questionable notion of equality suggested by a Round Table attended by a king and his nobility, he unwillingly, but apparently inevitably, betrays his king. Percival finds the Grail so as to heal his king for battle, but not to encourage others' spiritual quests: this secular if still spiritual Grail, not even the cup of Christ in the film, appears no more in the film once Arthur has drunk from it and regained his vigor. Arthur can't offer his world much protection without its best knight, nor can he offer it any knowledge once Merlin is gone, and he can hand down no strength once the ancient sword of kingship is gone. The transcendent, loving, anciently powerful quality of the Heart of Light (as contrasted with the consuming, self-absorbed, unstable Heart of Darkness) is missing from the film, replaced by present or potential magic, as magic replaces God in most of our modern imaginative recreations of the Middle Ages.[3]

The Grail quest, or its equivalent, has always lured us, even from our earliest stories. Not always though often as a promise of immortality, it always invokes a vision of the Heart of Light, something more powerful and better than we are, whether a holy mountain or a burning bush or a sacred cauldron or some other talisman. Gilgamesh travels to the end of the world, to the land of Utnapishtim the Faraway, to learn the secret of immortality. He returns mortal, as ever, but having glimpsed a certain light: to live well, joyfully to accept his lot, and to write his adventures so that others may learn from them. His quest, though not for a grail, aims at a source of immortality, a Heart of Light. The medieval Welsh Cauldron of Annwn, either gift or booty from the "Otherworld," can return dead warriors to life to fight again, but cannot restore the gift of speech, leaving them politically functional, but not fully human.[4] From those earlier examples we may leap to a specifically Christian instance: Spenser's Redcrosse Knight enables his success against the dragon upon seeing the light of the New Jerusalem in Canto 10 of Book 1.[5] Redcrosse has yet to defeat the beast, live fully, rejoin Una, and die gracefully, but as the knight of Holiness, having climbed the Mount of Heavenly Contemplation and having seen Eternity, he will no longer fall into the abyss, the Heart of Darkness, as he did in Lucifera's dungeon. A few examples appeared in Tolkien's dwindling century: Thomas Merton's *Seven Storey Mountain*, the mystic's spiritual autobiography, shapes the quest for the light of perfect faith and contemplation after the metaphor of Dante's Purgatory, but places the quest within a modern world realistic and tragic, yet still offering some hope of salvation and a belief in the Light unusual in serious literature of our time. Merton, as monk, mystic, and poet, balances the death of his brother against his own affirmation of faith, but Merton wrote under pressure to finish his account and intending to recount his own spiritual quest: the autobiographical milieu lacks the degree of choice available in fiction. That ability to choose seems more recently to turn our interest more to a Darth Vader than to an Obi-Wan Kenobi: what, after six films, do we know about Old Ben's internal struggles with the *Light* Side of the Force?

Amid the twentieth-century landscape Eliot's *The Waste Land* begins where Conrad's *Heart of Darkness* ends. Together they constitute, I think, the two most influential images of the century, and they set the tone for literature up to our own time. Conrad's turn-of-the-century quest has Marlow seeking the "blank spot" on the maps of his youth, a white spot on paper but a darkness to the European imagination. The imagination must then dare to look into itself and to emerge with a real-

2. Heart of Darkness, Heart of Light

ization of its own deep darkness: "The horror, the horror." From the brink of the abyss into which Kurtz descends, Marlow returns, after the fashion of Sir Bors in Thomas Malory's (and his French model's) version of the Quest of the Holy Grail, because someone must take the leap (of faith or horror, to God or the abyss), but someone else must remain behind to tell the tale. But Marlow returns, unlike Sir Bors, to light the way to the darkness rather than to point the way to the light. Similarly, Eliot's post–World War I mini-epic begins with the "Burial of the Dead" amidst a "heap of broken images," necessary in a post-war world, and then it traces a seduction, an unsuccessful attempt to discard desire in the noise and rush of the "Unreal City," an ambiguous trial by water as a kind of re-baptism, and a quest to find the prophetic answer to "What the Thunder Said" in a hurried and unsatisfying "*shantih.*" The culmination of the poem seems to laud almsgiving, compassion, and self-control (part 4) as it does the choice to renounce possessions and desires (part 3), but it follows the former with uncertainty and the latter with rape. Conrad's darkness, external but internal, and Eliot's Waste Land, internal but external, offer no hope but in our limited ability to examine and reproduce our suffering in artistic form. Though of course Eliot later returned to Christianity in a renewed search for the Heart of Light, his later poetry had less influence than his earlier disaffected work, because it speaks to a quest the larger society had already diminished.

While Tolkien did not, we as a culture yet neglect that quest or dilute it, or make ambiguous its end, especially in our popular entertainments. In *Saving Private Ryan*, for example, a group of soldiers quests to save another because Ryan's brothers have already been killed, and most of the questers die in the search, forcing us (and the saved soldier) to ask, was their sacrifice worthwhile? Ryan himself, the "grail" of the film's quest, asks, was I worth it?[6] We see a similar ambiguity in *Excalibur*, in the chiaroscuro that accompanies the period of Arthur's sickness until the green highlights that particularize the visuals of this movie highlight the return from ambivalence to action—though a choice of action that leads to Arthur's death and the loss of Camelot.

As *Excalibur* begins, the first frame we see reads, simply, "The Dark Ages." The first action, backlit in fiery gold but with dark, nearly black night in the foreground, shows Merlin appearing through smoke or mist, then soldiers rushing on foot or on horseback. The slight green tint that so characterizes the visuals in the film mixes in the smoke, and Uther responds to Merlin's call: "Merlin, I am the strongest! I am the one!" Then he calls, "A sword! You promised me the sword!" Merlin replies, more pleading than demanding, "And you shall have it, but to heal, not to hack." "Talk! Talk is for lovers, Merlin. I need a sword to be king!" Uther replies, set on achieving his own power, as the battle rages. Symbolically, Merlin emerges out of the light to call Uther to learn peace, but even Merlin's light is shadowed in smoke and haze. Uther, caught up in the darkness of the battle, refuses the light that Merlin offers; he turns to selfishness and to darkness as do, for instance, the Númenorean kings in "Akallabêth."

In the silvery green morning Merlin waits at a lake, where the ancient, magical sword that signifies kingship granted by the earth, Excalibur, emerges from the water, shining green in the rising sun, in the hand of the Lady of the Lake. Green, the color of growth and plenty and healing, suggests that the sword *should* symbolize the prosperity a good king's rule brings to his folk. Nonetheless, Excalibur is a sword, and a sword serves as an instrument of war, though it emerges into the light of day as if it had returned from baptism. The next scene shows the massed armies separated by a brook, and Merlin tells Uther, "Show the sword!" Interrupting their exclamations, Merlin explains, "Behold, the sword of power, Excalibur, forged when the world was young, and bird and beast and flower were one with man, and death was but a dream!" He commands Uther to speak, and Uther offers his enemies an ultimatum: "One land, one king: that is my peace, Cornwall." When Uther too yields something, the land from there to the sea, the leaders agree and make peace, the land shining green in the background. That green light remains after Uther's death, shining clearly from Excalibur even as it sits stuck in the stone where Uther thrust it years later as another tournament begins to determine the right to attempt to draw the sword. Because Uther uses the sword selfishly, the world is denied its healing potential, but the potential, the power of the symbol that connects the king and his people to nature and to antiquity, remains, waiting only for the proper king to regain it. For Tolkien the Sword that was Broken, Narsil/Andúril, serves a similar purpose, but its wielder uses it more worthily. He does fight with it, but to rid the world of tyranny, not to impose it, and he doesn't draw it needlessly or for personal gain.

2. Heart of Darkness, Heart of Light

After Arthur draws the sword, battle begins anew, and Arthur's first act as king-to-be is to pursue Merlin into the Green Wood. Arthur asks, "Merlin, why have you done this to me?" "Because," Merlin replies, "you were born to be king." Arthur asks, "What does it mean to be king?" "You will be the land, and the land will be you. If you fail, the land will perish; as you thrive, the land will blossom," Merlin explains. Here director John Boorman clearly connects Arthur to the Fisher King myth, but fertility glows green in the power of a sword (as it will again after he drinks from the Grail): the fertility comes with peace, just rule, and understanding "what is meant to be," but through a martial symbol and not implying any spiritual connection. The supposed Heart of Light in *Excalibur* is the power of the earth vested in a symbol used to rule by might and skill, not a connection to something greater such as spiritual achievement.

Later, when Arthur and Lancelot fight at the bridge, and Arthur is defeated by a stronger opponent and lying supine on the rocks above the water, he invokes, "Excalibur, I call upon your power," and he strikes down Lancelot and breaks the sword (more on this idea in a later chapter). The sword, its bright green glow intensified at Arthur's call, loses its light once it breaks. Merlin, watching, observes, astonished, "You have broken what could not be broken. Hope is broken." Hope equates to right governance through military might. "My pride broke it. My rage broke it," Arthur sadly replies, and flings Excalibur into the water, whence it is shortly returned to him, whole and glowing green again, by the Lady of the Lake, so that Arthur may retain his symbol of power of the land and its people—he has, for a short time, learned an important lesson. Arthur observes that Excalibur's "power was meant to unite all men, not to serve the vanity of a single man": democratic thoughts for a medieval Christian king and words of surprising social concern following a magical martial event dubious in a world of emerging Christianity.

Subsequently Lancelot, having defended Gwenevere's honor against Gawain's charges, lies in bed injured, shrouded in an odd, muted-gold light that seems to suggest some sort of sickness. When Arthur appears to comfort him, the green light shines off the mail on his right shoulder as he begs Merlin to heal his friend and chief knight. As Lancelot returns to life, responding to Merlin's Charm of Making, the green light shines about his head and Gwenevere's. Lancelot having recovered and departed court, Gwenevere rides after him through the Greenwood and finds him sleeping among green stones. The king and the land both have the power of healing, but as we saw in Arthur's fight with Lancelot, individuals may choose to use the power of nature for good or for ill. Nature itself makes no moral decisions. When Arthur finds them sleeping together and thrusts the sword into the ground between them, the sword passes directly through Merlin's heart, as the wizard exclaims, "Excalibur, into the heart of the dragon!" The sword, the dragon, and Merlin himself represent the power of nature which may be harnessed for good, exploited for evil, or misapplied to the destruction of the social fabric and the loss of strength and sanity among those who must uphold law, mete out justice, and maintain the land's fertility. Lancelot exclaims, "The king without a sword! The land without a king!" Here clearly *king* equals *sword* equals *order plus prosperity*. At this point in a medieval version of the story, we should see a holy person emerge from seclusion to interpret the events and advise the principles how to rectify their mistakes, usually by spiritual rather than military means, but in the strange world of *Excalibur*, now without Merlin and lost between a Heart of Light in which it doesn't believe and the Heart of Darkness to which it is unwilling to submit, we must turn to an odd, hurried, and unexplained version of the Grail quest for any hope of salvation.

Immediately Morgana, free of Merlin, bathed in the muted gold light, casts a spell on the sleeping Arthur so that he begets Mordred, that is, "murder." Then as Arthur and his knights attend mass, and a priest intones, "God save us from Morgana and save us from her unholy child," a bolt of lightning flashes through the altar window, striking Arthur to the floor. Where Merlin, now replaced by Morgana, has been the world's source of knowledge, priests and knights invoke God's help only to stay the Heart of Darkness, not to open the Heart of Light. In proper fisher-king fashion Arthur remains ill, and the green light that tints the knights' armor disappears.[7] It reappears unexpectedly shining from the dead knights' armor when Percival hangs from Morgana's gallows tree: as he nears death, he nears life, for the light of the Grail castle appears above him. In his imagination (Or is it spiritual fact? The movie doesn't tell). He approaches the drawbridge, the trees behind him glow bright green, and the Grail descends toward him, spilling blood. A voice

2. Heart of Darkness, Heart of Light

asks, "What is the secret of the Grail? Whom does it serve?" Percival flees back over the drawbridge, and another hanging knight's spur cuts the rope that has nearly choked him to death. Percival temporarily fails in his quest, lacking the courage to enter the Heart of Light, which he apparently equates with death, a step he isn't yet ready to take even to save his land and king. We see here that the characteristic green light, which signals the power of nature that invigorates us, does not equate even for the filmmaker with the Heart of Light. One may direct the power of earth or Nature for good or ill, as in the case of Morgana, who uses it for revenge, personal gain (extended youth), and to help her and her son to obtain power.

As Morgana enchants Mordred and his green-sheened golden armor, preparing for battle against Arthur, she chants, "No weapon forged by man will harm you whilst you wear this armor." Naturally she wishes to protect her son, but in doing so she intends to bring about the death of her brother, Mordred's father, thus gaining power for herself and him, not for the good of the land and its people. She also (recalling the witches from *Macbeth*) clarifies that Excalibur is a natural, not human creation and shows no awareness whatever of even a slight possibility of a Heart of Light—Mordred's golden armor has turned even light to evil use.

The quest for the Heart of Light remains, even after his initial failure, to Percival, since he is the last of the questing knights, the last "believer" even in the Grail's potential to exist. As he holds the dying Uriens in his arms, he realizes his loneliness as the last of the Grail knights, and he hears the magical voices drawing him again towards the end of the quest. The suffering people, led by the mad Lancelot, drive him into the river in a kind of re-baptism, the green glow encircling him. He nearly drowns, but sheds his armor, needing a different kind of protection that the film does not specify, and he emerges again at the drawbridge of the magic castle. The power of nature lies in and around him, but will neither help nor harm him of itself. He must willingly enter the Heart of Light and exhibit sufficient wit to answer the Grail questions and serve his king. Percival enters the castle, hears the questions about the Grail again, and answers, "You, my lord. You are my lord and king." And when the voice asks, "Have you found the secret that I have lost?" Percival replies, "Yes, that you and the land are one." He reaches for the

Grail, then, miraculously translated to Camelot, he immediately turns and hands it to Arthur, saying, "Drink from the chalice, and you will be reborn and the land with you." "I didn't know how empty was my soul until it was filled," says Arthur, regaining his strength, and the green light returns to him, to Camelot, and to all his knights as they ride forth to the stirring strains of the "O, Fortuna" from the *Carmina Burana*. The land, green and blooming, is ready for its king and his final stand. Percival has brought back the knowledge the world of *Excalibur* has to offer, which will sustain Camelot but briefly: if the king does well, the land does well. Tolkien uses a similar notion in the idea of "The Return of the King": the land revivifies when it has a king who rules well.

The Grail quest, in its medieval form, is the quest for the light of God, the vision and presence of God, which Galahad experiences fully in Malory's "Tale of the Sankgreal" and its French antecedent. In *Excalibur* Percival finds in the Heart of Light not God, but natural truth Arthur had already known, but forgotten, and forgotten not because of any tragic error of his own, but as the result of Morgana's whiles. While Merlin (a magician and no Christian) would turn his age to the use of nature's power to seek the Heart of Light, Morgana would turn it to the Heart of Darkness. Yet both derive their power as does Arthur from nature, not from God, and as we have seen, in the world of *Excalibur* nature doesn't always make moral decisions. The essence of the medieval Grail quest is a moral and spiritual decision, to seek not the powers of this world, but the light of God. That fact perhaps accounts for the strangeness and the unsettled conclusion of the film: it derives from a story about the quest for the Heart of Light, but appears in an age (ours) that believes more fully in the quest for the Heart of Darkness. As one might expect, the film ends with an ambivalence even greater than that of Malory's *Morte Darthur*, where we don't know whether or not to hope for a return of the king. *Saving Private Ryan* ends with a similar ambivalence; despite Ryan's own doubt about his worth and the heroic sacrifices made for him, we are glad the questers saved him, but we must doubt as he does the price they paid, their own equally valuable lives. Our Heart of Light in *Ryan*, the heroic soldiers' self-sacrifice, shines on one character alone and leaves him in doubt that his family can only partly assuage. *The Lord of the Rings* engages a quest to the heart of Mt. Doom, and the return of a good and peaceful king follows its successful completion: a distinct turn to the light, if not to the absolute Heart of Light.

In *Excalibur* Arthur tries to resolve his world's ambivalence for us. "I was not born to live a man's life, but to be the stuff of future memory," he explains to Gwenevere, who has got herself to a nunnery. "The fellowship was a brief beginning, a fair time that cannot be forgotten, and because it will not be forgotten, that fair time may come again," he opines hopefully. Gwenevere returns Excalibur to Arthur for what everyone seems to realize will be his final battle, connecting Arthur as symbol to the symbol of his power and focusing the theme of the film on the social implications of leadership and its connections to both nature and the imagination. Gwenevere can never again love Arthur as husband, however much he wishes it, and that fact constitutes her tragedy. Ours may be that we see (and are taught to wish for, as Malory recognized at the end of his book) the power of nature vested, briefly, in Arthur, rather than in the permanence of the Heart of Light; Malory concludes stating his belief that Arthur is dead and buried and asking for our prayers for his soul, so that he may seek the Heart of Light beyond his and all texts. Tolkien leaves us with an elegiac sense of loss but also a spiritual and humane sense of hope.

As *Excalibur*'s final battle draws near, Merlin appears to both Arthur and Morgana from the land of dreams. He encourages Arthur, but in the sensual red and gold light of Morgana's tent, tricks the sorceress into uttering the Charm of Making, raising a mist that uncovers her true self to her murderous son and masks the attack of Arthur's brave and true, but outnumbered forces. The green light flickers briefly both upon the matricidal Mordred as he exits toward parricide and then again upon the shoulder of Arthur's armor as he plunges Excalibur through his son's throat. The red, rising sun looms huge behind him, and blood covers his armor. Arthur encourages Percival to recommit the sword to the Lady of the Lake with this hope: "One day a king will come, and the sword will rise again," a small comfort for Percival and for us. As the arm of the Lady of the Lake rises to catch the sword Percival has flung, red still dominates the scene: the blood on the sword and the enormous sun appearing over the hill. The green light is gone; clouds dull the sunrise, and a red sail powers the boat that whisks Arthur away as Percival, Grail knight and the last hero of his age, watches Arthur disappear into the gloom. The dying strains of Wagner's *Parsifal* outlast the light. Arthur sails into the rising sun, but is he alive or dead, headed for the Heart of Light or merely into the long-lingering gloom? Either way, for us he dwells in darkness. The ambiguous ending typifies Arthurian legend as a whole, but not the Grail quest, which in medieval literature, though not in *Excalibur*, highlights the grand sweep of Arthur's kingship with the Round Table's single greatest achievement, its culmination in spiritual fulfillment.

Narratively the quest for the Grail accounts for only a portion of *Excalibur*, and not the largest portion, but it does mark the final turning point (the first comes with the consummation of the love between Lancelot and Gwenevere, the second with Morgana's imprisoning Merlin) in the plot. In Malory the turning point of the plot subsequent to the achievement of the quest hinges on Lancelot's choice: whether he will learn from Galahad's success and, as he has promised, turn to salvation, becoming a model of the "new virtue," or relapse into the material world and the physical loves of Gwenevere and feats of arms. In the Christian sense, not so important in the film as it is in Malory's text, he fails. By allegorical extension the reader must ask a similar question: whether we will follow Lancelot or Galahad. The audience for the medieval French tale must have been monks from noble families who wished to accept the holy quest without fully rejecting their families' chivalrous pasts. Comparatively, in *Excalibur* the achievement of the Grail quest heals Arthur long enough that he can defeat Mordred, but the audience departs with no particular spiritual choice to make: we can't believe in the return of Arthur, and we hardly believe that the king (or any political machinery) and the land are one, nor do we feel any more assured that we and the land are one. The heroic tale, without the hope for our own quest to the Heart of Light, or any further reason to believe in it, may stir our emotions, but to what result, to what action? We leave the film no better prepared to act or to live.

Tolkien would not leave his readers at that point. We do depart *The Silmarillion* and *The Lord of the Rings* with the sense that the world lies in the hands of weak and untrustworthy human nature. But humans have at least free will and the power to make good, even heroic choices if we learn well and find a place in the world. He does not deny either the heart of darkness or the heart of light: both remain, and both have power. But we may choose to seek the Heart of Light if we wish. Frodo departs with Gandalf and the remaining elves into their Heart of Light. Sam returns home to his beloved Shire and family. Aragorn will lead what will be for a time a better world. The quest to the Heart of Light *through* the Heart of Darkness has value, sacrificial and salvific—if temporarily and in the face of irreplaceable losses. Action in the world has value, but one can't escape sorrow and loss at last—though something better yet may come thereafter.

In denying or marginalizing the Heart of Light in so many of our stories perhaps we reject a romantic and limiting medieval notion; in pursuing the Heart of Darkness perhaps we unearth lurid desires, fears, and hatreds so that we may cleanse ourselves of them. But I can't help thinking (fearing?) that we have also acquired an unshakable disbelief in the possibility that good can at least balance (if not overtake) evil in our nature; I wonder whether we have given up the opportunity to learn if the Heart of Light may offer something more than does mere amelioration of the "dark side" and acceptance of the assumption that we must live amidst a constant, amoral struggle for power. Tolkien, accepting the evil in human nature, the persistence of our sinful behavior, and our every imperfection, still believed in the value of story to help make us better, to encourage us to find within ourselves courage, generosity, kindness, and appreciation for the beauty of our world beyond what we can make in it of dollars or pounds or euros. He believed both in the power of religion to improve if not heal us and in the amelioration of fairy story to give us secular strength to support the spiritual. If we must fail, we need not Fail. Story can bring both joy and wisdom.

Perhaps when we expect no greater quest of ourselves, we can't expect any more from our movies, either. *Excalibur* does raise some valid questions: where do we look for guidance when our old sources of wisdom seem lost to us? how do we heal a system of public safety and defense gone mad? can we realistically hope for leadership that can recognize embers of hope that the people and the land become one, when we scramble to develop our stock portfolios for self-interest rather than for the good of our world? We know we can quest for the Darkness, but is a quest for the Light even possible in an age devoted to irony but barely able to appreciate its kinder side, the one that looks for mutual learning rather than simply at recrimination? Beyond the interplay of light of darkness, the ambiguity and ambivalence about the source, use, and continuity of power make *Excalibur* an interesting and troubling film and a notable if finally unfulfilling incarnation of the varied and continuing Grail quest. The quests of Tolkien's fiction, by contrast, may lead us back to belief in good for its own sake, and they may remind us of the value—and the responsibility—of helping to preserve everyone's Shire.

Darkness, Light, and the Quest to Destroy the Ring

Frodo's quest takes him to the heart of darkness, to Mt. Doom; his reward comes when, because of the pain of old wounds physical and spiritual, another journey takes him to the nearest thing Tolkien's mortal world can provide to the heart of light: to Valinor, that land across the sea. The quest to the heart of darkness leads at least, though painfully and regretfully, toward the heart of light, and the reward comes with a greater sense of sadness and of loss than of accomplishment and joy. Frodo dwells for a time, particularly when he wears the Ring, in chiaroscuro, in a place between life and death, outside of normal time and place. There he is most vulnerable of all, most subject to Sauron body and soul.

Tolkien often casts evil or suffering as darkness: the garb of the Black Riders and their lack of clear bodily outlines, the darkness that precedes the battle of Minas Tirith, the darkness of Mordor, the dark men of the South who become soldiers of Sauron, the darkness into which Sauron intends to cast all creatures should he find the Ring and win the war ("One Ring to bring them all / And in the darkness bind them"). That metaphor has led to some critical responses accusing Tolkien of racism. But the choice of darkness comes partly from traditional symbolism and partly because of the fact that a dark atmosphere, either from night or clouds, often simply presents more danger: one can't so easily see and avoid antagonists as one can in clear daylight. The likelihood of finding darker skinned persons in hotter, more southern climates (particularly from the perspective of peoples of colder, more northern climates) is simply a fact of human existence, one that past generations have sometimes exploited to evil effect, but with which

2. Heart of Darkness, Heart of Light

Tolkien wholeheartedly disagreed.[8] In his letters he makes explicit statements against racism and apartheid. Most important, evil in Middle-earth does not devolve to southern or darker peoples; it plagues all sentient creatures equally, and for the same reasons. And darkness as a metaphor need imply anything about skin color; there American readers continue to fight a battle with our own horrific past that we need not impose on Tolkien's fiction.

Readers of *The Lord of the Rings* (or, more likely, film-goers) see only a small part of Tolkien's world. The most evil figures in *The Lord of the Rings* are Sauron and Saruman, neither of whom Tolkien depicts as having dark skin—Saruman begins, in fact, as The White. In the stories of the legendarium set well back in time, the greatest evils come, if not from Morgoth, from both elves and humans who turn away from the Valar; their greed and weakness and violence allow Sauron to gain sway. The humans of Westernesse fall in an Atlantean story of carelessness, pride, and selfishness. No people or race has a greater likelihood of goodness than another (though humans in general may most readily turn to evil), regardless even of more characteristic intention and preferences: the elves like woods and natural growth, the hobbits gently rolling tillable land, and dwarves mountains and caverns. Evil comes, when it comes, from bad choices, from failures of the will to do good, from desire to control others or to hoard. Isildur makes the greatest of blunders when he fails to destroy the Ring at a time when he may do so easily—at least in a physical sense. The Ring gains sway over him quickly, not because he desires to do evil, but because, despite his courage in battle and his presence of mind to preserve the fruit of the White Tree Nimloth, he hasn't the strength of will to destroy a weapon of power and an object of such great desire. Having suffered and conquered as he has, he still hasn't gained either by his nature or his learning the ability to resist its power. Gollum/Sméagol did not begin as a bad creature, but as a proto-hobbit with a will, as with so many humans, too easily swayed by greed, desire, and self-obsession.

As does *Excalibur*, Tolkien's fiction exploits ambient darkness throughout the quest to destroy the Ring: nearly all of it takes place in the darkness or at least under cover, to allow the members of the Fellowship to make their way to Mordor with as little likelihood as possible of detection. The journey through Moria takes place almost entirely in the dark; ironically, the greatest danger comes from light, by which orcs may discover the questers, or the fire of the Balrog, a creature who dwells in the dark but was born in and derives its power from flame. Lothlórien, too, though, is to outsiders a land of darkness, shadowed by wood and magic, not only because the elves are folk of the forests, but also because it must remain protected and hidden for their safety.

Frodo and Sam's journey into Mordor takes, with Gollum's advice, a disastrous turn, as they take the dark path of Cirith Ungol into Shelob's lair. But could any other path have succeeded? Without what we may have to term their deep-down spiritual strength and the help of Galadriel's glass, they would have failed and died horribly—and the quest with them and their world after them. The small lights of the Dead Marshes could lead them to drowning in its ubiquitous pools, but the small vial of elven light drives back a relentless adversary and returns them to the half-light or mere-light of Mordor, weakened nearly to death but still on course to succeed. At the fire of Mt. Doom Frodo does fail: he turns to his own darkness, unwilling at last, like Isildur, to destroy the Ring despite the pain it causes him. The same disease that caught Gollum from the first and Isildur quite soon catches Frodo at last. Only Gollum's monomania allows Frodo the opportunity to turn back to the light again, in the near darkness of the mountain's cavern, where, freed of the power of the Ring, he can return to himself. Even the safest of creatures to carry the Ring has an inkling of "darkness" of spirit within him, and the self returns when the obsession of the Ring has gone.

But that self has fallen. Frodo of all creatures makes the best choice to carry the Ring because he has the least desire for the powers it affords, yet even he can't remain entirely immune to its lure. All the characters of Tolkien's world have the potential to succeed, and all have the potential to fall. No one—no one—makes a good choice to carry the Ring. As with Gandalf or Galadriel, one might take it intending to do good, but the power at last would overcome, because it would allow even the best of creatures to impose his or her will on another. No one else could have carried it further than Frodo; probably no one, having got it that far, could have destroyed it. Isildur, a man of strength and courage and will, had the best chance anyone had ever had, because he had the Ring for so short a time and during moments when Sauron had no power over it. Yet he could not destroy it. Aragorn or Faramir (or someone like them, heroic yet unselfish and devoted to service and generosity) may have the character necessary, but could either have got into Mordor as unobtrusively as do Frodo and Sam? Wouldn't the fact of their own prowess and their strength of will have brought about their failure, exposing them to Sauron's armies?

The quest succeeds by sacrifice, the acceptance of an impossible task because it appears the "right" thing to do (and probably the only thing to do). That sacrifice leads not, as in Joseph Campbell's terms, to bliss, but to a sense of loss and sadness even in the victory it creates, a peculiar kind of darkness, lesser than that of bearing the Ring but an effect of having borne it. This story of great darkness broken by brief rays of light comes from a person who had seen war, loss, suffering, the needless destruction of a generation. Why did we fight World War I? At least for Tolkien the War of the Ring has a purpose: saving a world worth saving, though perhaps saving it in the dark: no one besides Frodo and Sam sees its real end, the destruction of the Ring, and they have then no hope of returning home.[9] Only the intervention of the eagles, creatures of the light and the air, with Gandalf's wisdom to guide them, can accomplish that miracle. But even the possibility of that miracle depended on another, and one filled not with good but with selfish and evil intentions: Gollum, having come from the darkness of his own cave beneath the mountain, pursues the Ringbearers to another mountain cave. His end comes in his own joy: he dissolves in the fiery lake having regained the prize that obsesses him. The message to Tolkien's time and to those to come couldn't be much clearer: in light or in darkness, we must let go of our obsessions or be destroyed by them. Yet the only evil darkness comes from within. That idea, driving the story of the Silmarils as well as that of the Ring, emerges as one of Tolkien's most important.

Complications of light and dark, from Smaug's cavern and the Arkenstone to Mordor and the fires of Doom to the loss of the Silmarils and the nightly rise of Eärendil's star, drive Tolkien's characters in as broad and intricate a weave of story as one can find. Scholes, Phelan, and Kellogg aver that the "greatest narratives are inevitably those in which the most is attempted" (16). Right....

3

The World of the Text and the Expanding Waste Land

Eliot's *The Waste Land* hints not just at his own internal landscape, but also at the post–World War I landscape of Europe and, in some ways, much of the world spiritually. He drew himself out of it to some extent (at least in religious terms) in his later poetry, returning to Christianity. Devotion to Christianity and the Greenworld, in which Tolkien never flagged, though they can't appear as such in Middle-earth, create tensions and terrors that inform Middle-earth and inflect his narrative. Tolkien grapples with a Waste Land of war and quest and duty and death that threatens disaster, but survives on the basis of a spiritual connection both of characters to a sense of something greater and of the author to his green and numinous creation. This chapter will explore further connections to T. S. Eliot along with issues of war and the environment. Eliot, along with Conrad and Joyce and sometimes Yeats and Woolf, appears in literary discussions as guiding voices of the time, but Tolkien as well as anyone addresses the problems that most shook the world and resonated through the early to middle part of the twentieth century. Apocalypticism, Christian, social, and environmental, has haunted our last hundred years.

Middle-earth and the Waste Land: Greenwood, Apocalypse, and Post-War Resolution

"There were giants on the earth in those days."—Genesis 6:4

Despite the Inklings' distrust of T. S. Eliot and his methods, we may draw some productive direct comparisons between *The Silmarillion* (plus

3. The World of the Text and the Expanding Waste Land

parts of *The Lord of the Rings* and *The Hobbit*) and Eliot's *The Waste Land*. Those divergent works exhibit rather extraordinary parallel concerns with the landscapes of "end-times" in personal, social, and cosmic terms. Significant commonalities emerge through various lenses—for instance, through extreme landscapes, concerns with hidden brutalities, and culturally precipitous moments. Together they create an intertextual sense of ambivalence buffered by differently but exquisitely textured confrontations with resolution. As Shippey has noted in *Author of the Century*, Eliot observed of Modernism that it allowed a writer to replace narrative method with "mythical method," and a concern with myth had provided the "whole drive of Tolkien's work" (313). Both *The Waste Land* and Tolkien's fiction find their particularity in non-realistic approaches to fully realistic feelings and ideas—and in the writers' responses to post-war devastation both physical, in the landscape of Europe, and emotional, in the suffering of individuals and nations worldwide. These authors grappled, as did many others, with loss on a grand as well as on a personal scale. For this discussion I will attend, of course, to both Tolkien's and Eliot's texts, but I'll direct my course particularly by means of Professor Shippey's notable commentary on Tolkien (such as his ideas of evil). Tolkien's use of both private and mythical landscape and Eliot's unfolding of both blasted and enervated human topography invoke similar themes through different literary modes and means. Both writers foreground the private and public creation of language and landscape to address post-war issues of loss, responsibility, and power.

As Shippey clarifies, many of the post–World War I generation of writers "saw in humanity a basic urge to destruction" and expressed quite clearly that "people could never be trusted, least of all if they expressed a wish for the betterment of humanity" (116–17). But as C. S. Lewis had discovered of *Paradise Lost*, "there was nothing at all grand, dignified and tragic about evil, which was instead tedious, sordid and squalid" (159). In *The Return of the King*, when Denethor in his disease foresees the end of the civilized world in a great fire, its ashes blown away by wind, his vision parallels a nuclear apocalypse, but that vision is also tempered by Frodo's assertion that the great stories never end, though the individual people in them do (Shippey 173, 153). We can resist evil through courage and with the help of luck, by means of the native virtue we can stir up. Tolkien would foreground—as would Eliot in his later work—that the world was made by a force for and of good. We must also persistently resist despair and even weariness: Shippey calls attention to the "French *défaitisme*, a word which came into being about 1918 to express the war-weariness of the Allies, the feeling ... that the sacrifices already made should now be abandoned for an inconclusive peace" (149)—Frodo is finally worn down by the Ring, but Sam must not be, and we must not be, since we, the audience, caught up in the story, have little choice but to see problems through to their end. The Hobbits must "scour" the brutally industrializing Shire before they can attempt to put the War of the Ring behind them. Readers of *The Lord of the Rings* had World War II behind them, but the Cold War before them. The great epic ideas, such as the need for steadfast courage that we find in *Beowulf*, don't relieve a people, an age, the earth of the necessity or fear of an ending; they do, though, allow a means of choice by which we may most likely persist through difficult and even horrifying times, best show kindness and compassion, and leave something behind that may prove worthwhile for ages to come. Tolkien and Eliot seem in *The Waste Land* and *The Lord of the Rings* both to have reached that conclusion, whether tentatively or with spiritual resolve.

Eliot's poem, which appeared in 1922, resolves into five sections: (1) "The Burial of the Dead"; (2) "A Game of Chess"; (3) "The Fire Sermon"; (4) "Death by Water"; and (5) "What the Thunder Said." Burying the dead, a complicated matter after the devastation of a generation that occurred in World War I, begins in the poem with an image of Spring lilacs rising from desiccated land. But the fragile image appears in the "cruelest month" of April: the "dead" are no longer so much the fallen soldiers as the displacement, decadence, and phony spiritualism that preceded and followed the war, their memory as fragile and intoxicating as flowers. Spring will not, should not, cannot renew them: a lost world needs something more permanently tangible and dependable to grasp. The chess game alludes to a distraction from a Renaissance play by Thomas Middleton: a seduction takes place offstage while the game occurs onstage. But conversation, music, parties, and drinking can't fully distract the memory of the dreadful losses of the war, which came about through a seduction by violence, the madness of a pre–World War I generation that feared it wouldn't have the chance for glory in war. Both before and after the war, the Waste Land remains barely below the flimsy

3. The World of the Text and the Expanding Waste Land

cultural cover that attempts to hide it. Part three alludes to Gotama Siddhartha's famous, concentrated homily on the destructive passions of the flesh, with the rape of Philomela, the continuing poverty of the slums, and the sickly fog of the "Unreal City" sifting up through the cacophonous gloom—even confessions of the war's horrors can't stop the City's remnant burning. "Death by Water," the brief fourth section, doesn't wash away the burning, but encourages compassion and meditation on the transience of life. It may refer to Noah's Flood or to the bitter, poisonous waters of Revelation 8:11, but it suggests more a baptism than another death: after the war we must cleanse and rebuild, regardless of how painful the process. "What the Thunder Said," the concluding section, refers to a prophetic utterance in the Book of Revelation that the Bible does not share: "Do not write what the Thunder said," the voice warns in 10:4. But Eliot's thunder calls us to give, sympathize, and exhibit self-control: the individual non-participants must find some way to respond to the horrors of the war that circulate constantly in their midst. *Shantih*, the call for peace that concludes the poem, may comprise simply an ironic, powerless refrain, or it may suggest that true peace comes only from recognition, compassion, purgation, and the will to persist anew.

The polyphonic uncertainty of the poem provides both its beauty and its difficulty, but it leads us either way to a similar point: when we come to an end, we must make an end—not avoid and distract, but bury our dead, create a compassionate peace, do our penance, find new ways to understand and improve our lot, and listen for the warnings that would keep us from repeating our errors. Eliot's Europe missed that last message, and they drew the rest of the world with them into another even more devastating conflict. Tolkien knew, too, as he showed in *The Silmarillion*, that evil and war persist: some people want them, and some may not seek them but can't resist them. The immense loss of World War I did not teach us the necessity of responsibility or the dangers of power and the desire for violence.

For Eliot growth with its trees, flowers, variegation, greenery—the restorative Garden—and accompanying spiritual regeneration doesn't return until 1930's "Ash-Wednesday": a specifically religious as well as a personal and cultural rebirth. Russell Kirk remarked that "Ash-Wednesday" "accomplished more to redeem the time—to attract support for a tolerable civil social order, as well as to restore a consciousness of spiritual order—than did everything Eliot wrote for his *Criterion*" (the literary review that Eliot founded in 1922), and it "turned toward Christianity many of the rising generation" (171). "To care and not to care" (from part I of the poem), Audrey Cahill observes, "reflects the heart of the Christian predicament" (82), and Eliot like Tolkien chose decisively to care and to try to change those things that writing can hope to change (perhaps finding difficulty in achieving detachment). Eliot's commitment to Christianity provides him a means to restore psychological as well as social landscape. The war brought death on a grand scale and the end of an age, but faith restored hope for at least a potentially redemptive apocalypse:

> Blessèd sister, holy mother, spirit of the fountain, spirit of the garden,
> Suffer us not to mock ourselves with falsehood
> Teach us to care and not to care
> Teach us to sit still
> Even among these rocks,
> Our peace in His will
> And even among these rocks [from "Ash-Wednesday," part VI; *Complete Poems* 67].

While, as James Miller points out, Eliot rejected the notion that *The Waste Land* expressed "the disillusion of a generation" and asserted that he "wasn't even bothering whether [he] understood what [he] was saying" (152), Eliot produced more than simply a "personal 'grouse against life'" (frontispiece). We may call the work both a "work of literary criticism" (ix) and, as with Prufrock, a voice that came to speak for a generation, its regrets and fears, whether Eliot intended it to do so or not. "Ash-Wednesday" adds a new chorus: affirmation growing out of the desert land. As did *The Lord of the Rings* with its broader fan base, *The Waste Land* embodied a landscape partly visible and partly invisible to the eye. As Michael North observes, "[t]he multiplicity and incompatibility of human points of view were never more unavoidably obvious than in the early twentieth century, when the Great War focused for the first time nearly the whole of human consciousness on a single event, an odious squabble the purpose of which almost no one could enunciate" (15); Eliot exploits that polyvocality to show how and to what extent, as Hamlet would say, the times were out of joint. "Ash-Wednesday" may have assumed finally,

3. The World of the Text and the Expanding Waste Land

in a smaller scale, the position that *The Silmarillion* did for Tolkien: the "work of the heart." As Eliot searched for spiritual resolution, Tolkien exhibits in his mythography the sense that the waste land will persist externally—we can fight it, but in the long run our hope of success comes only internally, particularly in a world before the Incarnation.

For Tolkien also humanity had got ourselves disjointed from Nature (as well as from God). Both *The Hobbit* and *The Lord of the Rings* foreground the green landscape (both *anti-* and *ante-*waste land), its beauties and dangers and its potential loss (in the war-wrought waste land to come). Tolkien noted that as a boy he loved stories of American Indians "and above all, the forests in such stories" (*Tree and Leaf* 41). The forests, along with vibrant towns and spectacularly architectural cities, evidence a sound heart in a living, breathing Age; their destruction, or their replacement by the rise and fall of blasted or infernal landscapes, marks end-times that we may not assume precede new, redemptive ages for Middle-earth and its peoples. Lórien, Fangorn, and even Mirkwood contrast markedly with the pre-apocalyptic Mordor landscape that Sam sees in *The Return of the King*:

> Hard and cruel and bitter was the land that met his gaze. Before his feet the highest ridge of the Ephel Duath fell steeply in great cliffs down into a dark trough, on the further side of which there rose another ridge, much lower, its edge notched and jagged with crags like fangs that stood out black against the red light behind them.... Far beyond it, but almost straight ahead, across a wide lake of darkness dotted with tiny fires, there was a great and burning glow; and from it rose ... the billowing canopy that roofed in all the accursed land [214].

Sauron took Mordor—"black land," but suggesting also Old English *morþor*, "murder"—in the Second Age, then reclaimed it in the Third Age. *The Silmarillion* records that when Sauron fell,

> the towers of Barad-dûr crumbled in ruin, and at the rumor of their fall many lands trembled. Thus peace came again, and a new Spring opened on earth; and the Heir of Isuldur was crowned King of Gondor and Arnor, and the might of the Dúnedain was lifted up and their glory renewed [365].

The landscape that could have engulfed Middle-earth collapses, but its grounds won't flower soon: evil corrupts the land as it corrupts human hearts, and it leaves behind reminders of ages past—a necessity, given the brevity and inaccuracy of memory alone.

The Silmarillion shares with *The Waste Land* a sense of periodic fragmentation and decay, of dwelling between two worlds, one of energy, desire, and hope, one of failure, destruction, and darkness. Verlyn Flieger describes Tolkien's great myth-creation as "permeated by an air of deepening sorrow, of loss and estrangement, and ever-widening distance from the light and all that it means" ("Matter of Britain" 58). In that sense Tolkien appears in the tradition of Milton and Blake, writers who focus "on the meaning and consequences of the Fall"; like them Tolkien establishes an "extended image of light diminished from its primal brilliance, yet still faintly illuminating the world" (58).[1] All three exploit thereby a lingering feeling of the *grotesque*, in the Romantic sense of that word, of creatures dwelling in the midst of metamorphosis, changing, becoming, uncertain of their direction or end. Frodo in *The Lord of the Rings*, Professsor Flieger adds, "is splintered light, and in his fragmentation he makes obvious the need for re-union with self, with world, and with God that Tolkien feels is Joy beyond the walls of the world" (143); not so much joy as relief and resignation conclude *The Lord of the Rings*, and the repetition of the motif of lost ages directs the course of all the tales of *The Silmarillion*. A sense of loss as powerful as that of Eliot's surreal post–World War I landscape pervades the book, and it has much greater magnitude. Frodo's world, like our post–war age, lay in fragments, and like Humpty Dumpty, we didn't know how to put ourselves, or the World, back together again. Tolkien's notion of "ages" suggests we must put behind us the old fragments: we connect simply reconstruct—what we have destroyed, tainted with evil, we must leave behind; we must instead build anew with new hopes, new leadership, and new ideas, without forgetting what we have known that was good and true and remains so. The greatest moment of renewal in all of *The Lord of the Rings*—which Peter Jackson transfers as Gandalf's words of hope to Pippin as battle reaches its climax in Minas Tirith—comes at its conclusion, as Frodo sales from the Grey Havens with the elves and Gandalf into the West, where "it seemed to him that as in his dream in the house of Bombadil, the grey rain-curtain turned all to silver glass and was rolled back, and he beheld white shores and beyond them a far green country under a swift sunrise" (*The Return of the King* 385). What Frodo finds we but glimpse: a healed landscape of sunshine and greenery where old cares can finally fall away. *The Silmarillion*, in contrast, shows

3. The World of the Text and the Expanding Waste Land

only serial rise and fall, and hope rests finally in the limited and occasional human and elven ability to eschew evil and seek good and in the knowledge of a kind Creator beyond the bounds of the world.

"Ainulindalë" ends with "the first battle of the Valar with Melkor for the dominion of Arda. "Valaquenta" concludes with the War of Wrath and the defeat of Melkor/Morgoth; the Valar thrust Morgoth through the Door of Night beyond the world, but "so great was the fury of those adversaries that the northern regions of the western world were rent asunder" (303), and the shape of the lands changed: Middle-earth's waste land. "Akallabêth" recounts another rise and fall, that of Númenor; when the Númenórean king Ar-Pharazôn sets foot upon the shores of the Blessed Realm, "claiming the land as his own." Then "Manwë upon the Mountain called upon Ilúvatar," who "showed forth his power, and he changed the fashion of the world; and a great chasm opened in the sea between Númenor and the Deathless Lands ... [a]nd all the fleets of the Númenóreans were drawn down into the abyss ... and the mortal warriors that had set foot upon the land of Aman were buried under falling hills ... [and] the land of Aman and Eressëa of the Eldar were taken away and removed beyond the reach of Men for ever. And Andor, the Land of Gift, Númenor of the Kings ... was utterly destroyed" (334). The images are Atlantean and the style Biblical. The Third Age ends as does the second, with the destruction of Sauron and a new Spring for Middle-earth, the course of which lies in the hands of humans, to preserve or to destroy. Each age recapitulates its apocalyptic motifs and unfolds its potential waste lands: the unveiling of a time of fall, followed by hope of renewal and warnings of the responsibilities and dangers that go with the gifts of land and life.

As Shippey observes in "Tolkien as a Post-War Writer," we can see Tolkien not just as post–World War I writer, but also "in essence as a post–World War II writer, one of that group "whose subjects were war and evil [and] ... who wrote in non-realistic modes essentially because they felt they were writing about subjects too great and too general to tie down to particular and recognisable settings" (235). We can see evil as an "addiction" (228), as W. H. Auden added, "defiantly chosen" so that eventually it "can no longer imagine anything but itself" (qtd. in Shippey 231). While the First World War led the parties involved in the Second to conceal their brutalities the more skillfully, the Second War vastly extended both the destruction of landscape and the Landscape of Destruction—any question of whether and to what extent the world had changed exploded in fire bombs, death camps, and the waste land of the Nuclear Age. As both world wars appeared to end all wars, they marked the turn from an old age of hand-to-hand warfare to a new age of mass destruction, Cold War, and terrorism. We exhibited a perverse desire for lingering lethality. *The Silmarillion* similarly shows a series of protagonists and antagonists bent, age after age, not only on rule, but also on destruction. Their desire for vengeance, acquisition, or domination deconstructs the earth around them, reshaping or eliminating much of what was beautiful, lasting, and good. And the scope and influence of the book extended far beyond its original intent; as Shippey points out in *Author of the Century*, "*The Silmarillion* centered ... on the sins of possession and mastery and the desire to exercise skill whatever the consequences," making it ultimately "less a mythology for England and more one for its own time" (260–610)—the book becomes not just of its time and place, but for its time and its world in the time to come.

While Tolkien never fell into cynicism, and while his narrative hardly shied from the darkness and evil of both internal and external landscapes, and while the resurrective quality of the greenwood lasts only so long, he located in Middle-earth's movement from age to age potential for both resolution and at least occasional comfort. Though the greenwood even as anti-waste land doesn't always provide a place of "goodness" or safety—Treebeard will not take kindly to anyone who threatens his forest or who even enters surreptitiously, and Old Man Willow is dangerous to anyone unwary—it allows natural growth. In the forest, as Marjorie Burns notes (quoting from *The Fellowship of the Ring*), "everything is 'very much more alive'" (85); that eminently living quality empowers the author's hope. Tolkien's sense of Christian optimism—not for this world, but for the world to come—translated in Middle-earth as a renewable landscape with fading, yet remnant and still-powerful greenwood. Eliot, too, recovered from the spiritual dryness of his fragmented waste land to find a garden of spiritual consolation not in a narrative world, but in a refreshing flood of imagistic hope. Tolkien and Eliot both realized that the resolve to replant the waste land must come from within; Eliot took longer than Tolkien to agree on the source of hope, but he came more quickly to believe that we could actu-

3. The World of the Text and the Expanding Waste Land

ally do something physically constructive with it. For both writers, so different in thought, method, and sensibilities, the end of an Age, the slow, painful step from the wasteland of World War I and post-war malaise to the briefest respite, filled with its own detachment and woe, unveils neither goodness nor eucatastrophe. Instead, what resolution we can find comes in the hope that a person and a people may breathe, look about, and gather strength for the mad gyre that spins itself into the Age ahead. In mutual song, complex and symphonic, though hardly harmonic, the two writers, not as far apart in their thinking as their divergent styles may suggest, chant for us the same message: find courage, find joy, and pray earnestly, and write what matters.

A Postscript to Tolkien and Eliot: Some New Leaves on Some Old Branches

Tolkien and Eliot were both in their own way "language writers." Tolkien not only created his own languages and used them to help develop his fictional world, but also worked in his dialogue with register and degrees of formality and solemnity to distinguish the emotional complexes of different peoples and events. Eliot, perhaps partly under the impetus of Ezra Pound's editorial hand, helped direct the course of the language—both verbal and imagistic—of Modernism. Most of us inevitably and aptly associate Tolkien with philology, a linguistic approach to scholarship and literary enjoyment that until after World War II required no defense. The nearly necessary way of academe's old—and still worthwhile—values pervaded university curricula and critical dialogue, a way not of effete gentility, but of tenacious rigor and tireless pursuit of understanding joined with love of the subject matter and good talk with anyone interested in it. Curiously, Eliot's interest in language and allusion drew (and draws) raves from Modern critics, but, even having heard that Tolkien was a philologist, the critics often miss the same qualities in his work. Like Eliot Tolkien was a "language poet," though more so in his prose than in his verse, which relies more on Old and Middle English sources and ballads and other songs than on linguistic play for its own sake. Tolkien's poems work better sung or chanted than if one simply reads them off the page.

Tolkien, of course, worked in the crease between his own fervent Catholicism and his admiration for the "pagan" Germanic "theory of courage"; the "'flavour' of Snorri and of Norse tradition as a whole" derives in part from its "endemic good humor," Shippey observes, and Tolkien adapted that tone in different ways but continually through his fiction (*Roots* 279–80)—the good humor in Norse materials often comes in the face of disaster. That familiar and somewhat familial sense of humor sets Tolkien apart from Eliot and much of the modernist generation and has probably contributed to some critics' sense that Tolkien's work lacks what Matthew Arnold might have called the "high seriousness" necessary for canonicity. But Tolkien also borrowed from that world a tension between heroic courage and the rising Christianity, its tendency toward proverbiality, and its fear of the corrupting influence of the "dragon-sickness" (greed, or the "disease of ownership," page 349), even as he echoed from the later Finnish *Kalevala* the sorrow of "dispossession and replacement" (34). His persistent attention to words and names, details that eluded most scholarship, led him on a mission of search and rescue; he felt himself "a kindred spirit of the poets, not only cleaning and restoring what they had written, but going on to use it in the way they had intended" (178)—that is, creatively, not merely scribally. Shippey hints at a nominal connection: from Old Norse *tulkr* to English *tolke*, "spokesman" (193)—close to *Tulkas* and not far at all from *Tolkien*. But he stresses that philology produces more than hints, if one pursues it correctly and energetically. A textual problem triggers imagination, because it is not, finally, merely a textual problem: it invokes a mythological explanation and implies an essential "real-world meaning," which, to be true to one's calling, one must pursue and refine over a lifetime (349). Tolkien was doing for language and linguistics what the Grimms did for story and fairy tale. Names, if we pursue them, as Tolkien knew and as Shippey so appropriately recapitulates, lead to stories, "myths," and to some extent modernism, as Eliot suggested, had "made it possible to replace narrative method with by 'mythical method'" (*Author of the Century* 313). War, the waste land, and the declining greenwood had highlighted the necessity of myth-making and the further, more intense interpretation of myth as a means—as Joseph Campbell would say—to throw ourselves into the midst of even the nasty bits of life with all its grit and gore. Our survival in the wake of our own destructiveness has perhaps come to depend on it.

3. The World of the Text and the Expanding Waste Land

The very first essay in *Roots and Branches*, "Tolkien and the *Beowulf*-Poet," focusing on Tolkien's constant fascination with names and place names in the Anglo-Saxon heroic poem, notes that "the conclusion he [Tolkien] drew from such continuities between ancient poetry and modern life" is that "the heroes of antiquity had not gone away. They were still there, in the landscape, in names, and probably in the gene-pool" (18). Heroism endemic in the landscape may help mend the waste land. We can only hope that the same holds true for the next generation of our most heroic scholars. In the final essay of the volume, on Peter Jackson's adaptation of *The Lord of the Rings* for film, Shippey asserts that while Jackson "may not have been able to cope with all the ramifications of Tolkien on Providence" [as, he adds, few have], he "certainly succeeded in conveying much of the ... narrative core ... the difference between Prime and Subsidiary Action, the differing styles of heroism, the need for pity as well as courage, the vulnerability of the good, the true cost of evil" ... while showing the courage to retain the "sad, muted, ambiguous ending of the original" (386)—more than one dare ask of any filmmaker or any novelist, however great and however scholarly. In an essay on "Heroes and Heroism," Shippey asks his readers "once again to reflect on *work*, what we do regularly for a living: it is the Great Unsaid of fiction, and of criticism" (268)—our daily work effects the embodiment of our creative impulse. Tolkien's sense of *work* included the "scholarly" and the creative" to such an extent that we can hardly separate them, and he approached it with the same critical incisiveness that Eliot helped resuscitate. Shippey concludes *Roots and Branches*, punning on his own earlier book's title, with the hope that Jackson's films will help "new readers facing a new experience, and finding once again Tolkien's road to Middle-earth" (386)—in a sense, to unveil to a new generation a world that can profitably absorb their attentions. Readers, filmgoers, and the next generation of critics may well follow both Eliot's and Tolkien's roads if we wish also to continue to build creatively our own gardens in the intellectual landscape.

Significantly, neither Eliot nor Tolkien stopped at the waste land, though both perhaps most famously paused there. Eliot went through his own personal and psychological Waste Land, from which the poem largely comes; from it he recovered sufficiently to regain his Christianity. Tolkien lived through his own Waste Land in World War I; he never lost his Christianity, if anything came to affirm it even more fully, but he lost something of the hope he may have had in his earlier life for humanity and our ability—or willingness—to regain the greenwood. One might suggest that *The Two Towers* (even more than the Mordor sections of *The Return of the King*) is Tolkien's *Waste Land*, and *Ash Wednesday* is Eliot's *Return of the King*. The former two describe landscapes on the brink of unrecoverable disaster; the latter two provide not a journey to bliss, but a means to healing, especially human spiritual healing. Whether by landscape or by journey or by our deepest psychological responses to either, Tolkien was no less a writer of ideas than Eliot, Greene, Orwell, or anyone else of his generation. His concern with the waste land and its aftermath place him in the center of the intellectual landscape.

4

Tolkien on Heroism
Beorhtnoth, Aragorn, and Arthur

Erich Auerbach's historical study of mimesis, the Greek idea of how art imitates nature, opened space for a narrative strategy that allows rapid juxtaposition, apposition, and addition of historical, spatial, imaginative, and aural elements. Tolkien's play with mimesis—an almost inevitable step for any writer in the Western tradition—led to one of the most important aspects of his success: the creation of a fully imagined world that yet seems to his readers true and compelling. It maintains internal consistency while exploring adventures that address some of the deepest concerns of his century and of literary history. The ideas of the mimetic creative world both reflect and inflect those of the physical world in which we live, and serious storytelling moves toward prophetic elements that interpret and comment on contemporary culture. Works need not be explicitly didactic to do so; the writer need only care about what he or she is doing, care enough about the reader to try the tell a worthy story, and grapple with ideas worth careful consideration.

Mimetic/Prophetic Heroism: Auerbach, The Battle of Maldon, *and* Beorhtnoth, Beorhthelm's Son

In the first chapter of *Mimesis* Auerbach contrasts the "realism" of the *Odyssey* with that of the Bible. While Homer produced "an externalization of phenomena in terms perceptible to the senses" (6), a constant foreground, a "uniformly illuminated, uniformly objective present" (7), concealing nothing, "no teaching and no secret meaning" (13), biblical stories aim instead "not to bewitch the senses," but to make concrete the "moral, religious, and psychological phenomena which are their sole concern" (14). Auerbach shows that both texts foundationalize the sense of "realism," a written text's potential to approach what happens in life, according to the assumptions and predilections of their age, and yet their claims to "truth" differ: "The Bible's claim to truth," wrote Auerbach, "is not only far more urgent than Homer's, it is tyrannical—it excludes all other claims" (14) and "insists that it is the only real world" (15). Both realism and truth value contribute to our sense of *mimesis*, luring readers into an agreement that a text imitates life in some way that has value and immediacy for us. But what authors attempt and what readers accept as mimetic varies from age to age; to some degree their approaches show us, Auerbach concludes, not only how their time understood imitation and how they used it in literature, but also how through imitation they interpreted reality (554).

In subsequent chapters Auerbach demonstrates how in the Classical tradition the use of objective detail, the acquisition of a "grand style" for "graphic dramatization" (39) of events, and the "recording"— or more likely *invention*—of precise, concise, and rhetorically powerful speeches lent credibility and stir to mimetic or "historical" texts. Later Christian tradition (not just in biblical text but also in commentaries, exegeses, and stories), borrowing much from the Old Testament methods, serves, for example in Augustine, "to explain the historical situation in rational terms and to reconcile the figural interpretation with the conception of an uninterrupted historical sequence of events" (75) in such a way as to teach a specific lesson. That is, the "real" to the Christian audience existed in the interpretive step by which "an occurrence on earth signifies not only itself but at the same time another, which it predicts or confirms" (555)—an essentially Platonic suggestion that something has reality to the degree that it illuminates to our imperfect perception the accepted truth of sacred texts or culturally central or necessary notions. We learn what Homer's heroes had to say to one another; what, though (to use an Old Testament example), Auerbach asks (11), did Abraham and Isaac talk about on their way to the sacrifice? We don't learn more than we need to know, because the reality of the story doesn't deal with the details of what they did or said, other than as they respond to God's command. The story attends to the moral and cultural meaning, where for writer and reader reality exists: in the permanent message rather than the ephemeral details. In either tradition heroism exhibits mimetic qualities, but they vary, and either audience would have found the other's something between peculiar and profane.

While someone such as Augustine could meld traditions, borrowing from Classical models "their precise gradation of temporal, comparative, and concessive hypotaxes," a variety of links, subordinations, and predications, his writing shows the "struggle in which the two worlds were engaged in matters of language" (Auerbach 75). The style of later heroic texts, the *Chanson de Roland*, for instance, exhibits no tendency toward "analysis or explanation," but rather a "paratactic bluntness" (101) eschewing rhetorical flourishes—though allowing for obvious typologies—without even the kind of commentarial "digressions" that we have in *Beowulf*. "For audiences of the eleventh, twelfth, and thirteenth centuries the heroic epic was history" and "[n]o other tradition existed" (122), Auerbach argues—audiences not so far removed from the time, subject, and approach of the Old English *Battle of Maldon*.

Of course the central theme of *Maldon*, adherence to the code of heroic duty, emerges pellucidly, and the poem's structure and style build toward that theme in the epic/historic mode that Auerbach describes. It has the strong sense of the elegiac that Tolkien borrowed, but it also engages another significant form of discourse: prophecy, not in its modern predictive sense, but in its more Old Testament–like aim to diagnose the present and offer its prescription for proper behavior. Geoffrey Shepherd, a younger contemporary of Tolkien's, elucidated this subject in several essays.[1] In "The Prophetic Cædmon" Shepherd notes that prophets were common to all early Christian societies (5) and that "prophecy is a common enough feature in the records of early England" (4). While the essay ties Cædmon to the tradition of dream vision and inspired song and expresses the point that speakers gain a recognized authority through public acceptance of the prophetic origin of their words (10), *prophecy* again means more than prediction of events or outpouring of religious sentiments. As Pope Gregory the Great clarified, Shepherd explains, "prophecy may be truth about the past: it can illuminate present mysteries also. Indeed prophecy is best defined as the disclosing of hidden things" (5). In Old Testament tradition most of the prophets deal with the problems of the present: they speak out God's displeasure with improper behaviors and warn about the consequences should such behaviors persist. "Many of the features of early English poetry, vernacular as well as Latin, may require interpretation in terms of this belief and in terms of the conventions which this belief in prophecy and the practice of prophecy engendered" (10), adds Shepherd: even the heroic poetry may yield satisfying readings via our considering them as prophetic as well as mimetic texts.

We may draw for comparison upon Wulfstan's *Sermo Lupi ad Anglos* (ca. 1010), the purport of which chastises the people for craven behavior and backsliding in the midst of troubles such as viking raids—a theme of course dear to the *Maldon* poet. The *Sermo Lupi* urges courage and preparation in God's name, but it addresses what may seem rather a social failing until we see the homily in the light of Auerbach's and Shepherd's approaches: the theme makes use of, as Auerbach would say, a "figural" conception, or what we might also call typology, in that the heroic/prophetic discourse appeals not just to church and military leaders, but to everyone—for Wulfstan, anyone who would wish to be numbered among God's people, and thus among those sufficiently brave and faithful to earn the title of Christian hero.

While *Maldon* (describing an event allocated in the *Anglo-Saxon Chronicle* to the year 991) does not proclaim itself as explicitly biblical in style or theme, it does, as Shepherd exemplifies in his essay "Scriptural Poetry," throw considerable focus upon Byrhtnoð's death-prayer, which uses predictable Christian rhetorical turns:

> Geþancie þe, ðeoda Waldend,
> ealra þæra wynna þe ic on worulde gebad.
> Nu ic ah, milde Metod, Mæste þearfe
> þæt þu minum gaste godes geunne,
> þæt min sawul to ðe siðian mote
> on þin geweald, Þeoden engla,
> mid friþe ferian. Ic eom frymdi to þe
> þæt hi helsceaðan hynan ne moton.

[Thank you, ruler of peoples, for all of those joys that I received in the world. Now I have need, mild maker, that you grant my spirit this good, that my soul may travel to you, fare with peace into your protection, king of angels. I implore you that hellish-enemies not hinder it] [lines 173–80].

The kenning epithets call to mind "Cædmon's Hymn": the rhetorical pattern follows that of a typical Anglo-Saxon prayer (with an interesting glance at the idea of Byrhtnoð's "traveling" to God). The term for the invaders reminds one of the monsters in *Beowulf*, and the *engla* may, as

4. Tolkien on Heroism

Gregory did, pun on "English." The prayer aims to make the hero's salvation even more real than his death, which follows immediately. Byrhtnoð is hewn down with two loyal followers, suggesting on one hand Christ on the Cross and on the other that those faithful to him die rightly and earn the same salvation he does. The scene significantly blends history with those elements Auerbach attributes to both Classical and Christian mimetic texts: specific detail plus direct recorded speech and the teleological appeal; it also follows Shepherd in that it prophesies the end of the English in that battle and sets a social standard that defines the Christian/warrior's courageous, sacrificial ethic. Tolkien employs a similar sense of commitment in *The Return of the King* as the small band of soldiers gathers before Mordor just as the Ring nears destruction.

As Shepherd asserts in "*Beowulf*: An Epic Fairy Tale," a fairy tale stands in relief against a good deal of historical and cultural information: along with verifiable names and events, we get the "strict court and military etiquette, with kin-structures and family obligations and with personal and social values" as well as constant reference "to the material objects of the culture, to halls, arms, ships, equipment and furnishings" (53). "*Beowulf* has," Shepherd adds, "sufficient scope and genius for it to be regarded as a summation of a culture" (54), and where we may expect the use of magic in the story, "the poet substitutes and emphasizes instead the efficacy of human virtue and divine providence" (55). The poet uses the past, Shepherd argues, not so much in the way of an antiquarian, but in that of a romantic, an aspect of the poem, Shepherd explains, that "Tolkien exemplifies much more powerfully in the *Lord of the Rings* than he did directly in his lecture about *Beowulf*. The poem is charged with evocation of an ancient unrealizable world of which the details may sound precise and solid, but it is their resonance that matters" (56). Auerbach might say that the *Beowulf*-poet uses the factual details mimetically, but that the true mimetic effect of the poem lies in its themes, of which the impinging Christian influence might aim to argue their timeless ascendancy. In "*Beowulf*: The Monsters and the Critics," Tolkien argues that "the theory of courage, which is the great contribution of early Northern literature," or the "creed of unyielding" (68) that dominates the mood and tone of the poem elevate it as a historical document, one of a "time of fusion" (70) when Northern imagination met Christian Scripture (71). *Beowulf*, however Christian or

Christianized, remains a poem of the "mortal hemmed in a hostile world" (72), and the poet "is still concerned primarily with *man on earth*, rehandling in a new perspective an ancient theme" (73). That theme, transience, and how we choose to deal with it, rivets the poem, fantastic elements or not, in a mimetic frame of reference. Now no one would call *Maldon* fairy tale, but it exploits the same themes that Shepherd and Tolkien ascribe to *Beowulf*, which does have fairy tale elements, suggesting that to the Anglo-Saxon audience, the mimetic quality comes not in the antecedent tale, but in the message and in the way the protagonists carry it out.

Maldon, despite Byrhtnoð's prayer, retains elements of what Tolkien would call Northern tradition interlaced with Christian rhetoric. Tolkien calls particular attention to the fact that while *Beowulf* may come from folktale, one stylistic factor in particular distinguishes it: its "high tone, the sense of dignity" that evidences a "mind lofty and thoughtful" (61). While *Maldon* derives from a historical event rather than a folktale, and thus we may at first suggest its purpose as more exactly mimetic, more importantly to an Anglo-Saxon audience it addresses a lofty, dignified, traditional theme, a theme that for the audience had probably a much greater reality and immediacy than the specific details recorded in the poem.

And the poem moves quickly, I would say paratactically, to that theme. The poet likes to take up narremes with *þa*, "then," or occasionally "when," which acts as a simple chronological connective: when one thing happens, then another happens because of that. The pattern somewhat mimics that of the *Anglo-Saxon Poetic Records*, where yearly entries often begin with *her*, "then" or "in that year," but *Maldon* does so with artistic unity. When their lord commands them, the English follow. When the viking messenger delivers his demands, Byrhtnoð only rhetorically asks for his soldiers' thoughts; he then commands their military reply. When the tide ebbs, the invaders advance. We learn the names of the English defenders, both those who stand their ground and fight bravely, and those who flee: part of the historicizing mimetic and paratactic necessity. We learn only what we must learn as exempla, with the kind of specific information that can convince an audience that the poet knew the facts. Knowing the facts, he may clarify his theme, which he does through direct speech. The poem has little waste, little in the way of digression, little if any hypotaxis.

4. Tolkien on Heroism

We may feel tempted to read the direct speeches as, at least narratively, hypotactic: they interrupt the flow of narrative. But, as in Classical models, for the Anglo-Saxon audience they serve as the points around which the narrative condenses, much in the same way that rubrics in New Testaments call our attention to their most important rhetoric, Jesus' words. As Byrhtnoð's prayer calls attention to a Christian/allegorical reading of his heroic demise as a martyrdom rather than a tactical disaster, so too does his call to the vikings to cross the causeway and allow God to decide the day, drawing us to themes of courage, faith, and fair play.

Similarly, after their leader has fallen and the English have lost hope of winning, the poet adds additional exemplary speeches to reinforce themes. In lines 244 and following Leofsunu (we may read the name allegorically as "beloved son" or "praiseworthy son" or "leftover son") vows that he will not flee one foot, but advance to avenge his *winedrihten*, "friend-lord." Even more powerfully Byrhtwold (whose name recalls his lord's) speaks what may be the finest lines in all of English poetry: "Hige sceal þe heardra, heorte þe cenre, / mod sceal þe mare, þe ure mægen lytlað" (lines 313–14). He adds, not sparing obvious detail, "Here lies our elder (or alderman), all hewn up, good one in the dust. Ever may he grieve (*gnornian*), he who would now think to turn from this warplay. I am grown old; I will not from it, but I mean to lie by the side of my lord, the man so dear to me" (315–19). The speech, of course, is not mere personal statement, but exhortation, and not to those at Maldon, but to the poet's audience, applicable both religiously and socially—Wulfstan himself might have written such a thing. The direct speeches, heightened as a poet hardly dare hope, culminate rather than interrupt the paratactic narrative: the story exists for them, not vice versa. The poet heightens the effect by closing (assuming we have the end of the poem) with references to two Godrics, one who stayed, and one who fled: one who accepted heroic martyrdom and one who must, unlike Byrhtwold, live with the memory of having turned away from the heroic moment.

The story, moving rapidly, provides the vehicle by which the terse speeches may deliver their tenor; we get little background, and little we need. Whatever we've lost in the first leaf or even leaves, we have everything essential to the history of *Maldon* and everything essential to its mimetic/prophetic purpose: a constantly illuminated foreground wherein the poet may speak out his word (and probably what he thought of as God's word) to an audience in need—at least so he believed—not of a Beowulf, but of a model by which to call up Beowulf's courage and upon which to place its remaining hopes. The Old English poem need not be a simple conductor of traditional heroic values to say something valuable about heroism, and Tolkien responds to its ambiguity by using both *Maldon* and *Beowulf* productively and ironically in *The Homecoming of Beorhtnoth, Beorhthelm's Son*. Both the poet's audience and that of Tolkien's time might resist the "Ragnarök spirit" that World War II had revived (Shippey, *Author*, 296) and that we have of yet not fully divested ourselves. We must admire heroism, but not sentimentalize it. Torhthelm, the young lover of heroic lays, says of Beorhtnoth,

> His head was higher than the helm of kings
> with heathen crowns, his heart keener
> and his soul clearer than swords of heroes
> polished and proven: than plated gold
> his worth was greater. From the world has
> passed a prince peerless in peace and war [*Tolkien Reader* 9].

The lines echo the conclusion of Beowulf, yet Beorhtnoth (Byrhtnoð) has not killed the dragon—though he may at least have clipped its wings.

Some of what we lose of the more quotidianly mimetic in the paratactic *Maldon*, we regain in Tolkien's *The Homecoming of Beorhtnoth, Beorhthelm's Son*. While the brief play ends with the Ely monks singing a dirge, the whole thing properly serves as a realistic coda to the Old English heroic poem. Two men must find and carry the headless corpse of the hero to the abbey for funeral rites—not Beowulf's pyre, but mass and Christian burial. The youth uses the alderman's sword, despite the remonstrance of the elder man, to kill one thief and drive off others pilfering treasures from the dead—a deed unnecessary, but who would be able to avoid it, fearing Danish raiders in the dark? Tolkien knew from his own experience that even after heroism—successful or failed—someone must clean up in the darkness and chant a prayer that, for those of us left, tomorrow will come and that we too may find, if not victory in battle, perhaps redemption at last. And like Bilbo most of us would join Torhthelm in soon adding "I wish we were back" (13), in this case not even home, but to their wagon, something they can recognize in the dark. "God guide our road to a good ending" (15), he will add shortly,

4. Tolkien on Heroism

and his companion "ever work and war till the world passes" (17) in another *contemptus mundi* that must have felt as common in World War I trenches as it does for anyone studying medieval literature.

Yet Tolkien's response in *The Homecoming* creates some more difficult and interesting problems yet. He undercuts the idea of Germanic heroism that he seems elsewhere to use and admire, and he also undercuts the poetic praise of it. Shippey has observed in it a "spiritual tension … which creates at once insecurity, apology, and power," a response to the "seductive" quality of the old heroic ideal"; but Tolkien was aiming to "reconcile a Christian attitude and a heroic attitude, and would have liked very much to feel that his ancestors … had tried to do the same thing" (*Roots* 339). Shippey sees in Tolkien's play a "highly personalized interpretation of *Maldon*" (339), and something like it had already appeared in *The Hobbit* in Bilbo's reaction (though of course it could not be specifically Christian) to the Battle of Five Armies: he may admire the heroism, but would rather stay far from it and would even prefer yet that the need for it never arose. Tolkien did create that heroic alternative in Aragorn, Faramir, and Gandalf. But though *The Homecoming* takes the form of medievalism, fantasy, it does so in quite a realistic way: two common persons searching the body of the dead for their lord so they may take it for proper funeral rites. Kocher notes, the play "drives home with utter immediacy the horror of a carnage that need never have happened" (*Master* 185), and, further, it focuses on how, as a "wasteful" act of war, it "cuts off the young" (187): it not only ruins the lives of those not ready for what they have tried to do, but decimates—or worse—the next generation, leaving it also depleted and mourning. Kocher calls the play "a warning against disproportion in the uses of fantasy"; while it may not serve as a "repudiation … of the heroic northern lays" (193), it does warn against "misreading and misapplication of them" (192). We must understand what we may and should take from literature and what we must not; while we read and write to improve our lives, we must weigh and interpret what we read and measure what we write with great care.

The play's narrative follows a simple pattern, more paratactic than hypotactic, though it is too brief to anything complex; it provides a brief scene of sadness with a silly incident of appended violence that ends in darkness and dirge. It aims quickly to make clear its point: we mustn't let false notions of heroism addle our judgment about the true nature of war, and we must remember and reject our human tendency toward rash and cowardly action. We must find instead compassion, the will to do what we must, and the faith to look ahead.

These readings do, though, overlook another potential interpretation of the poem that it is in fact heroic, but in a different way than we may expect, a way with its own practicality rather than planting its feet in Classical or Germanic heroism. A historical reading of the poem presents the possibility the local English had at some point to stand up to the viking raiders. Byrhtnoð might not have made the best choice of the who and the how, but he may have at least in part succeeded, slowing the raiders so that they might at some point be stopped rather than continuing their course of robbing and killing all the way down the coast. Such a reading makes historical sense without reducing the fact that to participants it would have seemed mad rather than logical. The paratactic poetics of both poems leads us to both possibilities; the play allows us less freedom to take our eyes from the slaughtered youth, a subject that arose powerfully in World War I and haunted the rest of the twentieth century.

Aragorn and the Twentieth-Century Arthur

The twentieth century literary landscape loved Arthurian tales, but it needed a new and better King Arthur, and the Arthurian world, like *Beowulf*, *Sir Gawain and the Green Knight*, *Ancrene Wisse* (or *Riwle*), and Norse eddas and sagas comprises an important part of Tolkien's intellectual landscape. Aragorn fills the role of the king who will come again (*rex futurus*) but without the evils that plague Arthur and destroy his reign. I once heard detective novelist Mickey Spillane, in response to an interviewer's question about why he wrote what he wrote, respond that he wrote what he wanted to read, but couldn't find. Tolkien provided in Aragorn the hero the twentieth century needed, but couldn't find.

King Arthur has undergone numerous transformations from Geoffrey of Monmouth's and Thomas Malory's warrior king to T. H. White's Wart; he has even, in the *Camelot 3000* comics, awakened in our future to fight invading aliens. He has had his great moments: defeating the

4. Tolkien on Heroism

armies of the Emperor Lucius to become, by "the dignity of his hands," as Malory says, a caesar himself. He has also had his horrifying moments: ordering, Herod-like, the deaths of male infants (to try to destroy Mordred before he grows to bring down the Round Table knights). Arthur has remained as fully present in twentieth-century fiction as he has ever been: books, films, poems, scholarship continually add to the already well-populated world of Arthuriana. To borrow a term from Chaos Science, one may say Arthur fills the role of a "strange attractor," drawing authors and tales to him as someone splendid, to give them a formational basis and an essential if individually variable shape. Needing a great king to unite the peoples of Middle-earth against Sauron and the power of the One Ring, Tolkien, I would like to suggest, evolved Aragorn as a rehabilitation of Arthur: not an avatar, but a courageous, loving, formidable, adaptable, and more appealing figure—someone his twentieth century desperately wanted and hoped for but could scarcely believe in.[2] Aragorn has Arthur's qualities of martial skill, courage, charisma, and hereditary kingship without his negative qualities or his moral/ethical debacles. He becomes, in the realm of the modern Fantastic, what England and Tolkien needed, but knew they couldn't hope to see in real life: a truly good, self-sacrificing leader with character, knowledge, wisdom, and strength. Despite his dangerous bad-boy looks when the hobbits first encounter him, Aragorn provides a guide to noble behavior and a stay against the cynicism the twentieth-century intellectual landscape could seldom avoid—two world wars turned any remnant of turn-of-the-century *Belle Époque* Romanticism to shrapnel. Not Arthur, but Arthur refined, Aragorn as literary character suggests that we should ask and expect a lot of our leaders and that we should ask and expect a lot from ourselves—a point Tolkien made for himself as well as his audience.

Critical response to Tolkien's views of Arthur and Arthuriana often derives from passages in the letters, particularly letter 131 (page 144), but the quotation often ends up truncated and therefore slightly inaccurate as an indicator of Tolkien's feelings about the matter. In the letter Tolkien sets out not to dethrone Arthur, but to explain the genesis of his own imaginary world—Arthur serves there only as a perspective point. Here's the passage more fully than one often finds it:

> Of course there was and is all the Arthurian world, but powerful as it is, it is imperfectly naturalized, associated with the soil of Britain but not with English; and it does not replace what I feel to be missing. For one thing its "faerie" is too lavish, and fantastical, incoherent and repetitive. For another and more important thing: it is involved in, and explicitly contains the Christian religion.[3]

Tolkien isn't dismissing arthuriana any more than he is denigrating Christianity. He wanted to create something fully *English*, not *British*—that's what he means by naturalized—with a land of elves not frivolous or childish or merely hinted at, but realistic, expansive, and still glorious. He wanted a pre–Christian world, because for Tolkien, after the coming of Christ myth recedes or even dies: one can create actual myth no longer. He adds, for further explanation,

> Myth and fairy-story must, as all art, reflect and contain in solution elements of moral and religious truth (or error), but not explicit, not in the known form of the primary "real" world.... I had in mind to make a body of more or less connected legend ... which I could dedicate simply to: to England; my country. It should possess the tone and quality that I desired, somewhat cool and clear, be redolent of our "air" ... and, while possessing (if I could achieve it) the fair elusive beauty that some call Celtic (though it is rarely found in genuine ancient Celtic things), it should be "high," purged of the gross, and fit for the more adult mind of a land long now steeped in poetry [144].

Faery exists in its own fictional world, not as part of Tolkien's Christian worldview. After the next couple sentences he calls his own aim "absurd" (145)—that is, he knows or believes he is asking too much of himself—but still he makes his thinking pretty clear. He wanted a work of high moral and poetic tone and mood in a Fantastic world complete enough to capture an audience's imagination, a world where heroes can fall, but where they have the moral strength to resist falling, where evil exists and has power, but good has free will and the fortitude to persist and assert itself. Such a world must have its own coherence, the telling must aim for beauty to attract and hold readers as well as clarity to makes its tales consistent and understandable, and the tales must show moral and ethical action as essential and always possible. A tale should have, or at least have the potential to reach—to use Tolkien's word—a *eucatastrophe*, or happy ending free of sentimentality. The tale must, to satisfy what Tolkien was searching for, have the feel of something fully English, neither pre–English nor Mediterranean nor Celtic.

4. Tolkien on Heroism

So Tolkien began not with a distaste for Arthur, but with a love for England, a belief that a collection of truly English tales had yet to be told expansively. Further, would someone who disliked Arthuriana go to the trouble of editing and composing a long essay on *Sir Gawain and the Green Knight*? And what of his own poem (which has now reached publication) *The Fall of Arthur*? Clearly Tolkien in fact had a taste for Arthurian material, but it didn't satisfy his creative urge for a more fully complete world with a more nuanced mythology. Nor did Tolkien write to bury Arthur, but to complement him, at least to fill in the lack of a fully English set of mythic fairy-stories that aim for both beauty and moral tenacity—no wonder two generations of post-war critics who believed in neither couldn't understand and appreciate him. Tolkien remained realistic, but not cynical—as a Christian must. He accepted humans as fallen and fallible, but believed us also fully capable of the good and the beautiful. Much of the literati of his time (as of ours) did not share those beliefs.

If Tolkien has a character more nearly Arthur (beyond, of course, *The Fall of Arthur*), he comes among the kings of fallen Númenor. Aragorn fulfills the promise that Arthur, locked in mutual death blows with Mordred, cannot: he is the king who *does* return, not from Avalon or from the dead, but from the remnants of a dead Avalon, from the marches, the shadows, from the promise of an earlier age, the Ranger from the almost-forgotten past who must regain a throne from which, with help, he can save the Western world. He wields the re-forged sword of kingship, a realistic rather than fantastic Excalibur, broken not by his own poor choice or ambition, but by that of his ancestor. Aragorn must regain the kingship that his ancestors lost, the one that has the potential to establish peace.

Like Arthur, Aragorn follows what Joseph Campbell calls the *monomyth*, the pattern that underlies all stories, the movement from some special origin through secretive training to emergence into public life to winning a boon and apotheosis. Aragorn enters the world miraculously, possibly (if events go poorly) the last descendant of the ancient kings of the Western World; he retreats from public life for training and unrecognized public service, returns at the time of greatest public need to prove himself, show his skills, and undertake a great quest, in this case the military defense against Sauron, Saruman, and their armies; he has the "meeting with the goddess," Arwen; he passes his trials—the Ring and the Palantir and Paths of the Dead—and achieves the quest of military defense of Minas Tirith; he acquires and shares a boon, peace, and provides an heir to rule in the next generation before his own apotheosis: passing, like Théoden-king, into the bosom of his fathers. His fills the "Arthur slot," but, to the degree that humans can achieve it, he perfects it: in typological terms, he's the antitype of which Arthur is the type, the fulfillment of an ideal of heroic kingship. He betters Arthur in every respect.

Arthur, of course, while he gains many great victories (as in Malory's "The Tale of the Noble King Arthur That Was Emperor Himself through the Dignity of His Hands"), learns a great deal, provides the setting for the Holy Grail Quest, and attempts to establish a just and stable court, fails in many ways. Arthur does not remain true to Guinevere (nor does Guinevere to him; can we imagine either Aragorn—even facing the love of the incomparable Éowyn—or Arwen straying?); he does not remain true to his principles (as in the slaughter of the infants at the close of part one of "The Tale of King Arthur" in Malory); he breaks the sword of kingship rather than using the re-forged sword successfully, as Aragorn does, to help win an essential battle; he dies rather than leaving an heir or returning to perpetuate a just rule. Aragorn as character achieves what Arthur as character only promises: that, I think, is what Tolkien meant by "purging the grossness" of the story and also what a post-war audience needed and wanted to read (perhaps without even knowing they needed it). Whether they could believe in it as realizable in our world or our time, readers needed to experience its fulfillment in fiction and to believe in its *possibility*—that's one of the major purposes of storytelling and perhaps the only way to recover from the horrors of war. One must believe that despite horrific human action, humans have the potential or can at least imagine the potential to learn to act not only courageously and with self-sacrifice, which world war had taught, but also morally and ethically and lovingly, which war had greatly called into question.

While Arthur undergoes a great quest, to become and remain a great king, he does not undergo the greatest quest of the Arthurian world: Galahad (or in some stories, Perceval) does, the quest for the Holy Grail—in Arthur's world holiness trumps kingship. While Aragorn

4. Tolkien on Heroism

undergoes a great quest in *The Lord of the Rings*, he does not undergo the greatest quest of Tolkien's world: Frodo does, the quest to destroy the Ring. Unlike Galahad's quest, which requires that he find something and which rewards him with salvation, Frodo must destroy something, and he suspects, probably believes and accepts, that his only personal reward for success will be death, perhaps with the knowledge that he has done the right thing. Even if Frodo can get to Mt. Doom and destroy the Ring, how can he escape afterwards? He aims to save Middle-earth, not to save himself. A better parallel for Frodo appears not in Galahad or in Arthur, but in the Gawain of *Sir Gawain and the Green Knight*. Gawain, youthful, brave, of good spirits, like Frodo, undertakes a task no one else will: to represent Arthur's court, to behead the Green Knight and seek the return blow a year after (and only with luck to return alive). While the Green Knight has magic, Gawain has none—though he has or should have his Christian faith—but he has, like Frodo, courage and commitment, and he also acts to save others rather than for himself: he rather than another must face the Knight's axe stroke. Gawain has no human or hobbit companions as he departs on his quest, but he has his shield with Solomon's star on the front and the Virgin Mary on the inside facing him—a far safer talisman than the Ring. And like Frodo he gets both good and bad guidance along the way. Each has helpers that will fail him and those who won't: the Fellowship of the Ring begin fully committed to seeing Frodo through, and Sam sticks with him throughout; Boromir fails in that he acts on his desire for the Ring, but he redeems himself in his defense of Merry and Pippin. The guide who rides briefly with Gawain and sets him on his way to the Green Chapel fails Gawain (either intentionally or not) by suggesting he run away: no one will know any better if you just leave, the fellow says, assuring Gawain he will tell no one. But neither Mary nor Christ, the companions of the true Christian knight, will fail Gawain, if his faith holds true (the real *magic* of belief on the inside of his shield should, but doesn't, remind him of that). Frodo has the real (in his world) magic of Ring (as opposed to the fake magic of the green sash), but he must not overuse it, or he will fall to its power and allow the destruction of his world. He, like Gawain, must remain *true*: he must keep his *trawþe*, as the *Gawain*-poet wrote, his courage his fortitude, his focus, his honor, his pledge.

Gawain, as the Romance shows, fails at the last: he keeps the magical sash that the lady of the castle insists will preserve him, though by the rights of the exchange game he should give it up to his host. As the Green Knight, Bercilak, that is, assures him, no human could hope to do better than Gawain has done. Gawain commits an understandable and pardonable sin—though he may not pardon himself for it. Frodo, too, fails at the last, and we must consider, though his failure is infinitely understandable, if it is pardonable, especially in what Tolkien would recognize as a pre-Christian world. At the Crack of Doom Frodo can't destroy the Ring—only accident and Gollum's monomania can do that. Probably no mortal could have done better. But Frodo alone would have failed. He returns home, like Gawain and Coleridge's wedding guest, a sadder and a wiser, but can he, does he, ever find personal resolution for that experience? The *Gawain*-poet suggests his hero also may not.

Must Frodo leave the Shire and Middle-earth because of the physical wound he received on Weathertop or because of the spiritual wound he received in Mordor through his own inability to act to destroy the Ring? To ask that question doesn't imply an assumption of superiority on the part of the asker; it goes to the heart of Tolkien's response to the human plight and also to the problem of Arthuriana. Frodo succeeds better than could anyone else in his circumstance: he least of all wants control of others, and that's the power with which Sauron hoped to imbue the Ring. But he doesn't succeed as Galahad does, or as Perceval does, or even as Bors does. But in the world of Middle-earth Frodo best can carry the Ring without giving in to the lure of power, far better than those who might, as Gandalf warns, have intended to use it for good. Frodo succeeds only in getting the Ring to the place of its destruction, as Gawain succeeds in getting to the place where he must accept the return blow of the Knight. As each story plays out, the protagonist—literally in each case the one who primarily must wrestle with the great problem—achieves praise from others, but feels most keenly the need for mercy, while he is not sure he entirely deserves it. There lies the great tragedy amidst the great eucatastrophe of each tale. Frodo's *world*, however, receives the mercy that circumstance does not permit Frodo himself. It survives; he lives with the knowledge of his own failure. Gawain's world, Arthur's world, does not receive that mercy: Camelot falls. Arthur produces his own tragedy; Aragorn averts tragedy, remains true, and

4. Tolkien on Heroism

finds for himself and his peoples a "happy ending"—something the true waste land may not allow.

Aragorn, unlike Gawain or Frodo, does succeed in his quest: he returns hope, law, kindness, and peace to his world, the promise in which Arthur (and even Frodo) fails. While we as audience are more like Frodo than like Aragorn, all the more reason that we need and want to believe in the possibility of an Aragorn. The World Wars of the twentieth century had uncovered a few Frodos—it had killed most of them—but it had brought to the forefront no Aragorns. I don't think Tolkien believed that result an acceptable conclusion—a fact, but not a necessity. Free will, the centerpiece of Christian doctrine along with Faith, allows us to fail, but it also allows us to choose to try to succeed, difficulty or not, temptation or not. And we should demand of our leaders a greater, not lesser ability to resist temptation, as Aragorn does. Fiction, particularly in the form of epic or Romance, moves us toward our better selves; it asks us to recognize where we as humans fail while urging us to do our best to succeed even beyond our hopes.

Aragorn's resistance to temptation need not and does not reach the level of Frodo's. That part of Aragorn's task is easier. He need not resist the Ring instant by instant, day by day, as Frodo must—and a good thing for him, too, since he does desire power, though not excessively or beyond his birthright. But he must resist despair if he fails to win Arwen or his kingship; he must resist weariness and the sense of being an outcast; he must resist taking the Ring when he knows that part of the quest isn't his; he must remain courageous and continue to lead; he must resist the will of Sauron when he looks in the Palantír; he must see the battle to its end; he must maintain good and generous kingship should he achieve it. Aragorn, unlike Arthur or Frodo, succeeds in all those tasks. He suggests—or Tolkien suggests through him—that heroic leadership is possible even in a world—like ours—where perfect resistance to all temptation is not possible (though like Faramir, one may have the will to resist the draw to power). But keeping one's faith and doing one's duty—in the Gawain-poet's term, again, one's *trawþe*—is possible and occasionally absolutely necessary. Aragorn becomes thereby the unexpected, new-and-improved twentieth-century Arthur, the once and present king *in* whom no one believed but *for* whom many, whether publicly or privately, hoped.

"The sword that was broken": Personal and Political Implications

The recurring motif of the broken sword allows the narrative to address private and public, moral and political flaws—and to suggest fixes for those flaws. Of all Tolkien's motifs it most effectively links him to the Arthurian tradition and to saga and epic, and yet it also places him more fully in his own century. The broken sword both requires mending and reminds the audience of the real and immediate dangers of violence; it connects characters and readers to their past and to the problems and needs of the present; it asserts our fragility in the face of the weapons of war.

Tolkien's Narsil/Andúril echoes but revises a significant medieval tradition of swords broken in battle. Some fairly typical interpretive notions accompany the motif, but, as we might expect, Tolkien refigures them as well as their narrative context to support one of the most important thematic vectors of *The Lord of the Rings*. Primarily, despite some popular criticism that asserts the contrary (largely based on films rather than books), Tolkien suggests that glory in battle has no virtue for its own sake: swords serve best only in their proper place. A great sword may have the worth of many soldiers in battle, but battle may well break it: it hasn't the endurance of the bravest hearts. First we'll turn to Tolkien's predecessors, and then I'll rehearse the remarkable number of references to broken swords in Tolkien's own texts.

While for this chapter I'll consider more thoroughly two Arthurian analogues of broken swords, one in Malory's tale of Sir Balin and one in Wolfram von Eschenbach's *Parzival*, for the sake of comparison I'll begin with a few Northern examples that deserve brief notice: *Beowulf*, *Gisla Saga Surssonar*, and especially *Volsungasaga*.

Beowulf breaks his own sword, Nægling, in his final battle, that against the dragon, on the worm's scaly hide. The narrator observes that the hero always had too much strength to wield conventional weapons anyway, implying more that the sword breaks because the hero swings it too hard rather than because of the dragon's natural defenses or any weakness in the sword or its wielder. That point has its own particular history within the poem. Against Grendel in Heorot, Beowulf, at his best, fights empty-handed. The hero kills Grendel's Mother in her lair

4. Tolkien on Heroism

with the use of an enchanted sword, the blade of which does not break, but dissolves on contact with her blood. Though Beowulf, having survived the Grendel-kin, dies after the dragon battle, he saves his people from further depredations likely to have been wrought by the fire-drake. Thematically that final episode supports Anglo-Christian notions of the "best" elements of heroism: they lie not in skill with weapons, but in steadfast courage, adherence to duty, and self-sacrifice. Human resolve, not sharp weapons, gets dirty jobs done best—a theme that Tolkien echoes.

Comparatively, in *Gisli's Saga* the sword breaks because Gisli, uncle of the character who gives his name to the saga, uses it when he shouldn't. Gisli must properly avenge his brother Ari by killing the berserker Bjorn, who has killed Ari to win from him his wife, Ingibjorg. Ingibjorg alerts Gisli to a special sword, Greyflank, in the possession of her bondservant, Kol, and with that sword Gisli slays Bjorn. But when the bondman claims back the sword, Gisli will not return it, and Kol attacks him; both men die, but in the battle Gisli breaks Greyflank against Kol's skull. The narrator doesn't explain the technical failure of the weapon, but the moral reason comes through clearly, if not explicitly: improper or unmerited use of the weapon may not just fail to help; it may also harm or at least lead to failure in battle.

By way of contrast, *Volsungasaga*, an obvious inspiration to Tolkien's narreme, employs the reforging and subsequent heroic use of the sword as well as the breaking. Oðin supplies the sword originally, thrusting it into the tree Barnstokkr in Volsung's hall, from which, after no one else can, Sigmundr easily draws it (note the parallel to two enchanted swords in the Arthurian tradition, Arthur's and Galahad's, drawn from stones by means of magical or religious enchantments). Later, when Sigmundr needs his sword most, it fails him. In Sigmundr's battle against King Lyngvi, as he defends his marriage to Hjördis, Oðin stands against him with his spear raised; when Sigmundr strikes the spear, the sword breaks, and Sigmundr, weaponless by Oðin's choice, believing his luck has passed, allows himself to be killed in the battle. Hjördis, pregnant with Sigurðr, saves the pieces of the sword, and later Sigurðr claims them. From them Reginn reforges the sword as *Gram*, which Sigurðr uses to slay Fafnir the dragon (as well as the treacherous Reginn) and to gain wealth and fame. In *Volsungasaga* the exceptional weapon serves whom and when Oðin wishes. Its wielder must not only be worthy, but also have the god's blessing plus luck and fate on his side—the ideas of luck and of the influence of outside forces appears periodically in *The Lord of the Rings*, and it forms a spiritual foundation even in *The Silmarillion*.

Arthurian examples occur in *Le Morte Darthur*. Not long after Arthur has established his reign, Sir Balyn, who has lost Arthur's favor, tries to regain it through a series of adventures. Perhaps the most luckless knight ever, Balyn pursues vengeance against the treacherous Sir Garlot, who rides invisibly and who has murdered an honest but less skillful knight. Balyn traces him to the castle of Pellam, the "Fisher King," where he receives welcome but agrees not to carry weapons. Finding his quarry, Balyn pulls another knight's sword and uses it to kill Sir Garlot, as it happens the king's brother. The sword breaks, and the king and his knights then pursue Balyn through the castle as he seeks either flight or a means of self-defense. He comes upon a bedroom with a seemingly dead body stretched out and a bleeding lance lying beside it on the bed; with that lance he strikes the king, who had been in hot pursuit of his own vengeance. Balyn's blow maims the king and reduces the castle to rubble and the kingdom to famine and disaster: unfortunately for Balyn and everyone else involved, the lance happens to be the one used to pierce Christ's side on the Cross. Balyn has unwittingly struck the Dolorous Stroke, partly as a result of a broken sword.

Malory's episode, rather like the failure of the sword in Sigmundr's hand, calls attention to the importance of luck, but more significantly it discourages rash action, particularly violence and vengeance, proscribed by Christian thought, though seldom do adventure stories omit it as a motif. Balyn had come into disfavor with Arthur because of an inability or unwillingness to still his hand, and while he tries to check his violence, except for cases in which he considers himself in the right, he takes action before knowing the full moral and social import of the situations in which he finds himself. The center of gravity of Malory's *Morte*, the quest of the Holy Grail, shows that knights at their best act out of piety and duty, and they commit no unnecessary violent acts, certainly no vengeful ones. Galahad best achieves the Grail because he best represents holiness, spiritual intelligence, forethought, and restraint: his martial abilities derive even more from spiritual purity than from physical power. Other knights succeed in the quest based on their degree of spiritual accomplishment—as we learn with Lancelot and particularly with Gawain, those who fail do so because they can't rid themselves of worldly concerns. Early in the *Morte,* refiguring Uther's sexual sin as a martial one, Balyn sets the paradigm by which we may judge the success of subsequent knights: the greatest of Arthur's knights up to his time, Balyn prepares us for those greater yet—Lancelot, Tristram, Perceval, Galahad—and teaches us to understand how they may fail or succeed. His sword, borrowed or stolen as it is, fails because he uses it in breach of an agreement and at a peaceful event, though in fulfillment of a previous vow. And the broken sword leads to the misuse of a far more powerful weapon, the lance, one that should no longer serve as a weapon at all, but as a symbol of the corruption that comes from violence, lovelessness, and poor judgment, the weapon once directed—paralleled pertinently in *Volsungasaga*—at God on earth.

The analogous episodes in Wolfram further a different purpose both narratively and thematically. Parzival, having reached the Grail castle and having seen the Grail itself (a stone in this version, yet still accompanied by a bleeding lance), receives from the maimed king Anfortas a bejewelled sword. The knight fails, however, to ask Anfortas the magic question, something as simple as "What troubles you?" Anfortas, the guardian of the Grail castle, failed in his duty of serving the Grail by fighting instead in the name of a lady; having suffered both a physical and spiritual castration as a result, he remains in pain, waiting for a death that won't arrive or for a knight to appear and relieve his pain by asking after his suffering. Parzival departs with the sword, but without achieving the quest, without either helping the king or rising to the position of new defender of the Grail. The first time he uses the sword in battle, it snaps, though the power of a magical spring later makes it whole, so that with it he wins subsequent fame. But the sword's fragility provokes the need for periodic repair—simply, it isn't a particularly trustworthy sword, possibly because Parzival isn't yet a fully trustworthy knight, certainly not sufficient yet to become guardian of the Grail. The decorated sword isn't the only one that Parzival breaks. Finally, and more notably yet, late in the Romance, as he battles a knight as yet unknown to him, the sword that he took early in the Romance from the corpse of Ither snaps. His fellow combatant turns out to be his half-brother, Feirefiz. Once they learn each other's identity, they make peace and become fast friends, and the quest may finally move rapidly towards its conclusion: Parzival's return to the Grail castle to ask the question and Feirefiz's conversion to Christianity and marriage to a Christian queen, all partly because of an aptly broken sword. Again, we see the sword as something the knight has won by significant accomplishment, and yet it fails; however, the author turns the weapon's failure to a different and significant purpose: the broken sword brings about a truce between the warring parties, the courtesy of whom leads to reconciliation and achievement of productive, even heavenly ends. Parzival has no need to reforge that sword—he can find better—and he accomplishes the healing of the maimed king and the attainment of his proper place as well as the salvation of the brother he hadn't known. As Mustard and Passage suggest, the break "betokens the snapping of the last strand of his youthful folly" (xliii). The thematic point in *Parzival* resembles that in the *Morte*, but with its own twist: we may achieve our quests best through peace rather than battle, and we do best finally to aim not for glorious heroics, but to heal, to do our duty, and to protect those values, earthly and heavenly, that mean most to us. The sword has value, but virtue has more—an idea that became a significant part of Tolkien's intellectual landscape.

The thematic resonances in Tolkien, to whom we may now turn, considerably favor the Arthurian analogues, even though the Narsil story (which appears in "Of the Rings of Power and the Third Age" in *The Silmarillion*) in narrative terms borrows more closely from the Norse tales. We should perhaps expect as much from a Christian novelist and mythographer who draws upon Christian texts while simultaneously loving and admiring medieval Northern ones. Narsil, though already broken when Elendil, slain by Sauron, fell upon it, still served Isildur eminently. With the hilt-shard as the means by which he struck the One Ring from Sauron's hand, Isildur scattered Sauron's spirit, ending the immediate threat of the destruction or enslavement of the peoples of Middle-earth. That the sword breaks presents no narrative surprise, and it also makes thematic sense: if we have such great weapons at all, we must restrict their use to the necessity of defending our lives, countries, and highest values, not in any less-than-apocalyptic event. Yet even there they may fail us. Only human resourcefulness and commitment can

4. Tolkien on Heroism

complete the task; there Isildur begins well, but ultimately fails, allowing Sauron to reconstitute himself, necessitating heroic/apocalyptic choices from another age. Even the broken sword doesn't inhibit the continuation of war; it merely suspends or redirects it for a time.

Perhaps the most interesting point in this tale of a broken sword comes in the fact that Narsil remains for centuries in shards, useless as a tool, but again eminent as a symbol of the memory of those deeds long past and of their gravity. Until Aragorn claims it, the weapon remains in Imladris, the house of Elrond, where "the shards of the sword were cherished during many lives of Men by the heirs of Isildur; and their line, from father to son, remained unbroken" (*Silmarillion* 355). That line offers a telling pun: though the weapon has broken, Isildur's line has not: human strength must outlast war and all its tools. Narsil's reforging as Andúril announces the coming of another new age, that of the rise of humans to pre-eminence among the people of Middle-earth, while warning us of our mortality and festering tendency to violence: the symbol of that rise is an object of destruction rather than of conciliation. In typological terms Andúril represents for Tolkien the antitype of the broken sword motif, the type of which appears in *The Silmarillion* and redoubles in *The Lord of the Rings*. In the "Of Túrin Turambar" in *The Silmarillion* Beleg cuts lose Túrin with the sword Anglachel, but the blade slips and cuts Túrin's foot, and so Túrin, waking suddenly, wrestles it from Beleg and kills him, not knowing his identity in the dark. The blade, Túrin says, mourns for Beleg, and he has smiths in Nargothrond reforge it, and he renames in Gurthang, Iron of Death (248–251). Later, having unjustly slain Brandir, at Cabed-en-Aras Túrin falls on the blade and kills himself. Before he dies, the sword speaks to him, "Yea, I will drink thy blood gladly, so that I may forget the blood of Beleg my master, and the blood of Brandir slain unjustly"—but the blade breaks beneath him, and rather than reforge it, his fellows bury it beside Túrin. That is the old *tale* that Aragorn must reforge with his own sword an age later.

Those instances presage the significance of Andúril as reforged blade, but the most significant narrative function of Andúril, oddly enough, isn't its actual use in battle—though Aragorn does that handily enough—but instead Aragorn's showing the sword to Sauron in the Palantír. The weapon that once harmed the Dark Lord threatens him again. The threat alone will not deter him, but it will distract him, inhibiting his ability to locate Frodo and Sam's quest to destroy the greater weapon, the Ring, which wears down the resistance of anyone who bears it until he *must* use it—again in contrast with Aragorn's sword.

Like the sword, the Ring, a far more potent weapon, lay in waiting. However, rather than serving as a symbol of strength and wisdom that had failed before and of renewed courage that must ultimately succeed in their stead, as the broken sword does, the Ring only plummets those who contact it into misery. It either gradually or abruptly wipes away the bearer, leaving him a shadow, utterly corrupt and entirely swallowed by the eruption of whatever potential for evil dwelt within him. Look at poor Frodo: the best of all possible bearers because he has least ambition, even he, standing at the Cracks of Doom, falls to the Ring's power: only chance, and Gollum's insatiable hunger for the ring, and perhaps a hint of divine mercy save him.

Unlike the ring, the sword Narsil/Andúril may have its greatest power when no one wields it. Though it serves Aragorn in battle, another fine sword might have done as well. It functions most powerfully as a symbol of the pending return of the king, the potential for order based on goodness and freedom rather than suffering and oppression to re-emerge in Middle-earth. It serves also as a fearsome reminder to Sauron of his vulnerability. The ring, which, if we borrow from tradition, should stand as a symbol of unity and mutuality, induces hopelessness; the sword, which by tradition should stand for divisiveness and violent compulsion, inspires alliance and hope. When Boromir reaches Rivendell, he recites a verse out of a dream:

> Seek for the sword that was broken:
> In Imladris it dwells;
> There shall be counsels taken
> Stronger than Morgul-spells [*FotR* 240].

The symbol of doom, as Elrond explains, is the Ring, not the sword; the sword draws together those who must do what they can to assure that the oncoming doom will bring an age of peace rather than destruction.

The broken sword motif recurs repeatedly, though never with such powerful thematic import. Even in *The Fellowship of the Ring* it fulfills several purposes. It appears first in the scene on the barrow-downs, the four hobbits sleeping in the cold tomb as ghostly arm of the Wight creeps toward them. Mustering his courage, Frodo grasps the short sword that lies near him and strikes at the Wight's wrist: the hand breaks off, but the sword splinters to the hilt. Frodo has daunted but hardly destroyed the Wight; his song then brings Tom Bombadil, who has strength more than sufficient to drive it away and rescue the hobbits (138–39). Another instance occurs during and after the attack on Weathertop. Strider finds the notched Morgul-knife blade of the leader of the Black Riders that has wounded and infected Frodo's shoulder. Later, when Frodo has crossed the Ford of Rivendell with the Ringwraiths on his heels, as he stands with his own sword raised, it spontaneously breaks in his hand. Not a spirited defense, but the raging water of the river scatters the Black Riders, the sword of little use anyway against these wraiths.

Then, during the time of the Council of Elrond, Aragorn identifies his sword as the one Elendil carried into battle against Sauron, "treasured by his heirs when all other heirlooms were lost" (241). Boromir replies that he came to solve a riddle rather than to beg a boon, but "the Sword of Elendil would be a help beyond our hope" (241)—he doesn't believe Aragorn, nor does he believe the counsels he hears about the Ring. He trusts only in martial solutions, even repaired ones, and so his own heart will betray him.

Before the Nine Companions leave Rivendell,

> The sword of Elendil was forged anew by Elvish smiths, and on its blade was traced a device of seven stars set between the crescent Moon and the rayed Sun ... for Aragorn son of Arathorn was going to war upon the marches of Mordor.... And Aragorn gave it a new name and called it Andúril, Flame of the West [269].

Presumably Aragorn could have had the sword reforged at any time; he carries thereafter not the old sword, but a remade one, because he is not one of the kings of old, but a new one who aims to resist the temptations that brought Isildur and Westernesse to destruction—people must follow not only a leader, but a symbol. Only a page later Bilbo returns to Frodo his broken sword, but replaces it for him with Sting. Frodo carries a weapon on the quest not because he has any serious fighting to do, but because it may serve in a pinch; he is the true "light of the West," and he and the West will survive not by his wielding a weapon, but by his destroying one. When Jesus says, "I bring not peace, but a sword," and when William Blake says, "I shall not cease from mental fight, / Nor shall my sword sleep in my hand," the sword image implies not traditional war aimed at peace through power, but the struggle of the spirit to create a world that finds peace without the need (or desire) for one to exert martial power over another. Tolkien's best swords, reforged or replaced, defend the same ends.

At the beginning of *The Two Towers*, Aragorn finds Boromir dying, his broken sword still in his hand and his broken horn at his side. He has broken the horn calling for help and has broken the sword defending Merry and Pippin—a mutually heroic and tragic end after his attempt to take the Ring from Frodo. Théoden's sword has not been broken, but it has been taken from him by Wormtongue; the king's strength returns with the re-grasping of his sword. Saruman doesn't carry a sword, but Gandalf breaks his staff—the event carries a similar point, in that it represents through a source of power the loss of power and a failure in character. In the Battle of Helm's Deep Gimli's weapon gets notched (by an orc's iron collar), but not broken; the weapon has taken what stress a weapon can, and the wielder has kept his courage and honor. The man who nearly falls on Sam during the battle with Faramir's soldiers in *The Two Towers* clasps the hilt of a broken sword even after his death ("Of Herbs and Stewed Rabbit"). Sam breaks his staff, not his sword over Gollum's back as Gollum tries to keep him from fighting Shelob—he swings a blow not to kill, but to discourage his attacker. In "The Passing of the Grey Company" in *The Return of the King* Aragron kneels beside the bones of a man, probably Baldor of Rohan, with a broken blade still lying beside him.

Broken weapons show both their usefulness and their limits: they don't solve all the problems of Middle-earth, but because they cause so many, they must also allay those they can. The broken weapons, and the lives that pass with their breaking, reinforce the idea of the transience of earthly things, the sadness that dwells in and sometimes nearly overcomes much of Tolkien's work, something akin to the German notion of Weltschmerz, but so exclusively internal. Acceptance of the sadness that pervades living experience goes a way toward recovering the value of the individual life in such a world. Courage, forgiveness, and healing must do the remaining work. As the Rohirrim fight in the Battle of the Pelennor Fields in *The Return of the King*, Théoden breaks his spear on a Southron chieftain. When Théoden falls beneath Snowmane at the Nazgûl's attack, and Éowyn strikes the head from the beast that carries him, Merry stabs him behind the knee, and the blade dissolves. Éowyn drives her sword where the face of the Nazgúl should be, and the blade shatters into pieces, the spirit disappearing with a wail. When Saruman tries to kill Frodo after the battle of Bywater, his knife turns and breaks on Frodo's mithril shirt. Curiously enough Tolkien says nothing of the blade that Wormtongue uses to slit Saruman's throat with the last stroke of the War of the Ring, right before Bag End; weapons that strike the most grievous or important blows tend to die themselves, but that one simply fades from thought and memory of a Shire that needs to rid itself of war, post-war, and all the troubles that come from exploitation, collaboration, and profiteering. The hobbits must break any desire for the sword to find peace, but they must remember what they earned by courage and steadfastness and commitment to one another—a significant theme from two world wars.

5

Epic, Faërie, and Myth
The Mortal and the Monstrous Body

Philology implies not only the love of words, but also a love of—and willingness to use—the matter of the great literature of the past. The ability to do so comes from language immersion. Tolkien borrows language and literary motifs not only from fairy stories and Romance, but also from epic poetry, and not from *Beowulf* alone. He applies the practice of using epiphany, so central to epic poems, refiguring it for the problems his time needed to address. Tolkien's epiphanies allow characters to gain knowledge or inspiration or face them with their greatest and most harrowing, monstrous challenges. As they have always done in the stories of the past with the greatest magnitude, epiphanies form an essential part of the experience and artistic power of Middle-earth.

Beowulf, Tolkien, and Epic Epiphanies

Tolkien's Middle-earth fantasy, while he saw it more as Romance than epic, appeals in its themes, motifs, and grandeur to the century's dearth of definitive epic poems.[1] It meets *Beowulf*, and epic tradition more generally, at what may at first appear an unexpected junction: *epiphany*, a facet typical not just of religious literature, but of epic and fantasy both. In its traditional sense epiphany would appear to be missing from *The Hobbit* and *The Lord of the Rings*, though present repeatedly in *The Silmarillion*. But Tolkien borrows the particular and peculiar form of epiphanies in his heroic fantasy directly from *Beowulf*, the poem he loved and knew so well. Epiphany typically means a meeting with a god, though it often appears more generally as contact with a different order of being, either higher or lower on, one might say, the Great Chain

5. Epic, Faërie, and Myth

of Being. Such a meeting in the history of literature stands at the gateway of a character's movement towards good or evil, toward boon or bane, and neither Tolkien's hobbit saga nor the great Anglo-Saxon epic makes an exception; in fact, Tolkien borrows the kind of epiphanies we find in *Beowulf* as most appropriate for his own fictional world, where, for a writer of his concerns, specifically Christian or Germanic instances would not fit. The model remains the same, but the application follows Tolkien's own path, which places epiphany right in the midst of twentieth-century fantasy literature.

Traditionally, epic has been "about" two things: what we know of heroism and how we meet our gods (that is, how we behave to reach epiphanies). For instance, Gilgamesh seeks immortality, but, failing Utnapishtim's tests, he accepts mortality; Achilles and Hector must meet in battle, the spoils to the victor and the victory depending on the help and presence of the gods; Odysseus must overcome all challenges and return to his kingship, both hindered and helped by gods; Aeneas must submerge his personal desires and do his duty to gods and country: such heroic deeds exhibit the demands of the epics' respective ages of antiquity. Beowulf must show steadfast courage in combat against monsters: that is the heroism of the Germanic Age. But in *Beowulf,* unlike what we see in the epics of the ancient world, God or gods remain disturbingly silent: we hear that "god" moves in the world or that *wyrd* goes ever as it must, but the only unusual beings we encounter are monsters: Grendel, Grendel's Mother, the dragon, and they are more natural than supernatural. Those meetings take place, according to Todorov's definition of *the fantastic,* in the realm of the fantastic rather than in sacred space. Anglo-Saxons believed, apparently, in literal monsters and dragons, but to modern readers, mostly because of those monsters, the world of *Beowulf* floats between what we accept as real and what we remit to fantasy.

The Anglo-Saxon *Maxims* tell us such indisputable truths as "Beam sceal on eorðan / leafum liþan," a tree must lay its leaves on the earth, "Fus sceal feran, fæge sweltan," a traveler must set forth, doomed to die (Krapp and Dobbie 157, translations mine), and "Draca sceal on hlæwe, frod, frætwum wlanc," a dragon must [dwell] in a barrow, old, proud of treasures (Dobbie 56). What to us dwells on the fringe of sanity to the Anglo-Saxon lived in the large world, if less than commonly, at least as naturally as trees and leaves.

Certainly the dragon even for the Anglo-Saxon is a super-natural if not a supernatural being, a grotesque with parts attributable to several other creatures, in some cases a man who because of exceptional greed or savagery has become a dragon—rather like the vampires we keep telling ourselves we don't believe in but who continue to show up in our novels, movies, television shows, and fantasies at large. The magic of *Beowulf* and its world makes possible and even desirable extraordinary beings within the bounds of nature, beings such as Beowulf himself, whom the poet calls *aglæca*, the same word he or she uses for Grendel and the dragon, which must mean something like "big, powerful, extraordinary (but not unnatural) thing." Meetings of or with such creatures constitute in the poem both the means by which the hero establishes his extraordinary courage and the only epiphanies that that world offers. Minus its magic, Beowulf's is a world not so different from that of our own time, which has found its own particular monsters, but which must still summon its wit, composure, and courage; with its magic, monsters, and great deeds, Beowulf's is much the same world that we keep employing in our fantasy games and tales of superheroes. It has the power to move readers to re-read and to study and writers to compose in appreciation or imitation.

Tolkien, one of the greatest *Beowulf* scholars, turned naturally in his epic-fantasy to Beowulfian epiphanies. Abjuring the person-meets-god epiphanies of ancient epics, the Christian or allegorical epiphanies of late medieval or Renaissance epics and of some contemporary fantasies, and the psychological or social epiphanies of the Romantics and Victorians, Tolkien, despite his own commitment to Christianity, chose, with the exception of *The Silmarillion* and perhaps the wizards in *The Lord of the Rings*, to have his heroes meet monsters and ghosts—and other peoples—rather than God or gods. His pre–Christian Middle-earth—like the Middle-earth of his readers—shares with *Beowulf*'s the same heroic necessity: steadfast courage from heroes and common folk alike in the face of enemies natural or supernatural. Even help from semi-divine representatives of good, such as elves or wizards, doesn't absolve hobbits or people of their heroic responsibilities. There Tolkien's world also parallels our own, where ghostly epiphanies are more commonplace and pressing than divine, and where we share a hero's and a hobbit's desire (in lieu of a good meal) for the courage to complete our appointed—and sometimes, seemingly, impossible—tasks.

5. Epic, Faërie, and Myth

There also Tolkien's world crosses from pure fantasy into *the fantastic*: the immediacy of his epiphanies pulls the stories from our imagination into the world of our everyday fears, hopes, and needs, where we too must meet our equivalents of stealthy orcs and peace-consuming dragon-fire with steadfast courage. Yet in Tolkien's world, unlike our own, magic, as an ability to skew nature rather than just to play on the limitations of human perception, remains, as in *Beowulf*, an accepted and expected part of nature. As Peter Beagle says in his introductory blurb to the Ballantine editions, Tolkien's Middle-earth was not his own invention, but what "was there long before him," waiting for "a great enough magician to tap our most common nightmares, daydreams, and twilight fancies." It is a world into which we cross regularly, for as Tolkien himself said, "'I am a hobbit myself ... in all but size,'" and "'[h]obbits are just rustic English people, made small in size because it reflects the generally small reach of their imagination—not the small reach of their courage or latent power'" (Carpenter 197). That comment applies normally to the rest of us as well, at least when our courage holds and when a magical writer gets hold of our imagination and shows us that we ourselves have the power to move the world toward evil or good.

Both epic poem and epic fantasy succeed because, as Rabkin says, we "participate sympathetically in the ground rules of [the] narrative world," because we participate in their, to use the Tolkienian term, *subcreation* (Rabkin 4, Tolkien, *Tolkien Reader* 49). Rosemary Jackson argues that fantasy, a "free-floating form" (1), provides not something transcendental, but an escape into nostalgia, for "it is literature of desire, which seeks that which is experienced as absence and loss" (3). In both *Beowulf* and *The Lord of the Rings*, our subcreation implies re-creation (and recreation), an effort or desire to return to a time when character, author, and reader can participate in a clearer heroic than contemporary times allow, a time when we knew what to do and, in fact, had little choice but to do it. In the "Heroic Ages" of *Beowulf* and *The Lord of the Rings*, heroes, whether Nordic warriors or hobbits, nearly always know what to do, what their situation demands of them, and they are not *confusticated* and *bebothered* by concerns of the Afterlife and how current deeds may affect the fate of their souls.[2] They are able to act heroically without confusion, something that the age in which both pieces were written wouldn't have allowed their respective audiences to do, when heroism clashed at least potentially with religious and social dictates that commanded peaceful suffering in the face of aggression.

As Shippey has pointed out (*Author of the Century*), Tolkien and other writers of his generation looked back to medieval models for their fantasy because contemporary thought provided no assurances about how best to deal with the twentieth-century "waste land"; because so many of their generation had fought in war and had known the potential of human atrocity, they saw that "the theme of human evil was not one which could be rendered adequately or confronted directly through the medium of realistic fiction alone" (221) because of the fog of contemporary politics and the difficulty in contemporary realism of not focusing the source of evil as "out there." The fantastic world allows for the connection between created and quotidian worlds, between the places that allow for a realistic shared burden of evil and a magical distancing from the finger pointing of politics. Following Shippey's argument, I would add that what Tolkien borrows from the medieval world to address the problem of evil he also borrows to create epiphanies in general (such as when hobbits or people meet elves or wraiths), those that involve special powers of good or evil alike and that those epiphanies dot the landscape of Middle-earth as necessary and natural steps in the Hobbits' journeys.

Tolkien's operative notion of *subcreation* takes over when the landscape of the text moves from our world into the world of Faerie, where magic is still an intricate part of nature. We move likewise into the fantastic in both Tolkien's work and in *Beowulf* when the boundaries between worlds become blurred, when we accept the proffered world as grounds in which we can fight the battles of good and evil.

Tolkien asserts in "On Fairy-Stories" that

> fairy-stories as a whole have three faces: the Mystical towards the Supernatural; the Magical towards Nature; and the Mirror of scorn and pity towards Man. The essential face of Faerie is the middle one, the Magical. But the degree to which the others appear (if at all) is variable and may be decided by the individual story-teller [52].

When magic is part of nature, we have stepped across a boundary into Faerie; we may not have left mysticism, scorn and pity behind, but we have certainly moved to a place where we will have to confront both good and evil in ourselves and outside of ourselves. Wherever magic appears, we will find creatures who will use it for good and creatures

5. Epic, Faërie, and Myth

who will use it for evil, and its effects will appear on a sufficiently grand scale that no one in the world, ultimately, can ignore it, as hobbits find out with the Ring of Power. We also find that since the magic must finally touch us (as when Frodo must carry the ring in Bilbo's stead) and since its physical power will be more than we ourselves can generate in defense, our only hope rests in steadfast courage, in the hope that courage will allow us to sustain what we believe to be good long enough to disperse the magic. We must find that strength or a power sufficient to counter it, or we must survive until it destroys itself or until we can find means within ourselves to eliminate it. We must succeed either by an act of will or, as in Frodo's case at the Crack of Doom, we must have our enemy eliminated for us by good luck, or fate, or powerful friends, or divine intervention.

Bilbo and Frodo do not have the power of Beowulf: Beowulf has the strength of thirty men, the very strength of his opponent, Grendel, slightly more than that of Grendel's Mother, rather less than that of the fire-dragon. But hobbits (and we humans) do have something special about them, something more than meets the eye, as several characters remark about hobbits in Tolkien's saga. What the hobbits prove to have, though, is in another way exactly what Beowulf has: sufficient resources to complete the task at hand. Beowulf defeats Grendel not because he has greater strength, but because he has greater courage: he simply hangs on as the monster tries to escape. He defeats Grendel's mother not because he has greater strength than she (though he does), but because he keeps his wits about him in battle and finds hanging above him a magic sword that he can use against her. He defeats the dragon, with Wiglaf's help, almost out of desperation, because he must do so or no one will, and he sacrifices his life in the process. No gods appear to help Beowulf, and he prays to none for help. As the hero himself has earlier observed, "*Wyrd oft nereð / unfægne eorl, þonne his ellen deah*"(ll. 572–73), "Fate [or just the course of things] often preserves the undoomed man, if his courage holds." Nor does Beowulf meet a devil, other than symbolically, in the monsters: they do not literally threaten his soul, which according to Christian doctrine was already forfeit, he being a heathen, but rather his life, his fame, and later his kingdom. The monsters are a natural part of his world, and he meets them as a natural if extraordinary man, most extraordinary because his courage never flags, and most successful for the same reason. Beowulf's epiphanies came against creatures of magic or at least of extraordinary powers—Grendel and Grendel's Mother, descendants of Cain and thus of murder, whose magic makes them impervious to all but magical weapons, and the scaled dragon that can spit fire and poison—and he uses not magic, but courage and attentiveness, even desperation, when necessary, to defeat them.

Bilbo and Frodo succeed similarly; they have no such strength as Beowulf's, but they have courage (Bilbo faces the dragon when the dwarves will not) and resilience, they have a willingness to take up duties that fall to them (Frodo offers to carry the ring back to destroy it), and they have an uncanny luck (Gollum's appearance to bite the ring from Frodo's finger at the crucial, culminating moment of the quest). Like Beowulf they neither meet nor call upon any god (contrary to what one might expect of a Catholic writer), though Gandalf is a kind of demi-god, nor do they meet directly a Satan, though Sauron, whom Frodo nearly meets, is obviously a Satan-figure. They do, though, meet plenty of extraordinary creatures, guides, monsters, and ghosts, everything from goblins to trolls to wraith-kings on the minus side and elves to forest-guardians to wizards on the plus. In each case what characterizes the epiphany is that the hobbit confronts a creature either able to use magic or a product of magic or some special power. The hobbit always has less strength than the character who provides the epiphany, except in the remarkable instance of the hobbit who possesses—but must not use—the Ring. In such cases other beings who meet the hobbit have an epiphany because of the magic associated with the Ring. The parallel with *Beowulf* holds up on this point also: people who meet Beowulf do not meet a being of another order or with strength beyond human limits (though Beowulf defines the limit), except when Beowulf uses the magical sword to kill Grendel's Mother. Hobbits with or without magic pose no special threat to any other creatures until their lives are on the line; Beowulf poses a threat only to creatures who use magic to do evil or to those (like the Frankish hero Dæghrafn) who threaten his life or his king's.

The difference appears in the characters' separate notions of what finally constitutes *good* in the world. Beowulf seeks *lof* and *dom*, praise and glory, whereas the hobbits seek a quiet and secure life with companionship and plenty of good meals. But Beowulf and the hobbits are not creatures of a different order of being than humans: neither desires to use magic or weapons at all, and neither has access to special or supernatural powers. Both intend to do what they were clearly born to do. Beowulf wants to become a hero, and he does, by means of steadfast courage—no problem there. Gandalf suggests that Frodo and Bilbo were *meant* to carry the Ring, without specifying who meant it. Hobbits don't set out to serve the other races, but they don't eschew that service when it falls to them.

The curious result is what becomes of the hobbits: they are creatures who want no more than long, quiet, gentle lives, but when those lives are interrupted by evil from without, they have no choice but to perish or to exhibit that same steadfast courage as Beowulf's, not out of a desire for the heroic immortality of praise and fame, but to return once again to their hobbit lives. The ends differ, except for the need to resist evil, which remains constant, but the means are the same, and the means call up for Tolkien, as they did for the *Beowulf* poet, the kind of epiphany necessary to their themes: the heroes must meet something within their worlds and beyond themselves, but not *unavailable* to themselves.

Having known war and having learned that evil arises from within as well as from without, and that one must *resist* it from within as well as from without, Tolkien went for his epiphanies to a hero, Beowulf, who fought magical monsters of chaos and greed and never gave in, but who may in the end have fallen to his own pride as well as to the fate of old age. Frodo nearly falls so, prey to the Ring and the pride of tyranny it offers, and only luck, or as the Germanic world might say, *wyrd*, neither luck nor fate, exactly, preserves him. As Frodo returns briefly and partly reluctantly, changed, to his old life, we must be prepared, Tolkien suggests, to meet our own duties and quests with the same steadfast courage, knowing that even should we survive, we will have been immitigably changed. Perhaps we will have briefly staved off evil and preserved by our deeds at least a small corner of the world we loved. That victory, finally, is the goal of epiphanies in *Beowulf*, Tolkien, or anywhere, "real" or imagined: to preserve something in the world worth keeping, as Sam asserts in the film.

Rehabilitating Aglǣcan and Faërie

To create his own characters, Tolkien had to push against disneyfied (and to some extent Shakespearean) public expectation of the character, size, and behavior of elves. He also had to deal with the Victorian and early twentieth-century vision of elves as cute little inhabitants of gardens.[3] He sought to return elves to characters of greater power and dignity, such as we find them in medieval stories. "The particular skill of the writer of fantasy ... lies in effecting the escape and still keeping the recognition," Flieger suggests (*Green Suns* 7): the world of the elves, or of Middle-earth more generally, must elicit enough interest for the reader to feel willing to move his or her consciousness into it. Once there, the reader must find that world consistent enough so that it feels "true" (honest, complete, consistent), and the characters must have some kind of dignity for us to follow their adventures with any commitment to the results. Notions of complexity, completeness, and dignity drove Tolkien beyond language creation to the addition of detailed maps, the histories of dynasties, and even to the lore of pipe-weed. World creation in fiction has particular importance in the case of a world that insists it is our own—we too live in Middle-earth—and that yet has extraordinary beings such as ents and elves, species not a part of our common experience, though perhaps part of our common imagination.

Tolkien also made some interesting turns of his own with respect to monstrosity. From the hobbits' point of view not only the "official" monsters, such as orcs and trolls, but also Gandalf and Aragorn (and Boromir and Faramir) and Treebeard and Tom Bombadil and Old Man Willow would be *aglǣcan*, that Old English world often translated as "monsters" but applying equally in the epic to Beowulf as to Grendel or the dragon. *Aglǣcan*, "large, scary, powerful, and potentially dangerous creatures," inhabit the hobbits' world, even if they choose to try to stay away from them. While Tolkien must have enjoyed the creation of his monsters, he had also to recover for his fictional world many dangerous "others," to make them either potentially frightening or potentially appealing—or both—to fill out his story and his landscape, both physical and intellectual, and to show the extent of the challenges the hobbits face.

The rehabilitation of ideas of the monstrous takes place in *The Silmarillion* and *The Lord of the Rings*, while of Faerie it occurs in his translation of *Sir Orfeo* as well as in *Smith of Wootten Major* and *Farmer Giles of Ham* as in *The Lord of the Rings*—though the theoretical grounding for all of the above appears in "On Faerie-Stories." Any number of commentators have mentioned the shift in tone that occurs right in *The Hobbit*, as it moves from the original intention of children's story to become much more. Yet it remains a fairy story in its sense of wonder and adventure and the presence of magic and the uncanny. But a fully reconfigured Faërie had already appeared in the early drafts of *The Silmarillion*, and *The Lord of the Rings* quickly grew from sequel to *The Hobbit* into something of its own, with strong vectors of epic as well as Romance that moved it toward a need for greater grandeur and what Matthew Arnold would call "high seriousness"—little place for the humor that both graces and restrains *The Hobbit*. "On Fairy-Stories" returns a sense of dignity to the fantasy story that determines the course of Middle-earth: the "realm of fairy-story is wide and deep and high and filled with many things" (33), Tolkien observes. "Spenser," he adds, was in the true tradition when he called the knights of his Faërie by the name of Elfe" (37), but Faërie contains also "dwarves, witches, trolls, giants, or dragons; it holds the seas, the sun, the moon, and the sky" as well as "ourselves, mortal men, when we are enchanted" (38). As in the Middle English *Sir Orfeo*, which Tolkien translated, the world of Faërie may come into contact with ours at any time, sometimes through our own actions (usually accidental) or because its inhabitants wish to come into contact with ours.[4] "Most good 'fairy-stories' are about the *adventures* of men in the Perilous Realm, or upon its shadowy marches" (38); they use magic, marvels, and tend to explore the "satisfaction of certain primordial human desires," such as to "survey the depths of space and time," to "hold communion with other living things" (e.g., to speak with animals), and, for a brief time, to escape mortality (41, 43, 85). In them we find the human as sub-creator (49), continuing God's act of creation, as they offer "Fantasy, Recovery, Escape, Consolation" (75); they allow for invention, for us to "clean our windows" and see more clearly, and as a "prophylactic against loss" (77). They tend to deal with the "fundamental things" of nature and living, but in a way that provides consolation for our sadness and failings in the world (78).

While allowing escape from the "rawness and ugliness of modern European life," it is not "escapist," in that it doesn't deny responsibility, rationality, suffering, injustice, and the possibility (even likelihood) of terror (82)—most traditional fairy stories are terrifying indeed, and hardly what most parents in our time would think fit to tell their children. While we find death terrifying, Tolkien adds wryly that the "Human-Stories of the elves are doubtless full of the Escape from Deathlessness" (85): for them not dying may feel as sad as dying does for us. Fairy stories provide the consolation of the *eucatastrophe*, the unexpected or even undeserved happy turn of events that brings joy and perhaps hope, a reward for reading or listening (86). Modernism in many ways turned away from beauty: fairy-story, Tolkien suggests, can provide beauty without sentimentality, in that it accepts suffering or sorrow without yielding to sordidness and despair. Beauty for him, and the potential to make good choices, to remain loyal, to find a place worth living in and work worth doing and leisure free of destructiveness, had great value, and fantasy or fairy-story could find grounds and narrative for it.

Once Tolkien has clarified that for him at least fairy-story meant not something minimal and patronizing, but something extensive and as true as life, a means to convey significant ideas with complex stories of dynamic characters who face enormous problems both internal and external, his fictional world has made its final move to adulthood: the charges that Tolkien's stories are simply for boys, that they pursue only a simple morality, or that they lack attention to the "real" world fall away because of the ideas that drive them and the complexity with which the characters approach their problems. Aragorn doesn't always know what choices to make; even Gandalf has no clear plan for what the Fellowship will do once they pass Moria or perhaps Lothlórien; neither Théoden nor Denethor is a flawless leader, nor is either an egregious tyrant. Each character has the potential to turn for better or worse, and the future course of the world depends on the choices of many, nearly of all, not just of one or two. Elves, too, can behave better or worse; they can help or hinder, save or kill.

The fairy story, Tolkien wrote in a 1955 letter, "is really an adult genre"—one, he added, "for which a starving audience exists" (*Letters* 209) and "one of the highest forms of literature" (220); most of twentieth-century criticism wouldn't agree with that point, but much of the reading audience did. *Faërie*, Flieger has observed, "may well be the most important word in Tolkien's creative lexicon, with its matrix of connections to place, enchantment, sub-creation, and a race of beings (*Green Suns* vii). Tolkien wrote *Smith of Wootten Major*, Flieger adds, "to correct what he

5. Epic, Faërie, and Myth

saw as a serious misapprehension of the word *fairy* on the part of George MacDonald" and "to correct the sugary Victorian ideas of fairies and fairyland as "little" and "pretty" as well as the "Disney concept of fairies as gossamer winged creatures living in daffodils "(67). He does so in nearly all of his work, making elves and all that goes with them more beautiful, more powerful, and more perilous—and more human in their ambivalence between achievement and frailty.[5] *Smith* and *Farmer Giles* are probably as good examples of pure fairy stories as one can find from the modern world. Alf Prentice, the Fairy Queen, the magic star, and Smith's rambles in Faërie provide explicit elements in the first, while the giant and the dragon do so for the second. They minimize the allegorical qualities that characterize "Leaf by Niggle," and they background any morals or themes. While *Smith* pretty clearly teaches humility and how to relinquish as well as how to accept, value, and use a gift, *Farmer Giles* remains much less explicit. There no one behaves exceedingly admirably: the Farmer shows some courage and wit, and Garm the dog shows some loyalty, but Ægidius (Giles) succeeds mostly by luck and by the power of the magic sword the tyrannical king unwittingly sends him, and though he shares his wealth, he acts largely out of self-interest. *Smith* and *Farmer Giles* are mostly about *the stories* or about the nature and execution of fairy stories: story for story's sake. The fairy elements serve not as cute attractions for children, but as means to enhance storytelling, to move ordinary characters into extraordinary settings and opportunities so we may see what they'll do and how they'll do it.

In medieval Romance elves or fairies share most traits with humans, though often they have heightened abilities or a firmer connection to the powers of earth. They often inhabit an "Otherworld," though not an "Underworld." Though some folk traditions attach them to the dead, literary tradition most often simply places them in parallel to humans with occasional interactions that may prove dangerous or instructive and productive. Most importantly, traditional elves or fairies have, like humans, good traits and bad, and they may act well or poorly. Like the elf king in *Sir Orfeo*, they may kidnap humans at their own whim, or like the one in "Pwyll," they may need help from humans and may reward them accordingly. They may take little interest in humans or may fall in love with them, or vice versa, such as Rhiannon in "Pwyll" or the elf princess in Marie's "Lanval." Tolkien's elves may take human mates

(Lúthien, Finduilas, and Arwen), and they may treat travelers kindly (they repeatedly help Frodo) or sternly (the Mirkwood elves imprison the dwarves in *The Hobbit*). Significantly for my study here they show free will to make a full range of choices from the humble and generous to the proud and the tragic, especially in *The Silmarillion*. The idea of free will drove Tolkien's creation as it has done that of so many other Christian writers, and it has implications in all of these stories.

While the single most tragic story in Tolkien's fiction recounts the trials of Túrin (the sufferings and suicide of his father, the unfortunate killing of Saeros and Beleg, the failure to save Finduilas from the orcs, the loss of his mother, the marriage to his sister and her subsequent suicide, his own suicide), the tragedy of Fëanor takes the central place in *The Silmarillion* partly because of the jewels and partly because it mostly fully represents the failures of the elves. The labor of Fëanor's birth deprives his mother, Miriel, of her strength, and her spirit passes out of her body and to the halls of Mandos. His father is killed by Melkor. In his pursuit of the Silmarils he divides the house of his father, and he orders the slaying of Teleri to steal their ships for the journey to Middle-earth. On their arrival at the ice of Hekaraxë, he again sunders his followers, bringing the most loyal but leaving the others stranded by taking and burning their ships. In his dogged pursuit of the Silmarils he dies in battle against the Balrogs at Dor Daedeloth, but he passes his oath, his obsession, and his curse on to his sons, who continue to seek the stones after his death—his choices create sadness even for those who follow him.

The story of Fëanor allows his craftsmanship, courage, tenacity, charisma, and skill in battle, but it also highlights his possessiveness, selfishness, obsessive-compulsiveness, and his lack of forgiveness. He dies not only because of Melkor's evils, but because of his own repeated errors of violence and because of his "addiction" to the Silmarils: they set the stage for similar responses to the Ring of Power in *The Lord of the Rings*, though the stones hadn't evil in their origin, as had Sauron's creation—all the more tragic a point for Fëanor.[6] Oddly, of all Tolkien's stories of the elves this one most rehabilitates them as fascinating, variable, multi-faceted creatures, far from Tinkerbell or Cobweb or the paper fairies of Cottingley. Elves can now have full-grown, complex stories full of good and evil and everything in between—and they do.[7] They can create and destroy, save and kill, fall and fail, persist and give.

5. Epic, Faërie, and Myth

Tolkien rehabilitates not only notions of elves, but also those of monsters—and humans, who may well turn out to be the worst of monsters. As Tolkien remarks in his essay on *Beowulf*, the problem with most fairy-tale dragons is that they aren't dragon enough. Tolkien's dragons don't have that problem. Chrysophylax Dives is pure dragon, as is Smaug, though both, like Beowulf's dragon, also embody the traditional idea of dragon as hoarder of treasure. In the Anglo-Saxon world the dragon is the worst of monsters, because it practices (and represents) the most socially destructive of sins: greed. When we live well and successfully, we collect wealth and treasures for gift-giving, not for hoarding, to reward others, not to belittle them by comparison. The dragon hoards for the sake of the hoard, then sleeps on it so no one can put it to proper use—bad leaders act similarly. And greedy humans can turn into dragons, as we see with Fafnir in *Volsungasaga*—that may even have been the case with the dragon in *Beowulf*, though no proof of that suggestion remains clear in the manuscript. Chrysophylax turns cowardly, as Smaug does not, in the face of a weapon of power, but he also shows a hint of honor at last, also as Smaug does not: Chrysophylax finally does keep his pledge with Ægidius.

Tolkien's monsters are not allegorical figures, but true monsters, part of the fabric of the world, perversions of their better alternatives or originals: orcs from elves, trolls from ents. Sauron, the most dangerous monster of all, was once, like Gandalf, a Maia. Saruman, once the best of wizards, undergoes the greatest fall, because he turns into the smallest of creatures in his petty hatred and desire for pointless revenge against the hobbits who have done him no harm whatever. They are simply ripe for exploitation, and he knows how to do it. Fittingly the worst, most horrifying, and pitiable of the monsters he has created, Wormtongue, destroys Saruman at last, having been kicked and degraded one time too many. No longer human, but cannibalistic and creeping, he outlasts his last murderous deed by mere seconds. Tolkien's world proves as horrible for its monsters as it does for those upon whom the monsters bend their violence. Their potential to change redeems them as fictional creatures worth study who can extend our human sympathies.

Even the notion of monstrosity has flexibility. Treebeard nearly proves himself monstrous to the hobbits—to Saruman he certainly becomes so. No one has greater potential for monstrousness than do

Gandalf and Galadriel, but they have the strength to turn away from its temptations. As with Beowulf we may reasonably call them both *aglæcan*: powerful, scary beings who may choose to cause great harm or to do great good. The rehabilitation of wizard, elf, and ent comes in the fact that they have both agency and choice in how they use it. Sauron's rehabilitation as monster (and Morgoth's) comes in the fact that he need not have turned to monstrosity: like Gandalf and Galadriel, he could have chosen to help rather than to seek power and domination. He becomes a true monster not because of anything in his nature, but because of the enormous horror and loss that accompanies his fall.[8] Galadriel has potential for monstrosity, but resists it: her generosity and self-control hold in the moment of truth. Boromir becomes a monster, then repents and "saves his soul," we may say, at last. Ted Sandyman and others like him in the Shire become monsters of a sort (and a horrible sort), collaborators who try to gain from rather than resisting a destructive enemy: Tolkien would have little sympathy for collaborators and profiteers. The word *monster* comes from Latin *monēre*, to warn: Tolkien's human monsters serve as a warning of what we may let ourselves become; his natural monsters warn us that the world remains a dangerous place, and we must resist adding to its dangers through perversions of our own better natures.

Monsters, Norse Tradition, and the Conjunction of Spirit and Flesh

Tolkien creates some interesting effects, both fantastic and horrific, by experimenting with the idea of monstrosity as it relates particularly to the conjunction or confluence of body and spirit. Many scholars have discussed the enormous importance to his work of the author's Christianity—its inescapable, central, and sometimes problematic connection to his thinking but seeming disconnection to his textual world. And Christianity certainly has its own long tradition of monsters. In this section I intend to explore the influence of some Norse tales and traditions with respect to how Tolkien created and depicted his monsters in *The Hobbit, The Lord of the Rings, The Silmarillion,* and *Farmer Giles of Ham*.[9] I'd like to suggest particularly that the relationship of body and spirit

5. Epic, Faërie, and Myth

implied in literary notions of monstrosity contributes significantly to the powerful effects of his fiction. Tolkien used gaps or disjunctures between spirit and body to provide means to indicate danger and inspire terror.

In one sense all Tolkien's monsters exhibit a "devilish" connection to Morgoth, virulent results of his fully intentional Fall from Ilúvatar's grace. A strong influence on how Tolkien elaborates them comes from medieval Germanic traditions, both folk and literary. Old Norse texts provide necessary and illuminating analogues that help with how the author adopted and adapted notions of monstrosity to the organic fabric of Middle-earth. Tolkien didn't so much borrow from Norse tales as parallel aspects of their conceptions of the monstrous, which often involve an ambiguous relationship between body and spirit; that very tenuousness makes his monsters horrifying both in a Natural—or *midgarthian*—and in a Christian sense. They raise questions about the nature of evil both internal and external: to what degree can we resist it, and how immediately and tenaciously will it persist in its efforts to destroy us even in our modern world?

Medieval notions of the monstrous often depend on the idea of the *grotesque*, the body bearing not a common, recognizable shape and constitution, but existing in a state of flux between forms and worlds. As Alixe Bovey points out, some medieval monsters represented spiritual dangers while others represented physical dangers (6); Augustine, for instance, "took seriously the question of whether or not monstrous races shared a common ancestry with humans" (10), implying that they must at least once have had souls. In the Old English *Maxims* the dragon, a grotesque of no less than serpent, eagle, and fire, appears with as tangible a reality as frost, wood, javelins, and gems. By nature it seeks a barrow and hoards treasure; a spiritual *symbol*, it is also, the verse suggests, a physical fact. Norse tradition adds to the traits of the dragon reason and speech: does it thus become, with the addition of human traits, more or less horrifying?

While Christian artists, especially later in the Middle Ages, "used monster imagery to demonize foreigners" (Bovey 11), the variety of monsters and their often explicit connection to natural phenomena allows no simple equation. Even the gods, in tales whose origins antedate Christianity, exhibit traits one may call monstrous: in *Volsungasaga* Oðin provides Sigmundr with a magic sword, then breaks it when the hero needs it most in battle. Oðin appears as an old, one-eyed man dressed in a long, gray robe and a tall hat, but he comes and goes in a blink. He shepherds the body of Sinfjotli—who had himself spent time as a werewolf—into the beyond. He may help or harm at need—one dare not expect one or the other. We see in Oðin of course one source for Gandalf and Saruman, but we also meet the potentials and dangers associated with the conjunction and separation of body and spirit: Oðin frightens us partly because of his intangibility. As in *Paradise Lost*, where the prelapsarian Adam and Eve interact easily with God and angels, whereas in the postlapsarian world they fear and hide from God and the Faithful, Tolkien's Middle-earth deities, wizards, and wraiths suggest a greater or lesser degree of danger depending on one's own intentions and powers and the current "state of the union" of one's body and spirit.

Germanic monsters tend, like the semi-allegorical figues Sin and Death in *Paradise Lost*, to hang about in fully corporeal forms. Glámr, an undead but nonetheless substantial monster in *Grettissaga*, and an analogue for Grendel in *Beowulf*, typifies Norse monstrosity: an irreligious loner as a live man, as a dead one he terrifies folk by killing their cattle and riding over their rooftops at night. Worse, anyone daring to glance into his eyes meets a fell light that chills his spirit. Grettir does fight him, and even though he wins their battle, ever after he fears the dark and must sleep with a light burning. Norse ghosts, unwilling to sleep in their graves, may in human or animal form glom onto passersby and ride their bodies right down into the earth, presumably all the way to the underworld. The relevant texts don't specify the continuing presence of any sort of *spirit*, but the lingering *body* has power not only to cause fear, but also to do great harm to both the body and soul of the living creature unfortunate or foolhardy enough to confront the dead one. Fafnir, the dragon of *Volsungasaga*, began as a man, but through greed and patricide he became the worst of monsters—worst because most disruptive to peace and stability—and his life ends with a curse: his violence continues beyond his own death, potentially indefinitely.

Tolkien's monsters often create their particular brand of horror because of their peculiar relationship to dis-embodiment. Orcs represent an especially interesting and problematic case, deriving from elves who through generations of physical and mental torture have had both bodies

5. Epic, Faërie, and Myth

and minds twisted and misshapen, so that the opportunity to "access" the soul that their progenitors had seems to have disappeared. Tolkien wrote in one of his letters, that he represent orcs "as pre-existing real beings on whom the Dark Lord has exerted the fullness of his power in remodelling and corrupting them, not making them. That God would 'tolerate' that, seems no worse theology than the toleration of the calculated dehumanizing of Men by tyrants that goes on today" (195). That is, orcs are essentially "like us," or, worse yet, like elves: originally better than we, now worse than we—the plunge terrifies. Trolls, however, as "counterfeits" that "return to mere stone images when not in the dark" (*Letters* 191), create part of their effect not only from physical strength and brute aggressiveness, but because little sense appears of a soul that might temper violence or cruelty with conscience (with the notable semi-comic exception in *The Hobbit*).[10] This notion rather contrasts with much of Norse tradition; Jacob Grimm observes that the word *troll*, "though often used of giants, is yet a more comprehensive term, including other spirits and beings possessed of magic power, and equivalent to our *monster, spectre, unearthly being*" (526). Grimm notes in general that giants, under which rubric he lists trolls, "stand as specimens of a fallen or falling race, which with the strength combines also the innocence and wisdom of the old world" (529); one senses there an influence of biblical as well as old Germanic and possibly even Indo-European traditions. As Hilda Ellis adds, though, "[g]iants and trolls play a large part in the *Fornaldur Sögur* ... it is not always easy to distinguish one from the other" (70). Martin Arnold has observed that in the Norse myths the troll is normally female and strongly associated with magic, but that distinction doesn't hold up in the sagas, where the usage more often implies great strength and capacity for battle beyond human abilities. Tolkien's trolls appear more as forces of nature, little more than stone in daylight, but at night or under the direction of an evil force such as Sauron capable of causing considerable damage. The fear they generate relies on physical rather than spiritual plight, and interestingly Tolkien seems to change his notion of them from *The Hobbit* to *The Lord of the Rings*: in the first they show the capacity to relent, while in the later book they don't.

One may create a critical counterpoint with respect to dragons and Balrogs, and on a grander scale. Dragons represent evil tied to greed and cunning, while Balrogs represent the most dangerous natural qualities that evil can corrupt for fully destructive purpose: fire that burns even beyond the normal potential of the natural element. Originally Maiar, and thus divine beings, Balrogs rebelled against Ilúvatar with Morgoth, who apparently drew out and heightened their potential for maliciousness (Duriez 172). Has a Balrog any remaining possibility of mercy? Ringwraiths, grotesques who have partly but not fully passed from physicality into spirit, have power largely (but not exclusively) through their ability to generate chilling fear. Sauron represents a mythological link to Balrog and wraith with the addition of Morgoth's desire to reshape good into evil: worse than what can arise from the physical nature of Middle-earth alone, Sauron becomes a lidless eye, a ghost beyond a body, or he acquires a series of temporary embodiments that serve only to spread fear, domination, and suffering. He achieves pure spiritual malignancy. He gives up bodily power to concentrate his physicality in an object, the Ring of Power; with it he would gain the ability to control others, both body and spirit, but through its destruction his physical power dissipates entirely, and his spirit loses the ability to re-establish itself in the physical world of Middle-earth. Sauron's "sin" recapitulates Morgoth's—the desire to create beings so as to rule them—and by the time of *The Lord of the Rings*, he represents the worst horror the world exhibits. As had Morgoth before him, he addresses all his effort to become something "wholly other" both from Ilúvatar and from all his creatures. As *The Silmarillion* tells, he has nominally repented only to turn once again to absolute evil: the desire to strip others of fee will and impose his will upon them. He replaces the original "diabolus"—Tolkien's term—and becomes the enemy, the shadow, the slave-master. Is Middle-earth's greatest horror then spiritual enslavement?

Converse examples of the problem of disembodiment come, of course, with Frodo and Bilbo, who leave Middle-earth with the Elves through the Grey Havens: much like biblical Enoch and Elijah, they exit quotidian existence with body and soul intact, reducing the audience's sense of fear and loss at their departure. We have grown so attached to them that their deaths would perhaps ruin the narrative. But they exist as partial grotesques, and so not without some sense of horror at their departing. Both have been "stretched" by carrying the Ring, Bilbo into great old age and Frodo into a version of himself with whom he can't

5. Epic, Faërie, and Myth

make peace: the hobbit who, entrusted with the Ring's destruction, at the moment of truth couldn't give it up. Middle-earth may be lesser without them, but, as they remain whole, we need not lament that terrifying event, the cleaving of body and soul of the characters central to the quest on which we have followed. Even Sam, who perhaps most strongly feels their loss, finds resolution in the completion of their story and in his return to Hobbiton: his "I'm home," even more than the ascent to the throne of the king, concludes that story of that Age and resolves what any story can of our human fears. Like Odysseus, we must put the hell of war behind and get back to life.

Perhaps the most troubling event of *The Lord of the Rings*, Frodo's inability to destroy the Ring inside Mount Doom, terrifies not only because of the landscape, the fear that Gollum may kill Frodo, and the greater fear that Sauron may at last recover the Ring, but also—and mostly—because Frodo, perhaps the least assuming of creatures, can't resist the Ring's power at last. After all he has done, he will still fall into absolute evil without the intervention of "chance" or, as Tolkien suggests in one of his letters, *mercy* (*Letters* 252). That is, Frodo can by choice— though under the influence of the Ring, of course—give up his own soul, the most terrifying choice of all. Gollum represents Frodo's double, Frodo as monster, having crossed over into total subservience to the physical object, the Ring. He can still fight his own monstrosity, as we see in the episode where "Sméagol" quarrels internally with "Gollum" for what they will do with "Master"; he may help him or kill him for the Ring. But the "monster"—having given up "spirit" to retain the existence of "body"—has already won long ago. The lingering battle only increases the immediacy of the suffering and the loss. Monsters don't necessarily suffer less for being monsters, and the truth that anyone may become a monster may be the most painful point of all: we can't entirely trust anyone, especially ourselves, and while a monster may gain power to destroy others, it most completely destroys itself—by choice.

So while Tolkien varies them, his monstrous models, with the notable exception of Sauron, come largely from Germanic sources, best documentable in the Norse or Old Icelandic tales: trolls represent natural, physical forces, enlivened versions of topographical phenomena such as rock outcroppings, waterfalls, rockslides, but anthropomorphized and imbued with magic. Icelandic ghosts and wraiths have physical, not spiritual presence: they terrify through remnant physical capacity, but also because they represent something dead or lifeless that gives the full appearance of life without any trace of humanity (spirit, conscience, mercy, justice). Perhaps Sauron, too, and "postlapsarian" Saruman like him, presents a demonized version of Oðin as a medieval Christian or convert might have seen him, one who lures the weak, unsuspecting soul under his influence and thus into horror and damnation.

A body separated from its "spirit" by death may create far more danger than it did alive with the spirit present; a body that never had a spirit, thus unsympathetic to those who have them, presents another danger; a body that denies or treats incorrectly the presence of its own soul may also provoke horror—compare, for instance, Kurtz in Conrad's *Heart of Darkness*. The dis-location of spirit and body creates horror by problematizing liminal boundaries: what am "I"? what does "death" mean? what shape will an enemy take? The "fallen" world of Middle-earth parallels without parody the Christian issues of in-body and out-of-body existence, exploits them to deepen sorrow and to expand the opportunity for glory. So we find here a great question: does the greater horror come from an enemy more like us—possessing soul and reason—or one wholly other from us—lacking both reason and soul?[11]

Back again to dragons: Smaug, the chief monster of *The Hobbit*, derives largely from the similar creatures in *Volsungasaga* and *Beowulf*. Fafnir of the saga is of course a man-dragon, a man become dragon by the ruthless murder of his father to obtain the treasure "Otter's Ransom." Regin, Fafnir's brother, recruits the young hero Sigurðr to kill the dragon, and even as he lies dying, Fafnir tries to find means to trick and curse the boy-hero. Some scholars, notably Raymond Tripp, have argued that the dragon in Beowulf is, similarly, a man-dragon, the last survivor of a race who climbed onto his people's treasure and through excessive attachment to it transformed into that worst of beasts in the Anglo-Saxon world.[12] The dragon hoards treasure, which one should give to secure friendships, to create and maintain the social bonds that support the society. Bilbo's dragon, like that of *Volsungasaga* rather than *Beowulf*, has reason and cunning, but he has no remorse about killing: the loss of even the tiniest part of his treasure will set him burning everyone and everything in sight until he has recovered the loss, quenched his

5. Epic, Faërie, and Myth

wrath, and terrified any survivors into generations of silence. For hobbits, dwarves, and humans Smaug is "wholly other" in the infernal sense, a different order of creature, either because he had no soul to begin with—if he represents a chaotic force of nature, something anti-organizational—or has lost it, a human who has given up his soul in favor of absolute commitment to greed. In *The Silmarillion* Morgoth breeds dragons as agents of terror, disruption, and destruction. The presence of reason accompanied by unrelenting violence makes the dragon among the most frightening of enemies: we fear the possibility that we may become like him, but not nearly so powerful, thus with the same drives but subordinate, forever at the mercy of a worse but stronger creature merciless to enemy and friend alike.

Tonally opposite, particularly for its use of humor, *Farmer Giles of Ham* uses both a giant and a dragon, the former contrastable with trolls and the latter with the dragon in *The Hobbit*. Though destructive, both monsters in *Farmer Giles* relent, and the story suggests that they do so not only because they fear pain and death, but because they can reason. Rationality implies the presence of spiritual substance, that as creatures they have or exhibit something more than a river or a mountain or a tree. The giant comes upon people rather accidentally than with the intent to do them harm, and when the dragon later explains how his own misfortunes came about as a result of the giant's misinformation—that away East he had found cattle undefended by knights—the giant can only say of the effusion from Farmer Giles' blunderbuss that "I thought it was horseflies!" (*Farmer Giles* 79).

The dragon, Chrysophylax Dives, by nature a hoarder and liar, immediately backs down from Giles upon seeing Tailbiter, the sword that essentially wields itself in the vicinity of dragons. He reneges on his promise to bring Giles his fortune in exchange for his life, but when Giles spares him a second time—along with an acceptable portion of his treasure—the dragon becomes a friend to the farmer and lives up to his promise to defend him against the king. Though both kill without compunction, neither dragon nor giant entirely lacks a sense of morality: that makes them at last partly comic characters and thus not ultimately sources of fear and horror for the reader. They notably complicate the body-soul issue by showing the power of comedy to turn horror into light adventure. They succeed in such a milieu partly because Farmer

Giles resembles them more than he differs from them: he, too, lacks a bit of morality, interested more in maintaining and expanding his lands, fortunes, and superiority to his neighbors than in doing anything an observer might call "the right thing." He fights mostly to avoid the scorn of folk such as the miller and the blacksmith, and he refuses, with the dragon defending his position for him, to share his treasure with the king. He finally becomes king of his own Little Kingdom, not by wisdom or right, but by luck, as the narrator several times repeats. The "monsters" in the tale are at last no worse than the people—for whatever comfort that truth allows.

Monstrosity in *Farmer Giles* resides, if anywhere, in the king, who governs by tradition and bluster rather than by wisdom, right, or even power, and who uses what influence he has to take what he wants at others' expense. Driven away by the dragon, he retreats into a sort of cave of unimportance, disappearing from the story and shortly from the world. Greedier even than the traditional symbol of greed (the dragon), but without any power left to enforce his greed, the king loses both relevance and the ability to inspire fear. That human monster, unlike the somewhat-redeemed dragon, dies before his death, monster no longer.[13]

Finally, then, Tolkien develops his monsters from different though interlacing traditions, but he allows them their own evolution though the course of his many tales: as with all other components of Middle-earth, they must organically fit the world. He develops his heroes by providing them with epiphanies from above and below: they meet the most frightening of challenges having been prepared by meetings with the most helpful advisers—or by finding the greatest of earthly loves. As essentials of Tolkien's world, the Norse-born monsters inspire fascinating and difficult questions about the nature of monstrosity and its capability to inspire fear, doubt, wonder, greed, and heroism.

6

Tolkien and Myth
Orientalism and Occidentalism

One of Tolkien's chief achievements lies in mythmaking. His "mythology for England" has inspired among less sympathetic readers (or moviegoers) more than a few cries of racism, sexism, and exclusionism. But his treatment of "differences" comes from battle fronts and a new approach to old notions of nation and empire that derive from Classical models, but show also the time's mixed fear and admiration of the "East." Brian Rosebury asserts that *The Lord of the Rings* "invests high value in the joyful acceptance of diversity, in the contemptuous tearing up of unnecessary Rules, in resistance to those who 'like minding other folk's business and talking big'"(148): this chapter will explore that idea as a question of "othering" and of finding one's own place in the world.

Tolkien, Classical Myth, and Said's Orientalism: Othering the East and the South

Tolkien's tales, both his own and as they appear in Peter Jackson's films, have touched off a few incendiary cries of racism, sexism, and exclusionism because of the interactions among some of his peoples. But the fictional impulses that some critics, typically those who would marginalize fantasy or, more recently, Western or male authors, have identified as exclusionary come in some respects from the battle fronts of Tolkien's time, from the World Wars and from academic or literary as well as international politics. They also come simply from the geography of Tolkien's imaginative world, with no political source or referent whatsoever. Tolkien's constructions of peoples, to the degree that he separates them at all, also show a new affective approach to old notions of nation and empire that derive from Classical models (epic poems particularly). Audience responses to orcs, trolls, Southrons, and woses, for instance, suggest a mixed fear and admiration of "Others" (in this case mostly peoples of the Middle East). While Britain struggled through the twentieth century with its failing "empire," notably in India and the Middle East, the twentieth-century world at large was gaining a greater sense of the effects of the confrontations and exchanges of different peoples through history: old ideologies met new ones, but in the remnant—and dangerous—context of old values of faith, heroism, and Classical traditions. England struggled with its own class system—so, however unwillingly American audiences may admit it, did the U.S.—and with prevailing economic and cultural models as well as educational traditions, based until then almost wholly on Classical texts and models. We can see some of those concerns amplified in *The Lord of the Rings*, with significant source stories in *The Silmarillion* and ramifications even in *The Hobbit*. This section will briefly consider Tolkien's feelings about and use of Classical myth, his treatment of the peoples of Middle-earth whom commentary has occasionally accused him of "othering," and Edward Said's salient discussion of Orientalism with respect to its bearing on Tolkien's world.

In *J. R. R. Tolkien: Author of the Century*, Shippey considers the political implications of Tolkien's fiction; some seldom enter discussions of his work, while some intrude on the criticism, often responses from those readers who bring to their reading their own literary-political positions:

> Tolkien not only poses questions about evil, he also provides answers and solutions—one of the things which has made him unpopular with the professionally gloomy or fashionably nihilist.... [H]is concern ... is not with the private and the personal (the themes of the "modernist" novel), but with the public and the political ... [because] the most important events in private lives (and even more, in deaths) have often been public and political [xxxi].

Shippey refers of course to the World Wars, not to the academic politics of who gets to critique whom and in what language. Tolkien addressed war and the clash of peoples and goals, the participation of high- and low-ranking folk equally; he sought to show the problem of evil action and evil intent regardless of one's rank or politics. He created stories in a mythic or fantastic realm to allow for the possibility of a solution at

6. Tolkien and Myth

once grand and simple, at once ancient and modern: whether we like it or not, we must resist evil, both internal and external, with steadfast courage, and we may not survive it. *Evil* means the attempt of those around us or those from afar, or even our own attempts, to enslave others to one's own selfish purposes. Through the twentieth century those attempts had become more pervasive, more wide-reaching, and far better armed than they had ever been, and they remained to some extent tied to racial (as well as cultural and economic) issues.

Because Tolkien set out to create a body of English myths, we may too readily assume that he had little esteem for the Classical or other mythologies: I don't believe that's the case. In a letter from 1951 he notes that he wants the tone and "air," the "clime and soil of the North West, not of Italy or the Aegean, still less of the East" (*Letters* 141). But that preference for tales dealing with his own part of the world doesn't imply a lack of respect for others. Later in that same letter he wrote that in Middle-earth the "better and nobler sort of Men are in fact the kin of those that had departed to Númenor, but remain in a simple 'Homeric' state of patriarchal and tribal life" (154); he is neither praising nor disparaging Homer or patriarchy, but commenting by contrast on the state of those "uncorrupted if ignorant" people who lived in the West of Middle-earth during the rise of Sauron in the Second Age—he adds later a comment on the "heroic 'Homeric' horsemen" as an essential part of *The Lord of the Rings* (159). In another letter from 1956 he wrote that Greek myth hinges more on its language than its plots (231): he was thinking as a philologist whose love of stories begins but does not end with the love of words and names. In 1953 he noted that he grew up studying Classics and first found "literary pleasure" in Homer; we shouldn't feel surprised to hear so from a philologist, finding joy in words, though for Tolkien the real discovery came in Anglo-Saxon (172). At King Edward's School in Birmingham and Exeter College, Oxford, he studied intensely Latin and Greek language and literature; what he gained there didn't inhibit his developing a preference for the Northern languages or literatures, but neither does that later preference negate the influence and enjoyment of the earlier.[1]

Tolkien got from Homer, and I suspect to some extent from Vergil as well, the sense of the Heroic World that encompasses the Classical epics. They touch very little on the life of "ordinary" people, focusing instead on the noble heroes whose skill in battle, whose wrath, whose duty to the gods, and whose fates drive them to the liminal boundaries of existence, to the constant cutting edge of martial achievement and mortality. Aragorn lives in that world, as do Boromir and Faramir. Homer departs from that world only for the briefest instants, such as when Eurycleia feels the scar on the leg of the newly returned Odysseus; Vergil can't depart from it, since he must tell the story of the divinely moved and heroically wrought origins of his country—he hasn't the license for the quotidian concerns of a servant washing the grime from a nearly exhausted, middle-aged soldier. Tolkien makes the significant move from the tight enclosure of the Heroic World with his hobbits: we find them as normal as cakes and tea, bread and ale. The presence of the everyday world in *The Lord of the Rings* doesn't deny the heroism that takes place in the big world around the Shire nor that of the hobbits who take part in it; it does show the realistic understanding of someone who knew the battlefield, who appreciated the actual sorrows of war more than its legendary glories, who preferred the life of a Bilbo to that of an Achilles. Tolkien's story takes place in a world comparable to Homer's, but in a part of that world about which Homer's audience didn't want to hear, but Tolkien's did. From him we gain an appreciation for the experiences of Sam, the Gaffer, and Farmer Maggot without losing any for Aragorn, Éowyn, and Éomer. Tolkien as storyteller interweaves, as he saw fit, in classic Anglo-Saxon style, the Classical with the Germanic with the modern. The Classical "South" is not "other," but part of the fabric of fiction's "world creation."

Tolkien has drawn criticism for his treatment of orcs and Southrons, and we may reasonably add to that list trolls; I have heard accusations of racism (from those who have seen the movies and not read the books) and sexism (from those who have read the books and not seen the movies). In some ways those assertions mirror the prejudices of our own times: we want every author of every time to show the same "enlightened" view we have and to make plain to the audience that everyone in the world of the text, regardless of race, gender, and preference, is equal and deserves the full range of human rights. In my recent experience, that means that more readers want something "relatable": I hate that word, but I'm hearing it more and more from students and from casual readers and even from some of my professional colleagues. That means, really, that they want protagonists who look and sound like them.

6. Tolkien and Myth

A few years ago I saw in the Sunday New York *Times* Book Review an essay (by a female critic) arguing that male authors aren't likely to find much success anymore unless they write for women: men who write for a male audience will be unlikely to find an audience greater than about 1500, so serious publishers should probably stay away from them. I hope that isn't true. Writing something like that is certainly sexist in its own way. The reading audience must then assume itself comprising almost exclusively females. Routinely I face questions from teaching colleagues at my home institution about whether women really read Tolkien or attend conference sessions on him, since he "wrote only about and for boys," or whether people of color find his work offensive. I explain as patiently as I can, and usually much to their disbelief, that at least half of Tolkien's current audiences and critics are women; that holds true, I think, because how Tolkien deals with the problems of evil, responsibility, danger, and mortality has as much applicability to women as to men. Those concerns constitute the eternal, pervading issues of living for all of us equally. Similarly, LGBT readers have found Tolkien's world congenial because, as I hear in discussions, they see the situation of characters who are or feel marginalized and yet have the courage or even power to assert themselves; they do so by means of who they are and what they do, as the equals of anyone more privileged in their world.

A useful way to approach those critical issues, at least in theoretical terms and for our time if not for Tolkien's, comes in Edward Said's famous and controversial book *Orientalism*. Said makes some pertinent formulations of the problem, though he addresses more an American audience than a British one, for example:

> One specifically American contribution to the discourse of empire is the specialized jargon of policy expertise. You don't need Arabic or Persian or even French to pontificate about how the democracy domino effect is just what the Arab world needs. Combative and woefully ignorant policy experts, whose world experience is limited to the beltway, grind out books on "terrorism" and liberalism, or about Islamic fundamentalism and American foreign policy, or about the end of history, all of it vying for attention and influence quite without regard for truthfulness or reflection or real knowledge.... The worst aspect of this essentializing stuff is that human suffering in all its density and pain is spirited away [xxi].

That passage clearly states the problem of American public discourse on the contemporary Arab "Other": we take greater interest in self-aggrandizement than in the issues of the Arab world. Writing later in the book about the state of "scholarship" on such issues, Said adds,

> One would find this kind of procedure less objectionable as political propaganda—which is what it is—were it not accompanied by sermons on the objectivity, the fairness, the impartiality of a real historian, the implication always being that Muslims & Arabs cannot be objective but that Orientalists like [Bernard] Lewis writing about Muslims and Arabs are, by definition, by training, by the mere fact of their Westernness. This is the culmination of Orientalism as a dogma that not only degrades its subject matter but also blinds its practitioners [319].

That statement addresses explicitly the problem of outsiders commenting on peoples and cultures about whom they're read—from polemical sources—but of whose cultures they have no personal experience. The term "Orientalism" applies to the matter that the ignorant and uncaring writers produce.

Said provides an answer to such questions:

> Modern thought and experience have taught us to be sensitive to what is involved in representation, in studying the Other, in racial thinking, in unthinking and uncritical acceptance of authority and authoritative ideas in the sociopolitical role of intellectuals, in the great value of skeptical critical consciousness [327].

We must, of course, avoid prejudice of our own and examine those of others. We must think for ourselves and learn on our own about persons and peoples different from us, and we must avoid quick judgments based on differences. He adds shortly ahead,

> The construction of identity—for identity, whether of Orient or Occident, France or Britain, while obviously a repository of distinct collective experiences, is finally a construction in my opinion—involves the construction of opposites and of "others" whose actuality is always subject to the continuous interpretation and re-interpretation of their differences from "us." Each age and society re-creates its "Others" [332].

The problem of construction of opposites enters the dialectic of many areas of scholarship and criticism in our time. But we should take care, before we judge others to be "Othering," that they are actually creating "Others" for us to critique—the problem that often comes up among the Tolkien "haters."

Said concludes, then, that

> it is extremely important to understand that the reason Orientalism is opposed by so many thoughtful non-Westerners is that its modern discourse is correctly perceived as a discourse of power originating in an era of colonialism ... [with a] chronic tendency to deny, suppress, or distort cultural context ... to maintain the fiction of its scholarly disinterest [345].

The problem comes, of course, in scholars' too readily making assertions about subjects we don't know, claiming sufficiently intimate knowledge to pass judgments without actual experience of the peoples and cultures—and in the sadly continuing enterprise to control other peoples for the supposed benefit of one's own.

What Said suggests about Orientalism, the study with obligatory polemical intrusion into the East, mostly the Middle East, by incompletely informed and often prejudiced Westerners, we might as easily say about gender- or race-based scholarship of many sorts. We may also say it about some of Tolkien detractors. Tolkien was writing fiction, not scholarship, about a created world, one with many peoples for whom interaction often proves difficult and dangerous, and not always because any one is good or bad. The concerns current in social or political scholarship readily invade literary criticism and have sometimes resulted in accusations that Tolkien treats creatures or races from the south or east as lesser than Westerners. So, and I ask this question of Tolkien's books, not the films made from them, what picture of "others" does Tolkien give us? He never set out to write orientalism, but he drew geographical distinctions among peoples and created in his fictional world "enemies" for narrative and thematic purposes.

First, since he was creating a mythology for England at the Western end of Europe, he builds his stories with a great sea and no inhabited areas to the west but the Undying Lands: thus no dangers will come from there in the hobbit stories (they do in *The Silmarillion*, which the critics often ignore). Second, we must remember that from the perspective of humans, hobbits, ents, and elves *are* others, and he hardly draws them as hateful beings. Further, anyone who has read *The Silmarillion* will know that elves and Western humans don't escape from accounts of their own selfish decisions, evil actions, and abuses of other peoples or their world—Tolkien does not treat them sentimentally. Orcs, from their own point of view, are also others among themselves, no group of them getting along very well with any other, as we see particularly in

"The Uruk-Hai," Book 3, Chapter 3, of *The Two Towers*, about the capture and escape of Merry and Pippin, and in Book 6, Chapter 1, of *The Return of the King*, where Sam must rescue Frodo in "The Tower of Cirith Ungol." Tolkien explains that orcs come from the perversion of elves to evil intention through evil treatment, so they do not begin as entirely other: they become distinct through evil use. He describes them in a 1954 letter as "fundamentally a race of 'rational incarnate' creatures, though horribly corrupted, if no more so than many Men to be met today" (190). Orcs are no less like us than hobbits. Though to humans and hobbits and elves orcs' speech seems foul, sharp, and aggressive, they use the Common Speech perfectly well if they want to, as when they capture Bilbo and the Dwarves in the Misty Mountains in *The Hobbit*. The language that disturbs the other peoples for its own sake comes not from them, but from Sauron, the ultimate Other, not because someone else chooses him so, but because he chooses so: "One Ring to bring them all and in the darkness bind them"—not exactly a generous and democratic principle. The people of Westernesse/Númenor we may see as worse than orcs, since they come to choose evil and bring about the destruction of their own civilization when they had every opportunity to know and act better. The Haradrim of the South, though they fight for Sauron in the war at the end of the Third Age, and though the one who dies at Sam's feet in *TT.* IV.4 has dark skin, descend also, at least in part, from the Númenoreans.[2] The Witch-king raises his realm in the North, not the South or the East, in the fourteenth century of the Third Age, and the people who join him are as bad as those from any other region.

Tolkien includes few details about the peoples of the East. In the nineteenth century of the Third Age the Wainriders, stirred by Sauron, attacked and conquered and enslaved people on its eastern and southern borders, and in the next century they made alliances with the Khandrim and Haradrim, but Eärnil's army defeated them, and many of them died in the Dead Marshes. Those tales make them warlike and subject to Sauron's corruption, but nothing that Tolkien wrote depicts them as inferior in character, courage, or soul to other humans, who have suffered similar failings. When Tolkien actually uses the word *other*, he does so in reference to Tom Bombadil, but with respect to other creatures with whom he comes in contact: "the spirit that desires knowledge of other things, their history and nature, *because they are 'other'*" (*Letters* 192).

The essential point to recognize here is that Tolkien shows no evidence in his stories of the prejudices against persons based on race, culture, gender, or locale: he does not give into the errors of twentieth-century orientalism any more than he rejected the value of Classical learning. He created a diverse array of creatures and peoples in a complex geography with an intricate and interwoven history, all of whom are capable of falling into evil—or resisting it. That point, perhaps, creates his most important theme and warning: mortality weighs on all of us, and we must resist evil within ourselves with all the heroism we can muster.

Myth and the Problem of Generational Succession in The Silmarillion

Combining the traumas of World War I and the mutual Christian and Germanic tendency toward apocalyptic cosmology, Tolkien in *The Silmarillion* also struggles with what I'd like to suggest is the guiding motif of any system of myth and an idea central to the movement of his own myths: generational succession. Many Occidental and Middle Eastern mythic cycles, Greek, Norse, Mesopotamian, Egyptian, or Cymric (as well as the narrative of the Jewish Bible, not only in Genesis, but in the passing of religious tradition and political influence from father to son), deal largely in the perennial cultural problem of passing wisdom and power from one generation to the next. Part of the problem of the twentieth-century waste land involved whether or not proper generational succession could even take place after the horrors of mechanized war. Tolkien the myth-maker explored the violent tensions as Middle-earth suffers various struggles of divine beings, elves, and humans among themselves and with one another. In the movement of *The Silmarillion* from Age to Age toward the coming to power (and implied ultimate failure) of humans, Tolkien suggests both the cultural upheavals of our own world to and through the "war to end all wars" and also each individual generation's grappling to understand and surpass its parents and to control and limit its children. That recurring theme in Tolkien mirrors aspects of history that produced the cultural implosion of World

War I; it also draws particular attention to the anxieties that trouble us as individuals seeking both continuity and identity.

In his 1934 book *A History of the Great War, 1914–1918*, C. R. M. F. Cruttwell explains the unique problems of World War I:

> In former campaigns, except during the comparatively rare incidents of battle, troops were generally withdrawn from the immediate contact of the enemy immune from danger. In the Great War a large proportion of the total forces were continually standing over against each other in trenches sometimes a bare thirty yards apart.... Men would live for long spells under conditions fouler and more horrible than the beasts that perish [628].

Yet, he adds, despite unprecedented misery, psychological stress, and doubt, English and French leaders succeeded in holding their peoples together by their ability to convince

> their countrymen by example, precept, and the fire of the spirit that the war must and could be won somehow.... "After every defeat," as it was written of the French revolutionaries, "they prepared for an impossible but certain victory" [628].

According to Winston Churchill in his 1931 history, *The World Crisis*, a similar mood was brewing in the United States, until President Wilson rose to recognize it:

> He underestimated the volume and undervalued the quality of the American feeling in favour of the Allies. Not until he was actually delivering his famous war message to Congress did he understand where ... the dominant willpower of the nation lay and had always lain.... [N]ot until then did he reveal to the American people where in his judgment world-right was founded, and how their own lives and material interests were at stake [702].

Churchill adds, then, lamentingly, what good Wilson might have done by acting two years sooner:

> And if done then what abridgment of the slaughter; what sparing of the agony; what ruin, what catastrophes would have been prevented; in how many million homes would an empty chair be occupied to-day; how different would be the shattered world in which victors and vanquished alike are condemned to live [703].

And those sentiments arose even before the rise of Nazism, creating a world where, as often in *The Silmarillion*, hope had to outlast reason. The tone of both pairs of historical passages has great importance. Topically the statements address the need for peoples to come together to

6. Tolkien and Myth

subdue a common enemy; emotionally they relate leaders' sense that morale and courage waxed sufficiently for millions of individual soldiers to endure torment and face death to keep a world from tipping over a brink into an age of unfettered destruction and international oppression on a scale as yet unseen in human history.

But while public and political hope and faith may have remained pragmatically high, the experience of the foot soldier was a different matter. Consider Churchill's reflections on the Battle of the Somme, in which Tolkien participated, and during which time *The Silmarillion* was taking shape in Tolkien's imagination[3]; note in the first passage a brief literary sally into the present tense and the subsequent gradual turn to cold, hard, horrifying, accomplished fact:

> A sense of the inevitable broods over the battlefields of the Somme. The British armies were so ardent, their leaders so confident, the need and appeals of our allies so clamant, and decisive results seemingly so near, that no human power could have prevented the attempt [660].

But when on July 1, 1916, "the British and French armies rose from their trenches steel-helmeted, gas-masked, equipped with all the latest apparatus of war" (664), while the French, after their "punishment" at Verdun managed to take the enemy by surprise, the Germans were "fully prepared" for the British assault (664). By that night "[n]early 60,000 British soldiers had fallen, killed or wounded, or were prisoners"—"this was the greatest loss and slaughter sustained in a single day in the whole history of the British Army" (667). Churchill adds, "The extent of the catastrophe was concealed by the Censorship, and its significance masked by a continuance of the fighting on a far smaller scale, four divisions alone being employed," only to continue and expand later (667 ff.). We know, of course, the end of that war, but Churchill concludes his book with these questions:

> Is this the end? Is it to be merely a chapter in a cruel and senseless story? Will a new generation in their turn be immolated to square the black accounts of Teuton and Gaul? Will our children bleed and gasp again in devastated lands? Or will there spring from the very fires of conflict that reconciliation of the three giant combatants, which would unite their genius and secure to each in safety and freedom a share in rebuilding the glory of Europe? [849].

We know, of course, the answers to those questions as well, and they must have shaped, indirectly if not directly, the evolution of *The Silmar-*

illion as a mythology because they shaped, or rather nearly disintegrated, the world that Tolkien's Europe knew in the early to middle 20th century. Churchill's call to the next generation has great importance here: "Don't do what we did," he implies; use what we learned and work together for peace. Tolkien's Middle-earth struggles with similar questions: alliances between groups of elves, elves and humans, elves and dwarves and hobbits and ents, all to face an enemy far beyond their individual strength and endurance in repeated, devastating wars. They work together because they must, and they succeed by doing so. When alliances fail, peoples fail, and the allies fail to raise a generation to follow them.

Similar questions undergird the development of many systems of myth. Though Tolkien didn't find himself drawn to Mediterranean myth, its cultural and educational ubiquity necessitated that it influence his imagination. In the Greek tradition first come Chaos, Gaea, and Eros, then Ouranos, Kronos, and the other Titans, then Zeus—Zeus, the wiliest of children according to Hesiod's *Theogony*. With Rhea's help he subdues Kronos and causes the father to disgorge the children he has eaten, and then he takes his father's place as king, sorting out the elder Titans according to whether or not they'll help him bring about peace. If we believe Shelley in *Prometheus Unbound*, Zeus, too, must eventually fall: nature changes, and even the gods must give way. In addition to the tales of the gods, Hesiod in *Works and Days* enumerates of the successive human races: gold (idyllic), silver (foolish), bronze (destructive), heroic (semi-divine) and iron (crafty, but decaying, and lost to pain and suffering). They show us the Greek preoccupation with the movement, perhaps more regress than progress, of generations.

In "Gylfaginning," which begins Snorri Sturluson's *Prose Edda*, the first living being, Ymir the giant, melts out of the primeval ice, and he gives rise to giants and Ogres. More frost thaws into a cow; her milk feeds Ymir, and from the frost she licks the first man, Buri, who begets a son, Bor, and he three sons, the first one Oðin. The sons kill Ymir, and from his body they make the world—a myth can conceivably begin any way, but this one begins like so many with succession and violent struggle. *Snorra Edda* also ends by dealing with succession: after Ragnarök, when the gods and humans have fought Loki and the monsters to mutual destruction, the children of the gods remain, and the earth rises anew

6. Tolkien and Myth

to be repopulated by Líf and Lífthrasir, two humans hidden away, presumably by the gods for that very purpose. The young gods will live well, along with the best of the old gods, recalling the adventures of the past under a new young sun—we may see that story as a metaphor for day and night or for natural necessity, which removes even the most glorious generations, replacing them with a bright new one with hopes of a better world. Those stories directly influenced Tolkien's imagination.

Not only Greek and Norse myths depend on generational succession: the Second-Millennium BC Babylonian *Enuma Elish* creates a similar pattern. It begins with Apsu, god of fresh waters, the begetter, and Tiamat, Mother and goddess of salt waters. From them come four generations, whom Apsu intends, against Tiamat's wishes, to destroy, because they disturb his rest. Ea, the skillful and wise god of flowing water, lulls Apsu to sleep and kills him. Ea builds his house atop his dead father and begets Marduk, for whom Anu, sky god, creates the four winds. The winds trouble Tiamat, who resolves to destroy the gods she earlier sought to protect. Marduk in his thunderstorm chariot defends the gods against her, defeating her and her army of monsters, but in exchange for his protection the other gods have had to give him sovereignty and the control of fate, which he accepts, setting the world in order according to his taste. Could we find a myth more obviously reflecting inter-generational struggles? We beget either from desire to do so or from the force of nature, but we struggle with the children, who must either destroy us or obey us and wait us out—they must either die or eventually rise to power to refigure the world in their own fashion. Sometimes, as we see in retrospect from Churchill's post–World War I questions, they fail, and Tolkien doesn't omit that truth from his fantastic world.

We find similar but demythologized concerns in the traditional Cymric tales of *The Mabinogi*. This body of tales, by the time of our receipt dealing mostly with heroes and their magical adventures, may comprise revisions of forgotten myths of Mabon, the god of youth: most of the stories teach something essential about one's coming of age, either skills or attitudes or rituals necessary for one to become worthy of and then deal with adult responsibilities. In its first story, "Pwyll Prince of Dyfed," Pwyll, hunting, pursues a stag into the "Otherworld," without knowing he has crossed its borders, and drives away the dogs that have brought down the beast. A horseman arrives and expresses offense—he happens to be Arawn, King of Annwfn—and he requires that, to atone, Pwyll must do him the service of exchanging places and shapes with him for a year, at the end of which time Pwyll must subdue a particular enemy of the king. Pwyll does so, avoiding lovemaking with the king's wife and completing the task assigned him. At the end of the year they exchange again, both having done well in the other's shape. In his next adventure, returned to his own world, Pwyll sits on a magic mound and watches a magic rider go by; eventually he stops her—Rhiannon, a magical princess—and they express their mutual love. After a year and a new test, he marries her; they have a son, Gwri Golden-hair, but the child is magically stolen. The court believes Rhiannon to have killed him, and as a penance imposed by the local wise folk, for seven years she must tell her story to anyone who visits court and must offer to carry visitors on her back. Eventually a lord, Teyrnon, manages to rescue the boy and return him to his parents. At Teyrnon's suggestion they rename the boy Pryderi, "anxiety," but a word also close to *prydu*, "to compose poetry." Pwyll has often been a dunce, if a decent one, through much of the story, but he rules well until his death; then Pryderi ascends and also rules successfully: together they transcend anxiety to become the stuff of didactic literature. That tale seems simple and secular enough, but I'd like to suggest that it also reflects the proper movement of generations. Pwyll, having without knowing it trespassed, must do penance to Arawn, the wronged father figure. Pwyll "replaces" him without breaching his relationship with the queen, here both his new ally's bride and a mother figure. He completes his assigned task by obeying the "father" *exactly*, becomes a trusted friend, marries, and has a son of his own. Significantly, he marries a figure for the beloved Celtic horse goddess; to grow up their boy must obey, show courage and obedience, master horsemanship, win a bride, reproduce, and fulfill his appointed social tasks. In time, if he's a good father, his son will fulfill his place and perform the same rituals to assure the next generation.

Tolkien knew well at least the Classical, Norse, and Celtic mythic traditions, and from them he incorporates language, characters, motifs, and themes. As Shippey points out, "*The Silmarillion* bears a kind of relationship to Christian myth" (*Author* 238); he adds that we may also

6. Tolkien and Myth

see it as a "complex tragedy of mixed blood, of the kind seen in several poems of the *Elder Edda*" (244); further, it embodies "a passion for family history" (242).[4] Thematically it stresses, especially in the Beren and Lúthien story, one of Tolkien's most important ideas: love's resurrective power (248), both in a romantic and religious sense. Perhaps the most consistent borrowing from all the mythic traditions comes in the repetition of the motif of generational succession and how love leads to successful succession. Possessiveness or dismissiveness, on the other hand, leads to the destruction of families and cultures—no surprise that he wrote *The Hobbit* as a bedtime story for his children.[5] Importantly, even *The Hobbit* doesn't shirk consideration of death: Bilbo faces it, and Thorin, Fili, and Kili die in the Battle of Five Armies. Death both tests and provides space for the next generation—in literary contexts it both stands for itself and symbolizes the changes necessary in the world.

Finally, with historical and mythical background in place, we may begin to examine the narrative movement of *The Silmarillion* itself, for which one of the most important organizing principles is the notion of Ages, what produces the movement from one Age to the next, and how Ages metaphorize generations.

The Silmarillion begins with "Ainulindalë," the story of Creation. Eru/Ilúvatar creates the Ainur, the holy spirits, as part of his cosmic song. The song creates a vision of the Arda, the world, and the generations to come. With a word, *Eä*, the world comes into being; those Ainur who enter it gain the name *Valar*, Powers of the World, along with Melkor, "He who arises in might," who will be renamed Morgoth, "Dark Enemy," and who will seek to turn the world to his own purposes. Lesser immortal spirits, the Maiar, join the Valar to aid them in their task. The book begins with the joys and problems of creation and of the begotten: all have wills of their own, but some will choose to support the one who has brought them into being, while others will resist, seek their own way, and aim to destroy anything outside their control—the situation that has haunted generations as long as humans have told stories.

The next segment of *The Silmarillion*, "Valaquenta," sorts out the powers and relationships of the various Valar and Maiar and with the rebellion of Melkor, who, when he can't possess the light, claims the darkness, who seeks to control all the world and who draws other rebellious spirits, such as Sauron, to aid him. "Quenta Silmarillion" follows next, from the "Beginning of Days" through the history of the Silmarils, the jewels in which Fëanor captures the light of the Two Trees of Valinor. In this section of the book, as well as in the next, "Akallabêth," we find the most significant stress on the problems of generational succession. The Vala Aulë, obsessed with the upcoming creation of the Firstborn, the Elves, cannot wait and instead creates his own race, the Dwarves, whom Ilúvatar puts to sleep until the rising of the Elves, who awake "first" to perceive the light of the stars. Even as they grow and learn as a people, Melkor captures some of the Elves and turns them into the fathers of the race of Orcs, perverting the Creator's purpose and continuing the process of severing kinships, which he began, not a maker but a breaker of generations. Melkor also provokes in the Elves fear of the Valar, damaging a relationship that should have been only healthy and refining for the Firstborn.

Eventually three elven leaders, with only a partial following, return to Aman to seek the company of the Valar—they win the new name *Eldar*, "people of the stars" (Tolkien 393), but the name clearly puns on *elder*, those older and presumably wiser. Following them come the Noldor, "The Wise," "wise in the sense of possessing knowledge" (416), then the Teleri, the "last-comers" (423), who remain outside Aman. The Sindar, or "grey-elves," stay behind in Beleriand in Middle-earth. The "History of the Silmarils" deals mostly with the Noldor and what happens to them with respect to the symbolic stones. Fëanor of the Nolder makes the Silmarils, greatest of jewels, embodying the remnant life of the Two Trees of Valinor, but Melkor, renamed Morgoth by Fëanor, steals them, and Fëanor and his seven sons swear an oath to destroy anyone who takes possession of any of the stones. When he leads the Noldor back to Middle-earth to recover the stones, they slay those Teleri who stand in the way of the Noldor who would steal their ships to make the journey.

The Valar then hide Aman from the folk of Middle-earth forever. However, Yavanna of the Valar (technically of the Valier, the female Valar) creates from the last fruits of the Two Trees the sun and the moon, which light the world for the Youngest Children of Ilúvatar, humans, who then awake and many of whom fall quickly under the sway of Morgoth. In Beleriand the Elves befriend the humans, whom they call the

6. Tolkien and Myth

Edain or Atani, "Second People"; from those early elf-friends come the greatest heroes of men and the greatest Romances, foremost the story of Beren, the human descendent of Bëor the Old, who marries Lúthien, the elf descendent of Elwë and Melian the Maia. She rescues him from Morgoth and later even from death itself, offering for him her immortality, that they might return to Middle-earth and share what life fate and the Valar have allotted them. The other tale deals with Tuor and Idril, the second marriage between human and Elf. Maeglin, an Elf who also loves Idril, in vengeance for her marriage brings about the fall of their city, Gondolin. But the couple escape. Their son Eärendil builds a great ship and, with a Silmaril to guide him, sails to Aman to beg the help of the Valar. He gets it, and the Great Powers subdue Morgoth and cast him into the emptiness beyond the world forever. Of Eärendil's sons, Elrond choses to become elf, builds Rivendell, and emerges as one of the great heroes of the Third Age, and Elros chooses to become human and the first king of Númenor or Westernesse, the greatest of human kingdoms and source of the family of Aragorn, who assumes kingship with the rise of humans in the Fourth Age.

This brief outline of the third Chapter of *The Silmarillion* illustrates its reliance on the guiding motif of the difficulties of generational succession. This problem arises not just because the book recounts a "history," but also because of the stresses of succession inherent in the individual elements in the story, both as myth and as products of Tolkien's imagination. The Elvish peoples form a hierarchy that mimics generations, and each generation provides both gifts and problems for the next to enjoy or solve, wills them both abilities and curses. We see the same pattern applied to humans in the fourth chapter, "Akallabêth," the "Downfall of Númenor," which after two thousand years had attained "The zenith of its bliss, if not yet of its power" (317), when messengers came to them from the Valar to warn them against seeking the Undying-Lands of Valinor. Subsequent generations of Númenoreans grew in pride and greed, until finally Ar-Pharazôn, the twenty-fifth and last king, misled by Sauron, commands a great fleet that sets out for Aman. They, along with the great island of Númenor, are destroyed. The story shows that as generations grow further from their contact with their immortal progenitors and teachers, they may advance in power in the world, but they also fall more readily and completely to pride, greed, hatred—each is in a sense both rising and falling at once, until the apocalyptic event that, after generations of warning, ends an Age. Consider the unprecedented military barrages of World War I: no one had ever seen anything such as the shelling that preceded and the machine-gunning that dictated the Battle of the Somme, not to mention aircraft dogfights. Consider also the at-once historically and mystically foreboding readings of the Apocalypse of St. John in the New Testament. Eschatology looms ever-present in Christian theology, so its resonances must have pressed Tolkien's to deal as part of his world with the truth that generations succeed one another—until they don't. End-times, wrought of whatever cause, disease, war, or divine intervention, shall and must call an Age to a close. Tolkien's stories seldom cease to warn of that concern and its contemporary implications for Europe, for Christian readers, for his colleagues, friends, and children.

The Silmarillion, for all its complexity and occasional prolixity, provides a necessary platform for one's understanding the range of ideas of Tolkien's other fiction. As Shippey aptly elucidates in *Author of the Century*, it is not only the "work of the heart," but also serves as a conjunction of Christian belief and pre–Christian understanding (259). "Centered as it is on the sins of possession and mastery and the desire to exercise skill whatever the consequences, [it] becomes less a mythology for England and more one for its own time ... a myth retold" (260–61), Shippey concludes. That myth, Tolkien's imaginative "center of gravity," speaks largely of the legacy we inherit and the one we produce, of the glories of generations past and of the escalating dangers for those to come.

The ideological question comes in the tension between what seems a lack of humility in the need to replace one's forebears and the necessity of doing so in a world bound by time and mortality. Tolkien once said in an interview that "tipping your cap to the squire may be damn bad for the squire, but its damn good for you" (qtd. in M. Burns 16). We do well to show respect for others, but the others may too readily feel they deserve it and so use it exploitatively; we must find a way both to maintain respect for others, those of and before our time, while emerging as ourselves in our own time. Aragorn best exemplifies the idea of respect in the face of disaster or destruction in *The Lord of the Rings*; he treats everyone else with kindness and even deference, not asserting himself or his position until the time comes, when others feel willing to accept and acknowledge his position. It takes full shape for Tolkien in life both as Christian duty and secular participation in the world of work and ideas, and the twentieth century desperately needed to remember it.

7

Good and Evil, Choice and Control

The twentieth century had much to say and much to show about the nature—and practice—of good and evil. It had much to teach about leadership—and about how we follow leaders, good and bad (mostly bad). Tolkien saw a great deal of evil, and of leadership problems, in person. As a Catholic, or simply as a concerned, thoughtful person, he thought deeply and on many levels about the problems of leadership and about what it meant to be a follower of Christ and a subject of a monarch. Tolkien once wrote that "one must face the fact that the power of Evil in the world is not finally resistable by incarnate creatures, however 'good'" (*Letters* 252)—a cynical opinion had it come from someone irreligious or, in the modernist sense, guardedly realistic.

This chapter will first consider Tolkien's work in the light of leadership theory, a field growing in recent years in academia and in pop culture. It will then turn to an additional consideration of what Tolkien says about good and evil and how leading or following (or demanding leadership or obedience from others) affects the course of spiritual and quotidian life.

Tolkien and Leadership Theory

The study of leadership has grown over the last twenty years. It has evolved, I feel sad to say, into an "academic discipline," which probably won't do it any good. That means we've gone from trying to conceptualize and appreciate it to trying to teach it without really understanding it. So students with little interest in books or theory eagerly sign up for courses that, they hope, will without much reading, traveling, thinking, or suffering of any kind immediately prepare them to take on high-profile, high-paying management jobs at Fortune 500 companies where they will lead other human beings of whom they know nothing.

While the gulf between our needs and our practices may look hideous, the leap from the abstract idea of leadership to the quotidian practice of management may not be so wide as we may fear. John W. Gardner wrote in *On Leadership*, one of the better books in the field, "Every time I encounter utterly first-class managers they turn out to have quite a lot of leader in them" (4). Successful "management," he suggests, may emerge from good "leadership"—not necessarily an obvious conclusion. The wider, perhaps impossible leap, at least for those of us who have lived longer than our students have, tried to circulate in the world, and regularly read the New York or London *Times*, comes in the notion that one may study leadership in such a way as to prepare a detailed, practicable program for personal use on the job by post-baccalaureates. My own observations tell me that leadership comes more from personal magnetism—force of personality, charisma, or a commitment of will—a person's willingness to take charge of situations and the ability to remain confident that others will follow even when he or she errs obviously. As we look at history and our tendency to lionize personalities, don't we often observe in practice that leadership comes more from built-in qualities than from learned strategies, despite the current deluge of self-help books? Often leadership comes simply because a person sits in a position of wealth or power, not because he or she has sterling qualities that should by themselves earn trust and obedience.

Not surprisingly for devotees of Tolkien, *The Lord of the Rings* directed our attention to those and related issues long before the emergence of Leadership Studies as a discipline, and despite or perhaps because of its setting in a fantastic or partly imagined world, it explores them in an informed and instructive (because controlled) way. As powerful literature with the capability to move our thoughts and emotions, it can, in the Sidneyian sense, urge us to concordant action. And story may work as well as (or better than) theory to improve our understanding of a growing field of study.

In this section I'll aim to show that, though they show no sign of knowledge of or interest in Tolkien, several of the most important, even foundational figures in Leadership Theory could as well have drawn their best examples from *The Lord of the Rings*: what they have discovered or illuminated, he had already put into narrative, and that element of the narrative—what it teaches about leadership—may indicate one of the most significant reasons why Tolkien has moved from almost guilty pleasure-reading to a staple in our classrooms and scholarship. I'll start by enumerating the tenets of three of the major theorists, then I'll turn to *The Lord of the Rings* to show how Tolkien's major charismatic leaders, particularly Gandalf and Aragorn, already exemplified the best of Leadership Theory's principles long before the subject nominally accrued public interest.

First, let's consider three prominent volumes common to Leadership Studies curricula: James MacGregor Burns' *Leadership* (New York: Harper & Row, 1978, 2010), John W. Gardner's *On Leadership* (New York: Free Press, 1990), and Robert K. Greenleaf's *Servant Leadership* (New York: Paulist Press, 1977). Each book describes a discrete, detailed examination into the sources and successes of leadership; together they may not canonize that sought-after simple program for students, but they do provide some useful tools for behavioral, textual, and thematic analyses that may help us comment on examples of leadership whether we find them in life or in texts.

Burns combines *crisis* plus *charisma* plus the *representation of an essential idea* as central to leadership. In times of crisis the person with charisma will emerge into leadership if he or she can clearly articulate and lay claim to embody an idea that his or her people find essential to the time. Only times of crisis call for real leaders, and only the charismatic person—or the person spun as heroic by campaign charisma-doctors—can emerge successfully into public view. Others will simply not capture sufficient attention to lead. And the nascent leader must be in tune with the ideas the public most wants further publicized—any others, however important, will not attract sufficient attention.

Next on our list of theorist, Gardner employs a list of traits, each fairly self-explanatory, to define leadership in action:

1. envisioning goals;
2. affirming and regenerating values;
3. motivating and managing;
4. achieving unity and trust;

5. explaining circumstances;
6. serving as a symbol;
7. representing the group;
8. bringing about renewal.

Up to the last one, which requires not just any leadership but successful leadership and effective followers, we can see all the other traits as typical of political campaigns, ingenuous or otherwise. Without a statement of goals and values, the ability to explain current problems, inspire trust, and motivate others to act, and the willingness to present oneself at once as the fulfillment of a symbol and as the embodiment of the group's identity, the likely leader would have difficulty gaining and retaining office—barring, of course, military coup, gross misrepresentation to a fragmented public, or outright theft, none of which can actually produce the desired renewal.

Third, but equally important among our theorists, Greenleaf argues that we will and should trust only that leader who first demonstrates the ability to serve: leadership evolves *from* service and *as* service. When leaders attempt to emerge with agendas other than public service, if we have sufficient information about them we must and will reject them. *Leadership* means no more and no less than living to represent and improve the lives of one's constituents. For Greenleaf the term *servant leadership* is both a redundancy and a specification of power and greatness: servants must be willing to come forward to lead and leaders must see themselves exclusively as servants. The alternatives are folly and fascism.

I suspect we can find few better literary incarnations of those ideas than in Tolkien's work, particularly in *The Lord of the Rings*, where the quest to destroy the Ring of Power depends on three points: (1) luck, which has great importance, but for which I can't account in this argument; (2) Frodo's ability to endure bearing the ring to Mt. Doom and to part with it once he gets there, which has to do with individual character and has been the subject of much excellent scholarship; and (3) the leadership of those who must support Frodo and try to create a space ad opportunity through which luck and his character may shine.

As *LotR* begins, we find Middle-earth confronted with leadership problems. The single most powerful and most committed leader, Sauron, is bent on subjugating the world and all its creatures to his will and to destroying all of the beauty and freedom invoked in the world's creation—for the background of his story we must turn to *The Silmarillion*, the *Unfinished Tales*, and appendices. No equivalent source of leadership power exists, since Sauron has concentrated his energies toward acquiring tools and armies with destruction and enslavement as their only goals. We learn that the strongest nominal opposition to Sauron, Saruman, sent into the world along with Gandalf and the other wizards to resist the remnants of Morgoth's power, has fallen under the sway of the Dark Tower. Tom Bombadil, though incorruptible, will neither lead nor join any organized resistance—such an act isn't part of his nature. At the level of Sauron, only Gandalf leads through service, with equanimity, and with willingness to sacrifice himself for the general good. He will not take a nominal position of leadership, but will counsel others willing to listen and to resist tyranny.

The strongest remaining folk in Middle-earth who will fight evil, the elves, have allowed their numbers and power to diminish; yet strong, they haven't sufficient faith in people as allies to lead them or follow them—though of course they do renew the old alliance at the time of greatest need. Elrond and Galadriel and Celeborn retain power and persuasiveness as leaders of elves, but they have not sought and will not seek similar influence over humans. The Dwarves constitute a force with great will power and some wealth and strength, but they have retreated from the larger world into an isolationism that leaves them the furthest of all the free peoples from most immediate battlegrounds. Regardless of the "nodes" of influence that the elves have because of their protective havens, those havens have to some degree, like the dwarves', isolated them. Hobbits have remained isolated all along largely because the larger peoples have taken little interest in them. Ents, as powerful in themselves as any creatures but the wizards, take too long to communicate—even when they wish to—to have any potential as leaders of others. Who among the other peoples could respond to hobbits or ents as *leaders*? That truth says a lot about what we expect of leaders: we want them to be like us, but *larger than life*.

For leadership positions, then, that leaves humans who, as Elrond points out, have greater aptness to turn to evil than to good. The great peoples of the past have, like the elves, diminished; the remaining leaders

7. Good and Evil, Choice and Control

have lost their ability to lead, have lost access to leadership positions, or have abandoned themselves to Sauron. The last descendants of the Númenoreans, the Rangers, perform an essential function as guardians of the marches, but they hold no position of leadership. Gandalf, the greatest source in the world of wisdom and of knowledge of Middle-earth's peoples, desires to counsel, not to lead, but he will and does use that role to help human leaders. As *LotR* begins he is not the head of his order; further, because of his semi-divine nature and commitment to preserving the free will of the peoples, he resists any transition from counselor to leader. He leads the Fellowship as they begin their journey, but by consensus, not by command. From the Rangers and the Wizards must come leadership—they are the only possible sources—so Gandalf, first "the Grey," second to Saruman, and then "the White," successor to Saruman, emerges from their ranks, and Aragorn, descendent and heir of the Kings of the West, emerges among humans. They lead because of their nature and lineage and because of their willingness to guide without oppression.

Aragorn has willingness to serve and eagerness to lead—the tasks to which in Tolkien's world he was born—but he will not take power except with the consent of the governed and having proved himself worthy of it. He needs only the right circumstance to allow him to pursue his throne—notably, a circumstance unlikely to occur in his lifetime but that "chance" or "fate" (or divine purpose) brings about. Gandalf, similarly, has in his nature both to serve and lead, but knowing the dangers that leadership engenders for one as powerful as he, he tries instead to inspire others to lead, aiming to gird the proper leaders of the peoples for their own tasks rather than to control them himself.

We have left, then, those two sources of leadership: Aragorn and Gandalf. Burns' understanding of leadership applies remarkably to them as they step into the foreground. *Crisis* lifts Aragorn from border guardian to rightful king. And while, at least early in the tale, neither hobbits nor other humans would call Aragorn "charismatic," they feel the force of his personality; they don't recognize it as charisma because of Aragorn's dress and the fact that he shrouds from them his true nature. From his labors in the Wild "he became somewhat grim to look upon, unless he chanced to smile; and yet he seemed to Men worthy of honour, as a king in exile," says Appendix A of *The Return of the King*. Certainly to Arwen he has charisma: she gives up immortality for him. And while he defers to other leaders (for example, Gandalf, Elrond, Galadriel, Théoden, and even Denethor within their own realms), when the time comes for him to rule Gondor, his presence has grown beyond anyone's desire to keep him from it. While his accoutrements change, the idea that Aragorn represents remains constant. With the exception of the Steward of Gondor, the free peoples of Middle-earth believe that the right and true king should, as protector of the people, rise to power and govern justly within his realm, reaffirming peaceful and prosperous alliances with the other peoples. Tolkien's world, like that of the *Beowulf* he loved so well, not only allows for but also wishes for good kings, and Aragorn even better than Beowulf embodies that ideal.

No one questions Gandalf's charisma: his dramatic and even intimidating presence acts upon everyone from hobbit children who love his fireworks to kings who need but fear his advice. His function in Middle-earth is to prevent or assuage the crisis if he can, to master it if he must by engaging the peoples to conquer it. The idea he represents—that we need people of learning and virtue to acquire knowledge and wisdom and apply them to counsel us honestly, courageously, and selflessly—has informed not only our educational systems, but also our religions for at least two and a half millennia.

We may apply Gardner's criteria as aptly as Burns'. Once Gandalf identifies the Ring of Power, he knows what someone must do with it, even if he must sacrifice himself in the process. Neither does Aragorn have trouble envisioning goals; he knows his lineage, his doom, and his limitations, but no one could lead—but to defend and assist them toward peaceful ends. He even gives up authority to Gandalf when he should.

Both Gandalf and Aragorn affirm and regenerate the values of ages past, of the Valar who made Middle-earth and affirmed order and peace. Their participation in the War of the Ring aims to regenerate not only the values of heroic resistance to tyranny the alliance of peoples, but also the purpose of those values: the re-establishment of a world worth inhabiting, free of Sauron's desire for control of others' wills.[1]

Gandalf serves particularly as motivator—that task he acquired from the Valar—and until his battle with the Balrog, he "manages" the Fellowship on the quest to destroy the Ring. After Gandalf's fall, Aragorn, who has served under Gandalf as a sort of chief warrior on

7. Good and Evil, Choice and Control

the quest, becomes its manager—until the fellowship is broken by the attack of the Uruk-hai and Frodo's departure with Sam for Mordor. Once the war has ended, Aragorn rises as chief "manager," as king of Gondor and hero of the West of Middle-earth. His task completed, Gandalf need not motivate nor manage any longer, so he departs with the elves for the Undying Lands. Gandalf shows that one can lead without becoming a Sauron, and Aragorn seconds the point by showing that not only an "angel," but a human can do so, too. He need only have respect for others as individuals and to know, so to speak, *his place*.

Both Gandalf and Aragorn throughout the story promote unity and trust: they work particularly to join all the free peoples as allies against Sauron, not by force or guile, but by reason and example. Aragorn will not enter Gondor as king until he receives the invitation to do so: he wants to achieve his position not by taking it, but by having been given it. He rules finally not by blood and insistence, but by having proved he has the character and ability to lead with kindness and generosity and the willingness to give praise as well as receive it—much like Beowulf as the poet describes him in the final two lines of the epic (kind and gentle, generous, eager for fame, but also eager to praise). Gandalf, too, leads by consent and consensus, and he does not take on himself others' responsibilities. For instance, he doesn't return to The Shire with the hobbits to participate in its liberation: having learned what they must do and having gained the experience and strength to do it, they must act on their own, with Gandalf's guidance but without his physical presence. They must move into free decision making and take responsibility for their own homes and lives: they must at last lead themselves.

Gandalf particularly spends enormous effort not only to research and discover the truth of current circumstances, but then to travel to explain them, along with the great events of the past that have brought them about, to the various peoples. Aragorn must exhibit how the history of Númenor has re-emerged in him. Even hobbits have an old saying, half joking, half longing, about the "return of the king"; Aragorn must both explain and show, through stories, icons, and deeds, how he comes to claim the throne.

Gandalf, the living symbol of the Valar among the elves and mortals, symbolizes the desire of the elder, greater creatures to help the lesser. He looks as though he belongs among the mortals, but he represents the value implicit in the sacrifice to sustain all that the creators wrought. Aragorn symbolizes the greatness that mortals can achieve; though Númenor fell long before, with him it gains re-invigoration, and the ancient glories spread to all those allied with him. Through him, as through Gandalf, they stretch their roots to the beginning of Middle-earth.

All the members of the Fellowship of the Ring represent the group from which they've come: that's one of the main points in the formation of the fellowship. Gandalf and Aragorn have particular importance because they lead among leaders: the representatives of other peoples look to them for guidance and safety. And each of the peoples, with the exception of the elves, who will see their powers diminish in Middle-earth, so that they must at last depart to the Undying Lands, sees a renewal in the completion of the quest. The hobbits must reclaim the Shire from Saruman and Wormtongue and their minions, but in doing so they finally and fully (and to some extent sadly) grow up. The dwarves through Gimli have reconnected to the other peoples whom, in their solitary delving, they had come largely to ignore. The wizard himself experiences a renewal as "Gandalf the White," returned from death following his battle with the Balrog, and so does Aragorn, risen to kingship after his long days as a sometimes-despised Ranger, serving sentry duty on the marches. With his "renewal" and the fall of Sauron comes a new age, a renewal for Middle-earth. But then no renewal comes without loss, and each new age involves a passing as well as a rising—Tolkien allows no sentimental romanticizing of that sad fact. With the renewal of the power of humans comes potential for great good and great tragedy; meanwhile, hobbits will fall into, if possible, greater obscurity than before.

Finally, the ideas of third of our theorists, Greenleaf, have perhaps the fullest flowering in Tolkien's world. Both Gandalf and Aragorn exemplify "servant leadership" better than anyone short of sacrificial deity could. Gandalf has no personal ambitions whatever—he turns down even the leadership of the "White Council"—marshaling knowledge and power exhaustively and even giving his life for the quest, a life miraculously restored by the Valar until he can complete his task. I assume we may forgive him his pipe of tobacco and cup of tea—and taste for occasional fireworks. Aragorn, too, has given his youth to protect and serve the other peoples who as a rule either don't know him, fear him, or even despise him, as we see at the Prancing Pony. As king he represents the opposite of Sauron: the safety rather than enslaving of the peoples, the acceptance of war to free them rather than the love of war to bind them.

A brief chapter can but turn the first page in considering such a large issue that plays an essential part in a sweeping and epic work. I think we may say confidently that Tolkien, through his experiences in war and Academe, must have sounded issues of leadership and drawn particular conclusions about what it meant—and should mean—to his time and in the age to come. Perhaps not remarkably, nonfiction writers, who have dealt with the twentieth century through a theoretical rather than fictional lens, came to similar conclusions. They found, like Tolkien, that, while leadership may not bring each of us wealth and power, proper foundational principles may help create more stable and equitable societies. We keep, though—all of us together—the capacity to choose to use those principles to build or destroy.

Finding the Nature of Good and Evil

These questions perhaps more than any other plagued twentieth-century philosophy, politics, and religion: what is evil, what is good, and what causes or provokes either? They rather faded as concerns of fiction—one of the points for which Tolkien fell out of favor with some critics. For those who came to prefer what we came to call "literary" or even "mainstream" fiction, such questions may seem simple, even simplistic; we humans spent most of the century proving they weren't and aren't. Moral authorities have often decried the "moral relativism" that followed both World Wars, while critical and theoretical authorities have often decried the "moralism" and didacticism of previous ages. I'm not sure we've seen so much *relativism* as an almost post-apocalyptic desire for the kind of tolerance that relieves persons of the desire to *impose* their moral particulars on everyone else. Writers and philosophers began to back away from what they saw as the great flaw of earlier writing: its devotion to didacticism. Nearly everything in literature up to the twentieth century has at least a hint if not a heavy load of it. Writers and readers alike saw that as their purpose. We saw literature, following

Horace, as *sweetly useful*, which more often than not translators rendered as serving to teach and delight. Despite his own conservative views on religion and morality, Tolkien didn't use his fiction to preach, yet no one in Middle-earth may remain neutral (Kocher 67). Because they choose, and because in *The Lord of the Rings* the good win a victory, Tolkien may appear to have imposed a simple notion of good on his fiction where in fact he has not.

Yet as difficulties in leadership plague Middle-earth, so problems of leadership similarly emerged in the twentieth century, from oppressive regimes to infantry charges, from the trenches of World War I to how populations felt about monarchy or democracy. Our political difficulties led us to question whether good or evil come from ourselves or from our leaders: whom do we hold responsible for either, and to what effects? With the trepidation of the *writer* in matters of teaching came also a failure in humility of the *reader*: we came to see ourselves as above what a writer could teach us, about traditional questions such as how to determine right or wrong. What right had a writer to try to *teach* us anything? We readers hadn't really got any better at thinking about the great and troublesome questions; we had just got, for a time, more literate, a little more widely educated, more consumerish, and more the subject of pandering by those who wanted to sell us a simple feel-good philosophy. Tolkien didn't buy into that trend; he held to the earlier line not, I think, because he believed himself better than reader—or even other writers—but because he believed himself *like* other readers: we can all choose to do better, or we can choose to do worse. So he devoted a great deal of his literary work to finding and exploring where, how, and why we do well or poorly. For him that subject made better stories than those that treat lighter concerns—though of course he would not dismiss those either. He simply wouldn't settle for them alone.

The key here comes, I think, in the idea of *finding* the distinctions between good and evil in choices and in actions. The major characters in Tolkien's world often seek the good even when they fail and fall into evil. The characters unfold their own ideas by means of their choices. Ted Sandyman, supposedly to Hobbiton pub-goers a voice of common hobbit-sense, makes fun of Sam before he leaves on the quest, yet Ted turns collaborator at last—one can imagine he did so with little difficulty or compunction, believing that good sense meant he could benefit from

7. Good and Evil, Choice and Control

it. Bilbo must find within himself the strength to part with the Ring; without Gandalf's help he probably couldn't, but then many of us need the advice—sometimes the firm advice—of counselors, friends, colleagues, or parents to gain the means to do the right thing (in our time, we might say Gandalf has an *intervention* with Bilbo). Frodo must find the courage and strength to carry the Ring into Mordor: he knows from the Council at Rivendell that he must, and he admits he hasn't at ready the courage to do so. But he must summon that courage. The rewards he gets for getting the Ring so far are fleeting and few in Middle-earth: he must find consolation across the sea, lost to the world of his beloved Shire.[2] Tolkien wrote in a 1956 letter that he believed it "*quite impossible*" for Frodo to drop the Ring: "He was honoured because he had accepted the burden, and had done all that was within his utmost physical and mental strength to do" (251). He survives by "Mercy ... the supreme value and efficacy of Pity and forgiveness of injury" (252), predicated partly on his own ability to learn and show pity and partly on the presence of mercy in the world, coming from a higher power. The idea has both religious genesis and secular significance and perhaps Anglo-Saxon resonances: *wyrd* often preserves the undoomed one if his courage holds, we learn from *Beowulf*; mercy, Tolkien suggests, may preserve the deserving one, if his pity holds. Then again, in either case they may not: something inscrutable remains in a world created by but not bound to kindness.

Frodo deals after the quest with a sense of taint; Tolkien observed that "it was not only nightmare memories of past horrors that afflicted him, but also unreasoning self-reproach: he saw himself and all that he [had] done as a broken failure.... That was actually a temptation out of the Dark, a last flicker of pride: desire to have returned as a 'hero,' not content with being a mere instrument of good" (*Letters* 328). Tolkien's judgment of Frodo is both very Christian and harsh: Frodo's world hasn't the hope of Christian salvation, nor does Frodo give any apparent sense of feeling himself an agent of some outside power that is working through him for good. Who can blame him if some desire for heroism or recognition had remained with him, since he had endured the quest that probably no one else could have. His "failure" calls to mind, as I have discussed above, that of Sir Gawain in *Sir Gawain and the Green Knight*. There whole situation is a game, of course, to tempt, test, and probably embarrass Gawain, and it succeeds; Frodo, however, is playing no game. The Green Knight assures Gawain he has done as well as any human could, but Gawain remains unsure and unsatisfied with himself. Regardless, he can no longer consider himself the perfect knight he hoped to be. Frodo would hardly have had Gawain's pride or self-obsession, but he would certainly have come home with better mental health (regardless of the physical wound he received on Weathertop) had dropped the Ring in the Fire of his own volition. He has shown a very small imperfection—the Ring, after long wearing him down, overcomes him at last as it reaches the place of its greatest power—but one that could have caused the destruction of Middle-earth, rendering it entirely under the power of Sauron, had the Ringwraiths caught him before the Ring fell. Small failures can yet cause great pain, even for Frodo, who has no pretentions to perfection. In the world of *Sir Gawain and the Green Knight*, Camelot will fall; in the world of *The Lord of the Rings*, a new age comes in which the power of humans will rise, but the elves, the dwarves, the ents, and the hobbits will fade. Neither reduction comes through the protagonist's failings, yet they come: one's own imperfections reinforce the weight of mortality and add to the sum of our sense of loss.

Arwen chooses to lose her immortality for the sake of the love of a mortal man; she chooses the course of loss that so besets human nature for the love that ennobles it and makes the idea of mortality tolerable. Galadriel accepts the loss of Middle-earth to the elves and the departure into the West after all she has done to preserve her land, her people, and all the beauty and wisdom they brought with them and for so long preserved. Each has the potential for good that they believe those choices represent, but each has also the potential to turn away from that good. They must find the will to Good when their own good seems to drive them otherwise: a pretty traditional religious message.

Tolkien's fiction writing really began with the early drafts of what became *The Silmarillion*. Its stories consistently explore the gaining and losing of knowledge, friendship, spiritual insight, power, and love. Good comes in pursuing them with a generous heart; evil comes in exploiting them or forgetting them. Each of *The Silmarillion*'s stories raises those concerns, from the Creation story that begins the book to the destruction story that ends it. The stories point to and lead to a kind of eschaton:

7. Good and Evil, Choice and Control

the fall of Númenor, wrought by the failure of its own people. The love of the Creator allows them even after great evil yet to find glory in Middle-earth and to have a new age, a new chance, to regain not their former glory, but a stronger and better commitment to the Good. The elves have, in some sense, even a greater opportunity for good, as their chief joy lies not in acquisition and possession, but in the perpetuation of life, of the Greenwood, of learning, and of understanding among peoples. While not so complete as the fall of Númenor, their own fall in the story of the creation, loss, and war to regain the Silmarils shows the inherent ease of corruption if one fails to resist it, the dangers of possession and the possessiveness that can come from it. Even the failure of the ents represents a choice: the entwives take their lives in the direction they prefer, straying so far that their mates can no longer find them. As a species the ents suffer a slow and sad demise, an eschaton not of fire or flood, but of drift, self-absorption, and forgetfulness.

In *The Silmarillion* problems begin not long after Creation begins; Ilúvatar brings into being creatures with free will, and among his first creations Melkor already desires to turn aside from his Creator to a make on his own something that he may control—if anything a rather kinder trope than that of Satan in the Christian stories that have grown up around him. Problems hardly end, though with the destruction of Númenor in the "Akallabeth" that ends *The Silmarillion*: the fall their merely leads to other falls and makes the return to a state of blessedness all the more hazardous and difficult. While Melkor's fall begins the process of creatures bound to their wills failing to pursue the good, it does not relieve responsibility from those creatures for their own errors, which they often make willingly—just as Isildur does in failing to destroy the Ring, having achieved the chance to do so.

Impatience and desire to take control of creation drove Melkor, and his music turns quickly to discord and wrath until he contends with it against Ilúvatar. The music of each of the Ainur contributes in its own way to creation, but Ilúvatar shows them how each originates in him. Each one as subcreator shapes elements of the world more wonderfully, executing part of the Creator's plan. Serving as part of that plan didn't satisfy Melkor, and though "in the powers and knowledge of all the other Valar he had a part ... he turned them to evil purposes, and squandered his strength in violence and tyranny. For he coveted Arda and all that was in it, desiring the kingship of Manwë and dominion over the realms of his peers" (*Silmarillion* 23). Melkor, "he who arises in might," becomes Morgoth, "the dark enemy": much like Milton's Satan, he wishes to become both God and the opposite of God, both creator and destroyer, and he fails most fully of all creatures to perceive the nature of good (freedom and protection of others' freedoms) and evil (desire to control others). Aulë nearly gives in to the same error as Melkor, creating on his own without the approval of Ilúvatar in the making of the dwarves, but he submits and allows his creation to fit into Ilúvatar's larger plan. Similarly, elves and humans also fail when they focus first on acquisition, possession, and self-service rather than on the good of creation.

Such focus leads to decline and ends in a fall; one resists the fall by generosity, labors that share their fruits with others, and genuine love for Middle-earth and its creatures—a message traditional in any kind of moral and ethical thought, but no less true and valuable to Tolkien, his time, and his readers for that fact. The symphony of Tolkien's fiction is very classical, and he uses it to promote the idea that we don't create the nature of music, but we can participate in it joyfully, faithfully, and productively. Leadership proves so important in Tolkien's work because he knew how easily it can evoke good or evil and how easily and quickly it can turn from one to the other.

8

Teaching Tolkien and His World, and Why He Matters

In the last twenty years Tolkien scholarship has grown energetically, as has the number of college and university courses that include Tolkien's work or even study him exclusively. We do scholarship to share knowledge and appreciation of texts with our fellow scholars, but that work finally returns with us to our classrooms and our students: the scholarship of pedagogy is also growing. Tolkien's work perhaps better than any other author's features world creation as an essential technique, and discussions of world creation or even individual or group exercises with students on world-building can prove both enjoyable and illuminating, and they can often inspire the students to creative projects of their own. This chapter will explore ideas of mythopoiesis and pedagogy with respect to Tolkien's work and their continuing value as part of our literary study.

The World of the Text

In a brief headnote to the Ballantine edition of the *Lord of the Rings* (added to the 1965 edition, printed in 1973), Peter Beagle intuits that "in the end it is Middle-earth and its dwellers that we love, not Tolkien's considerable gifts in showing it to us," for "the world he charts was there long before him" as part of "our most common nightmares, daydreams, and twilight fantasies." Beagle adds, "He found them a place to live, a green alternative to each day's madness here in a poisoned world." Middle Earth appears before us as a world we already know and, despite its dangers, love.[1] Somewhere between the printed product of Tolkien's imagination and the active, organic, semi-responsive world of our own, we meet in a compelling place, as Beagle suggests, of our mutual construction, or, as Tolkien might say, of our subcreation. Despite its originality, that world feels familiar and, despite its challenges, it feels appealing—in many ways more so than our own. A good part of that familiarity both comes from and leads us back to the medieval literature that Tolkien himself so loved; particularly for younger readers Tolkien and his world build a bridge from modern literature to the medieval literature they may otherwise miss. That bridge of thought forms an essential feature of Tolkien's intellectual landscape and stimulated a great deal of today's popular medievalism.

With our students we enter Tolkien's Greenworld not only for pleasure, but also to learn something about how to deal with evil, so that we might return better prepared to deal with our own "Waste Land" or to create a better alternative to it. We also aim to understand—theoretically and practically—how a writer can create such a complex and compelling milieu for story-creation. The sources for many of Tolkien's motifs and images come from the Middle Ages. What we learn about world-creation from Tolkien, a writer nearer our time and of what we often call *medievalism*, we can carry over to discussions of texts from the medieval world. Tolkien sails to a shore that for our students may at first seem too far away, too difficult to reach: the world of the Middle Ages. Medieval writers, too, had to build their own Romance worlds: they didn't find them at their doorsteps anymore than Tolkien did, yet the most successful medieval tales found that place of twilight fantasies, as Beagle wrote, that seems, as we read, not a discovery, but a rediscovery of something that, deep down or long ago, we had already glimpsed. And as many insights as we gain from Tolkien about how to read medieval stories, we gain from medieval stories hints about how to read him.

This section will examine some possible methods for teaching a Tolkien course not only as a pleasure in itself, but also as means to introduce students to world-building in medieval literature or in medievalism. All successful fiction hinges on the writer's creation of a world readers want or at least feel willing to inhabit, a place if not beautiful at least strangely attractive. Tolkien's popularity validates medieval litera-

8. Teaching Tolkien and His World, and Why He Matters

ture not for those of us who already love and teach it, but for many of our students: they love him, and he loved those old texts, so they may be worth studying, too. And medieval literature can key us to many of the ideas that filled his thoughts and his fictional world. An examination of the texts and writers that influenced Tolkien and whose methods he echoed or revised so effectively in his fiction helps open both Tolkien's work and the medieval world to more careful and complex reading. Students find a comfortable means to reach books and ideas that may otherwise daunt or elude them—older texts that may simply seem, because they have less cachet in pop-culture, beneath their notice. But the world of Tolkien's fiction can capture them and lead them to the equally exciting worlds of the actual texts from the Middle Ages—they move more comfortably from Tolkien to his sources and influences than they would if they were to take up the early texts without the bridge of fun and (for them) legitimacy that Tolkien provides.

The idea of "the world of the text" proves a powerful one regardless of the time and texts one chooses. "What is the world in this story *like*, and how did the author build or realize it?" make interesting and useful technical questions for reflection in any literature course. Paul Ricoeur, in a response to Northrop Frye's *Anatomy of Criticism*, asserts that between the author's product, the text, and ourselves as imaginative respondents moves a multi-dimensional "world of the text":

> I see Frye's second phase [in his theory of symbols] as the nexus or turning-point between suspended reference and recreated reference, what I would call, in a vocabulary close to Hans-Georg Gadamer's, reference to the world of the text. To the extent that the poem unfolds in some hypothetical dimension, it also projects a world that we might inhabit.[2]

That is, the world of the text makes no special claim to "reality," nor does it detach itself from reality; it acquires an especially useful kind of applicability as a connection between a potentially instructive symbolic system and the daily life in which we often need, despite modern reluctance to admit it, instruction. And a symbol, or a text, or a world, may simultaneously attract and repulse:

> this polar structure is itself unified by the strength of the desire that configures both the infinitely desirable and its contrary, the infinitely detestable.... [A]ll imagery is inadequate in relation to the apocalyptic imagery of fulfillment and yet at the same time in search of it.[3]

Any "real" world must have, according to any given author's or reader's taste, positive and negative attributes, and because any real world must come to an end, its inhabitants may prophesy and prepare: from our reading we can learn how they do that and how we may do that.

In a second essay, this one on the process of interpreting narrative, Ricoeur, emerging from a background of Monroe Beardsley's work, writes,

> I assume that it is the task of an hermeneutic to disentangle from the referential claims of any literary work the kind of world it displays.... [W]hat is to be interpreted in a text is a proposed world that I might inhabit and wherein I might project my own most possibilities [sic].[4]

Essentially, then, all literature aims at something "fantastic" and expansive, the creation of a shared world of mutual becoming. A literary world must have its languages, its limits, and its sources. That world expands as we read it and come to participate in its realization.

As Shippey argues in much of his critical work on Tolkien,[5] Tolkien wrote not as an escape from our quotidian world, but as a way of moving into a realm where he could explore and grapple with the problem of evil—I would say as a response not only to World War I (and II), but also to the devolving sense of the twentieth century as a Waste Land both physical and spiritual. Tolkien's world grew, as many critics have commented, from a combination of philology and a desire to create for Britain its own mythology, free of Mediterranean influences foreign to English sensibilities. Its rationale, geography, and inhabitants take full shape in *The Silmarillion*,[6] but its human heart fully emerges in *The Lord of the Rings*. Only in the story of the destruction of the One Ring amidst a crumbling world do we bury the dead, retake, for a time, the greenwood, and exchange our spindly *shantih*, as we have already discussed, for the smithy that the modern world has demanded we build: we learn that with *making* (ποίησις or *scopcræft*) comes the potential to un-make, for ill or for good.

Though "Tolkien himself did not approve of the academic search for 'sources,'"[7] source study has always influenced Tolkien criticism, and the works he studied inevitably influenced how and what he wrote. The practice of determining sources and influences presents difficulties both practical and theoretical, but successful searches can help illuminate the texts we study and can say a lot about the process and facets of an

8. Teaching Tolkien and His World, and Why He Matters

author's world-creation. Northrop Frye notes that the writer's choice "is inseparably bound up" with our acceptance of "cultural heritage"; not just literary works, but everything that has built the culture in which writers live and work necessarily influences one's imagination.[8]

As a professor of the early periods of English language and literature, and especially as a philologist, Tolkien shows an especially strong influence from languages and primary texts, not only from Old and Middle English, but also from Old Norse, Finnish, and medieval Welsh—the latter two as "sources" for his elvish language—and even from the Classical world, if less directly. So of course did his family background, the powerful sense of his own Englishness, his war experience, and his devotion to Catholicism all inflect if not guide his work, as did a school curriculum that foregrounded the study of languages ancient and modern.[9] We have a wealth of sources to study influences, and we can introduce students to them in our teaching of Tolkien: Tolkien's professional essays, editing, dictionary work, and translation, along with his letters, but also the great texts from which he drew ideas, characters, and inspiration. The energetic research of such scholars as Shippey (see especially Appendix A, "Tolkien's sources: The True Tradition," in *The Road to Middle-Earth*) and Anderson calls attention to the profoundest influences on his "creative" work: *Beowulf* and everything else in Old English (especially "The Battle of Maldon," *Exodus*, "The Wanderer," and "The Ruin"); the Norse eddas and sagas (especially *Voluspá*, Snorri's *Prose Edda*, *Fáfnismál*, *Skirnismál*, and *Volsungasaga*); medieval Romance, Arthurian and otherwise, but specifically *Sir Gawain and the Green Knight* (and *Sir Orfeo*) as well as other literary products of the English Northwest Midlands (including *Pearl* and *Ancrene Wisse*); *Mandeville's Travels*; *Kalevala*; *Mabinogi*; Gibbon's *Decline and Fall of the Roman Empire* and Saxo Grammaticus' *Historia Danica*.[10] Those examples affected Tolkien's thinking and his fictional world only slightly less than the Bible (perhaps more in Latin and Gothic than in English), fairy tales, fables, and folksongs, such as those collected by the Grimms and by Svend Grundtvig. We may also consider border ballads such as those edited by F. J. Child, the work of William Morris, George MacDonald, and perhaps Kipling, and Classical myth (though he may have found much of it unappealing). The readings and discussions with his fellow Inklings kept him writing and adjusting—and re-writing. Noticing such sources may not, as Shippey points out, change one's reading of Tolkien, but it "always brings out Tolkien's extremely keen eye for the vital detail,"[11] and it may lead a reader to other pleasurable reading and a better understanding of the author's imaginative processes and responses to the creative, historical, and religious work of others. It certainly draws readers into a wide array of medieval texts and concerns: a great value to those of us who teach the Middle Ages and its more recent offshoots and hope that students' readings do not end, even if they begin, with Tolkien.

Tolkien—and his whole generation—met societal convulsions that neither the wisdom of the ancients nor current authorities could explain: the devastation of modern warfare and the addictive nature of evil.[12] What no one could accomplish through "realism," Tolkien's generation sought to explain through fantasy—an important idea for students who believe only realism can deal with real problems. Good fantasy works not because it provides an escape from our "real world," but because it creates an alternative world in which we as readers and critics can attend at least the confrontation if not the solution to the "great problems," neither finding ourselves excluded by politics nor dying in the process of fighting them. Medieval literature—the best of it, certainly, but most of it, at least in part—serves the same purpose, but often with more concentration than the modern. By sharing them we can work through them together alongside appealing (and sometimes appalling) characters in a world we believe worthy of saving. We may even carry over something of the answers or solutions that we find in that world into quotidian life. The secret, I suppose, is that one must love both worlds and find them worth saving. As Shippey shows in *Author of the Century*, Tolkien's creation of a whole world, full of maps, languages, and peculiar local customs, beyond the adventures in which we share through all its significant history, teaches us "what it would be 'like' to be there," not just in Middle-earth, but also in the trenches of World War I or in the midst of a council of the Mighty as they seek not to ignore or profit from our problems, but to solve them.[13] There, I think, lies a major key to Tolkien's success and to students' understanding *Beowulf, Sir Gawain and the Green Knight*, or *Volsungasaga*: if they can reach the world that the text creates, they will find themselves caught up in the stories and what they say. They need both to know and to *feel* the world, to accept its conventions for a time, to suspend disbelief and live there with sufficient attention and investment so that all the facets of the story may come to work for them.

Tolkien (more in *The Lord of the Rings* than elsewhere) responded to his own understanding of the between-wars Waste Land with a vision of Middle-earth that resists entropy: no world can defy it, but Middle-earth at least impedes it. Less cryptic than Eliot's world, it retains a greater capacity to seem present and alive, and it stimulates hope despite what loomed between the wars as a decaying and perhaps even hopeless future.[14] The Shire, Rivendell, Lothlórien: in the text they resist Mordor and its growing waste lands, and outside the text they continue to inspire readers' imaginations in subsequent generations. Gandalf, Elrond, Galadriel, and the Fellowship: they resist Sauron, Saruman, Ringwraiths, and the internal spiritual waste lands of the text, but they also remain for audiences models of service, generosity, and courage. Most importantly, unlike Boromir the hobbits together resist the desire to use the Ring, and they do have luck on their side—anyone who hasn't noticed the value of luck in our world has simply not been paying attention. As Shippey argues ("Post-War" 228), the potential for the greatest evil of all occurs when within Mount Doom when Frodo nearly fails to destroy the Ring: without Sam and, most ironically, Gollum, he probably would have failed, as might any of us in such a circumstance: the apocalyptic moment, Tolkien might have said, comes for all, even the smallest of us, and tests each one. The apocalyptic world is as much personal as it is cosmological. Each of us will find ourselves, at our greatest test, lacking something that would make success easier or more likely. But a world with the potential for goodness and good luck always offers another opportunity for hope: we need not fail, despite whatever we lack, despite our imperfections. These points have great value for teaching, because they reinforce that heroes come from human backgrounds and experience human flaws: they simply do their best and face what others fail to face.

Like the Old English heroic verse that formed the centerpiece of much of Tolkien's study, the thematic, ethical center of *LotR* emerges quietly as steadfast courage, blithe persistence in one's code of conduct, belief in the glory one wins through laudable behavior, and willingness to sacrifice personal gain to share peace—students still respond to those themes. As a Catholic writer who created a pre–Christian world, Tolkien allowed his creation to remain free of dogma, but not of moral or ethical imperatives. They come largely from those texts that most influenced him, and we do well to study those works to understand the genesis of Tolkien's world. And while Tolkien kept his world clear of religious holidays or Christian allegory or even explicitly and exclusively Christian symbols, he echoes many moral concerns with Christian thought and practice.[15] Students may see such points as driven by religious morality or simply by characters' desire to find and do good—either point works well in the classroom.

Middle-earth shares with our world violence, horror, suffering, perversion, weakness, death; it also shares with ours kindness, self-sacrifice, courage, and the love of things that grow, companionship, a good meal.[16] We inhabit his world with only the briefest hesitation—and most of us who have entered once re-enter it often—because there courage and goodness can win, if one has a bit of luck to go with them. Whether that fact represents in the long run fantasy or truth remains for us to prove, but most of us, I think, wish to live in a world that has at least that much potential. Of that potential our best fiction, Tolkien knew, aims to convince us—a non-cynical message that we may include in class discussion without introducing it artificially.

With that "theoretical" background I have begun "Tolkien's World," a course I've now taught twice at St. Norbert College—and from what I can observe from discussions with colleagues from other institutions, interest in Tolkien courses continues to grow in colleges and universities nationwide and even worldwide. Together we delved into *Beowulf, Volsungasaga, Sir Gawain and the Green Knight, Mabinogi,* and *Kalevala* (with references to other primary, critical, linguistic, and biographical works, including Carpenter's biography of Tolkien) to discern the elements upon which Tolkien drew to construct his world, its moral as well as physical and intellectual space. Those elements prove essential to one's understanding of Tolkien's creative process and to our fuller appreciation of the complexity of *The Lord of the Rings* specifically. With a background of some of Tolkien's own reading we could move into the study of Tolkien and his work with a better sense of the genesis of his fictional world and the value of its literary "parents."

We read Humphrey Carpenter's biography to establish the influence of his parents' deaths, World War I, and his religious background, and his linguistic and literary studies on Tolkien's fiction. We proceeded to several important literary antecedents or influences: for example, as Welsh and Finnish provided the model languages for Tolkien's Elvish, *Mabinogi* (in its mix of human and supernatural and its attention to coming-of-age issues) and *Kalevala* (in its development of wizards and their mediation of the human and natural worlds) influenced major elements of his "world building" (the components, laws, and "feel" of Middle-earth).[17] Similarly *Beowulf* contributed not only a dragon, but the Anglo-Saxon worldview colored by blood-feud and the ideal of steadfast courage, and Tolkien's essay on *Beowulf* shows how a writer's literary criticism (which of course they must write as part of their study) may influence his or her fiction. *Sir Gawain and the Green Knight* instilled a sense of nature as worthy of reverence and full of both dangerous and salvific surprises (it also created a moral basis of *The Lord of the Rings*—we learn that no matter the quality of our character, we may well fail at last with or without outside intervention). While Tolkien's essay on *Beowulf* exemplifies his own critical methods, which we could employ in our own reading of his fiction,[18] studying the poems shows another productive kind of criticism: writing creative responses to one's readings rather than expository or theoretical ones. Prepared with that toolbox, we covered a number of Tolkien's works with special focus (six weeks' reading, plus a bit, of our fifteen-week semester) on *The Lord of the Rings*, aiming to develop readings that satisfied us in both scholarly and aesthetic terms. Our Tolkien readings included not only *LotR*, but also *The Silmarillion* (which students have proven to like better than one may expect, some even terming it their favorite for the semester, even beyond *LotR*!), and "Leaf by Niggle" (which shows them his use of allegory despite his oft-stated distaste for it). We didn't use *The Hobbit* for class, but most students had read it before hand, either on their own or at my suggestion, so it occasionally entered discussions.[19]

At the middle and end of the semester the students composed substantial papers, one "critical" and one "creative," following Tolkien's own models for how to respond to great texts. They had the freedom to take notions of criticism and creativity as broadly as they might, so papers included a range of approaches from fiction of their own to art work, proto-movie scripts, Middle-earth "products" to market, and traditional papers as well as more personal, reader-response essays. Tolkien's creative freedom can inspire the students' as well.

One can, of course, vary the syllabus in any number of ways to focus more on Tolkien's texts, more on his sources or his criticism, more on other writers of his generation, more on other fantasy writers. But finding means to attract students to the serious study of Tolkien's work or subsequently to the study of the Middle Ages (and perhaps the Renaissance, Classical age, or other early European classics) yields positive results; students begin to look through Tolkien to the endless world of pleasurable reading and productive study beyond. One must adjust the syllabus for the length of term (semester, quarter, summer term), student population (literature and/or language majors, general education students, students already versed in fantasy and science fiction), and one's own strengths and interests (some teachers may prefer to stick with Old and Middle English influences, some may want to explore linguistic influences more extensively, some may want to introduce children's literature or folk tales and fairy tales).

Mythopoiesis and *cosmopoiesis* (keys to understanding Tolkien's world) imply not only story-creation, but also world-building. Tolkien draws us in not only through the story of the Ring (and its antecedents), but also with elves, ents, Tom Bombadil and Goldberry, Moria, and even barrow-wights and Old Man Willow. Along with the hobbits we like to eat bread and butter and mushrooms and drink hot tea and dark beer—each element contributes breadth, sense, presence. The Norse medieval world has warrior maidens, a cursed ring (and a huge, useless treasure to go with it), human interaction with gods and monsters, werewolves, magic trees, and family feud and revenge by the cartload. The fourteenth-century England of *Sir Gawain and the Green Knight* foregrounds knights and ladies, connections to ancient dynasties of epic stories, and tests (both passed and failed) of morality and courage, and it uses but perhaps satirizes quests. The fourteenth-century (or perhaps earlier) Cymric *Mabinogi* introduces giants, magical music, the value of crafts, and a sense of closeness to the land. Not in itself medieval, but perhaps *medievalism*, *Kalevala*, assembled from older stories by Elias Lönnrot in the nineteenth century, shows how a committed scholar-editor and storyteller can acquire and assemble a mythology for a people, one that resonates with an ethos so fully that it becomes embedded in a culture as though it were much older and more complete than it is. Tolkien borrowed from all of them and from many other aspects of the medieval world, and more than anything else he found and incorporated into his creative process their *feel*: what a writer can do with narrative, language, character (individual and national), landscape, magic, and courage to build stories that will last as long as those that inspired them. The world of Tolkien's fiction comes partly from them—it did not rise *sui generis*, and fiction never fully does. Once students get that idea they not only read better, with more sophistication, but they also have a far better chance of writing better, both in critique and in their own fiction.

From *Beowulf* and from Tolkien's essay on *Beowulf* students can learn how scholars' love for and knowledge of their topics can lead to successful fiction writing. Many of our undergraduates take up English majors because at first they believe they want to be writers, not medievalists, and looking specifically for Beowulfian echoes in Tolkien's fiction and closely examining his critical approach to the poem shows them how by absorbing works past they can create more powerful works of their own. No one escapes literary influence, so we ought to do our best to acquire and harness the most powerful influences we can. *Beowulf* provided that influence for Tolkien, and it can do so for our students as well. *Volsungasaga* similarly offers a dragon and heroism and, like *Kalavala*, a wizard figure; *Beowulf*, too, brings heroes and monster, but it adds romance, betrayal, and extended examples of familial and national conflict to students' critical and creative vocabulary—not to mention Old Norse and its linguistic relationship to Old English.[20] The Norse material adds the trickster figure in Oðin—he shows both potency and unreliability—particularly if one introduces Snorri Sturluson as well, and it presents a world that mixes grim, matter-of-fact realism with imminent enchantment. *Sir Gawain and the Green Knight* provides students another of Tolkien's favorite texts, this time, if an instructor chooses, in his own translation (so one can address issues of translation theory productively). *Mabinogi* adds the magic of the "Otherworld"—Faerie may lurk just at the local liminal boundary, such as a wood or a tor—and humor plus, for the doughty professor, an opportunity to introduce a bit of Medieval Welsh and another angle on philology. *Kalevala* adds serious and potent wizardry, the powerful sense of a lost age, a means to look at how compilers or editors assemble texts, and again an unusual linguistic opportunity.

These texts of course merely scratch the surface of Tolkien's connections and influences—they get the older ones rather than the newer, such as George MacDonald or Andrew Lang or William Morris or even C. S. Lewis and Charles Williams, which one may easily enough add—but they offer a range of motifs, ideas, and languages that show students the complexities of creating effective fictional worlds: points we often miss in our early attempts at fantasy fiction. Through them students learn a lot about older and newer literatures and about careful, dedicated *making*. More importantly for most of them, they begin to grasp the range, depth, power, and pleasure of medieval (and Modern) literature relatively painlessly, thoroughly organically, and even joyfully, and they see how influential the thought of the Middle Ages has been in spurring later re-creations: that is, medievalism. Appreciating and valuing the products of the medieval world can in other contexts prove difficult because in so many instances students receive encouragement to think of relevancy only in terms of contemporary issues presented by contemporary writers (even our colleagues who should know better will use *medieval* to describe something unrefined or closed-minded or brutal). If they themselves wish to become fiction writers, though, few studies can help them more than the idea of building a textual world in which their own readers will want for a brief time to live.

The Problematic Tolkien: Social Conservative, Political Liberal, and Practical Theorist

Marjorie Burns, noting that the chief negative responses to Tolkien's fiction hinge on claims of "moral simplicity," remarks that

> Tolkien's fiction seems unquestionably to have been created along these lines [of clear demarcation of class, rank, morality, and good and evil]. It is not difficult to identify Tolkien's likes and dislikes, his values and preferences, his sense of who belongs where. All the usual clues mark his partialities: light and dark, ugly and fair, black and white, high and low, up and down ... the superiority of North over South, of West over East, and the unadorned over the ornate [30].

8. Teaching Tolkien and His World, and Why He Matters

While Burns goes on thoroughly and effectively to defend Tolkien as a writer, I think one may say more about these issues, both for Tolkien and by studying what he says for himself: in his letters. Tolkien's show of sympathies for the Germans (for the *people*, not for the leaders or the Nazis) as World War II came to a close has raised charges of Fascism—charges a reading of the letters can easily set aside. Tolkien admired certain virtues (e.g., loyalty, courage, fidelity to duty) which he saw in the peoples of many countries, not among the Allies alone, and he saw atrocities among the Allies as well as the Axis powers. Tolkien believed, for instance, in "hierarchical loyalties" and in "traditional roles" (43), in, for instance, tipping one's hat to the squire, however bad that might prove for the squire, because showing respect to another does one good by promoting humility. For Americans issues related to class and traditional notions of faith or heroism can prove particularly thorny, as I have found regularly in discussing the relationship between Frodo and Sam in *The Lord of the Rings*: some readers—or mostly viewers of the films who haven't read Tolkien—can't imagine Sam willingly calling Frodo "Master" and showing affectionate deference. For Tolkien such thinking has personal, social, cultural, and religious significance. And the letters, for instance, show a number of ambiguities that deserve mention—though often not those ambiguities of which one finds Tolkien accused.

Tolkien's letters offer interesting if occasionally troubling insights on his views of all sorts of issues, many (but not all) more prominent in public discourse now than they were in his own time. Based on his fiction some critics have accused him of sexism, racism, or simply of persistent adolescence. While I can't help feeling that reading them constitutes an inappropriate intrusion, since he didn't write them for us, and that commenting on them exacerbates that rudeness, the letters do expound personal opinions that help us address such "charges" in the author's own words—and so perhaps put some of the "hating" to rest. While, given the ideas Tolkien expresses in the letters, we may not simply clear him of all complaints of offending our contemporary sensibilities, the letters show us a complex person dealing with complicated influences: that is, a human being of extraordinary gifts and achievements who to some degree suffers as each of us does from the limitations of his time. In this section I intend to address some of the specific ideas that Tolkien expresses in several of his letters and to show the curious way that conservative socio-religious views combined with liberal political views directed him to an approach to literature both practical and realistic, at once pessimistic yet hopeful, at once traditional yet liberating. I believe that while a contemporary reader may occasionally feel "disappointed" at Tolkien's personal opinions, the judicial reader will depart them believing that he or she has met a person of genuine kindness whose life and work encourage freedom and liberation rather than the oppressive values of which some critics have accused him.

In a draft of a 1943 letter to C.S. Lewis (number 49, pages 60–62 in the text), Tolkien mentions a wedding he attended in which the couple married twice: once in a Catholic church and once in a civil ceremony. The first ceremony, he notes, included mutual pledges of fidelity and the woman's vow of obedience; the second took place before a female registrar—an "impropriety" he calls that—with no vows of fidelity or obedience—an "abominable proceeding," "ridiculous" and redundant and perhaps insulting in that it apparently ignored the earlier church service (*Letters* 62). In the same letter, criticizing Lewis's idea of a "two-marriage" system, Tolkien suggests that "sexual continence" requires the sanction and control of religion to invest a relationship with sufficient "awe" to inspire and demand it. While the idea of lifelong fidelity upheld by religious decree hasn't now the cultural force (at least nominally) that it had, the problem many readers will find here comes in the use of "obedience" as a necessary part of the woman's vow. "Toleration of divorce," he adds, "if a Christian does tolerate it—is toleration of a human abuse" (61). Tolkien maintained thoroughly traditional views of marriage.

More of that sort of issue comes in an earlier letter (number 43, 1941, pages 48–54, addressed to his son Michael, on marriage), and with greater elaboration. He answers the *When Harry Met Sally* question that men and women can seldom maintain a true friendship without sexual desires and intentions intervening. He asserts that while chivalric tradition remains "strong" (a doubtful assertion, though perhaps truer then than now), though under greater influence of Christianity and "inimical" to the times, its separation of "love" from marriage and God places the woman dangerously on a pedestal and produces "at best make-believe." However, Courtly Love's alter-ego, Marianism, gives warmth and color to "our hard, bitter religion," ennobling it, though not without its own dangers, falling short of theocentricity. It may draw "the young man's eyes off women as they are, as companions in shipwreck not guiding stars," and so may turn a man "cynical" so that he forgets women's "desires, needs and temptations," exaggerating romantic love and separating it from "age, childbearing, and plain life," steering one away from the idea that relationships take effort and commitment (49).

Women, he asserts further, show less selfishness, but more sympathy and understanding; they will enter more easily into a man's interest than men will theirs, and they more gladly take up the their partners' interests. Falling in love for the "unspoiled natural young woman," he suggests, "means that she wants to become the mother of the young man's children." He opines that women turn more to the practical than the romantic, and they tend less to bawdry and don't need much "glamour" to fall in or remain in love, and that they retain a "delusion" that can "reform" men. Women are "instinctively, when uncorrupt, monogamous. Men are not.... No good pretending." He adds, I'm not sure if with humorous intent, "Faithfulness in Christian marriage entails ... great mortification. For a Christian man there is *no escape.*" From Tolkien's point of view married persons may not and cannot search for a soulmate: they have found that person already. He continues, almost ominously, that "nearly all marriages, even happy ones, are mistakes," since "both partners might have found more suitable mates." He believed marriages would more likely turn out happy if the young persons had only limited choice: family authority would choose better as long as the social structure promotes fidelity. This long letter has much more, but those excerpts provide enough for us to sink our teeth into the argument, and one can see readily enough why some readers may find those thoughts troubling or even "oppressive."

I don't want to make any assertions of my own about the truth value of Tolkien's statements—anyone can do that as well as I. They appear in the context of a letter of advice from father to son during wartime and both following and preceding times of social upheaval, and they come from someone who as a baby lost his father and barely a youth lost his devotedly Catholic mother, leaving him in the guardianship of a priest. We may say that he allows "romanticized" stereotypes about women, but he also utters less-than-flattering—and equally stereotypical— apothegms about men. We may accuse him of dogma, but he endured early loss and near poverty, fell in love at eighteen with the woman he would later marry, for three years at his guardian's insistence did not see or write to her, married her at twenty-one, survived the trench warfare of World War I, sold the last of his meager inheritance to get her special nursing care to bear their first child, apparently remained entirely faithful to her for his whole life, and lived long enough to see and experience a lot of life. He concludes the letter by recommending to Michael—who later became a priest—"the one great thing to love on earth: the Blessed Sacrament." Doubtless some readers will find parts of the letter insulting; one may even find the religious turn at the end facile, an abdication of a necessary conclusion to issues with personal, secular implications as well as religious resonances. Yet the ideas fit perfectly in the thought and practice of twentieth-century Catholicism; they are in no way peculiar or outlandish in the midst of Tolkien's time or traditions.

But I suspect that we all hear in those words *honesty*, a struggle of emotion with hardship, belief, and ethic—and points with which we'll individually agree, though which they are will differ among us. I suspect, too, that, while we don't hear what our age would feel willing to term equality, we do hear *equanimity*: a calm balance that aims at a fair and truthful rendering of experience. Women and men may view romance similarly or they may see it rather differently; women may well through weakness (or even evil design) get corrupted from societal expectations; men may turn into cads who abuse women as objects or may remain in a weak adolescence of dangerous idealization or unwillingness to make adult commitments. Some critics have faulted Tolkien's fiction as devoid of adult responsibilities and relationships or even as overtly sexist, but they forget or ignore the circumstances of Aragorn and Arwen, Beren and Lúthien, Tom Bombadil and Goldberry, Galadriel and Celeborn, and even Sam and Rosie. We see few women take center stage in the action, and the one who does most fully, Éowyn, at last turns from the life of soldier to that of wife and healer. He does not single out women for a different morality and ethics than men: both, he firmly believed, should remain faithful in marriage and to God.

But we do find females of power, both for great good—Galadriel—and disgusting horror—Shelob: little romanticizing there, but a clear sense that good and evil choices and actions are the equal province of women as well as men. And we can hardly expect a male writer of

8. Teaching Tolkien and His World, and Why He Matters

Tolkien's time to strive for gender equity in stories that largely create the objective correlative for his own experiences in World War I, where he would have had few interactions with women good or bad, only the love of one urging him to survive to get home. While his opinions of women to some degree reinforce problematic and oppressive ideas, they do recognize potentials for good and bad equally, and they place responsibility for good relationships equally, if somewhat differently. And they may well adhere to the realities of his time better than we would wish to believe, as we try to revise our notions of human character and eliminate stultifying boundaries. How easily we could have had tales with no Galadriels or Éowyns at all, allegorical islands of boys worshipping pig-headed gods. We see in Tolkien conservative views of women, but also conservative views of how men should behave. We see clear awareness of male exploitation of women and ideas pointing toward the value of responsibility and kindness, free of selfishness, if not urgings of complete social equality.

With respect to religion, as the previous step in the argument partially demonstrates, Tolkien remained unabashedly, devotedly, exclusively Catholic, with no Mertonian leanings to Buddhism, but also with few if any outright attacks on other beliefs. He did, though, point out unequivocally any abuse of Catholicism that he observed in friends or foes, as he does notably with Lewis's bias against Catholics in letter 83: "There is a good deal of Ulster still left in C.S.L., if hidden from himself" (page 95) and "if a Lutheran is put in jail he is up in arms, but if Catholic priests are slaughtered—he disbelieves it (and I daresay really thinks they asked for it)" (96).[21] He doesn't so much focus on apologetics as he does on practice informed by careful thought and a willingness to let his own religious opinions take shape. In a 1944 letter to his son Christopher, he says, "I fancy that Our Lord actually is more pained by offences we commit against one another than those we commit against himself, esp. his incarnate person" (letter 86, page 97): not standard theology, but an interesting and fairly liberal interpretation of the suffering of Christ, one that allows space for the creation of a fictional world beyond (or before) specifically Catholic influence. And he does express sympathy for ecumenism, not always current in Catholicism or any denomination; in a 1968 letter to his son Michael he wrote that he found at least sympathy in ecumenism, in any group that could truly call itself Christian—

however he might wish for Christian re-union in Catholicism. Any "increase in 'charity' is an enormous gain," he added (394). He would like to have seen all Christians return to the Catholic fold, but probably didn't believe it likely or even possible and didn't press for it.

Tolkien shows also notable sympathy for Jews in a time and place where those sympathies were hardly universal. In a response to a German publisher who inquired in 1938 about Tolkien's ancestry, he replies: "I regret that I am not clear as to what you intend by *arisch*. I am not of *Aryan* extraction: that is Indo-iranian.... But if I am to understand that you are enquiring whether I am of *Jewish* origin, I can only reply that I regret that I appear to have *no* ancestors of that gifted people.... I cannot ... forbear to comment that if impertinent and irrelevant inquiries of this sort are to become the rule in matters of literature, then the time is not far distant when a German name will no longer be a source of pride" (37–38). Tolkien maintains a love of "northernness" alongside a hatred of Nazism: "There is a great deal more force (and truth) than ignorant people imagine in the 'Germanic' ideal.... You have to understand the good in things to detect the real evil.... I have in this War a burning grudge—which would probably make me a better soldier at 49 than I was at 22: against that ruddy little ignoramus Adolf Hitler.... Ruining, perverting, misapplying, and making for ever accursed, that noble spirit, a supreme contribution to Europe, which I have ever loved, and tried to present in a true light" (55–56). Tolkien had no sympathy for warmongers or selfish, violent tyrants.

Tolkien's work has often elicited charges of encouraging militarism, but his own thought—and textual examples—stand as far as possible from any desire to urge violence. After Michael volunteered for the army in 1940, Tolkien wrote him that "in times of peace we get ... too engrossed in thinking of everything as a preparation or training or a making one fit—for what? At any minute it is what we are and what we are doing, not what we plan to be and do that counts. But I cannot pretend that I myself found that idea much comfort against the waste of time and militarism of the army" (46). He had aimed to do his part in military service, but had no desire to do violence.

While he suggests a willingness to fight, he expresses an absolute hatred of war, and despite its horrors Tolkien manages a realistic optimism: "All things and deeds have a value in themselves, apart from their 'causes' and 'effects.' No man can estimate what is really happening at the present sub specie aeternitatis. All we do know, and that to a large extent by direct experience, is that evil labours with vast power and perpetual success—in vain: preparing always only the soil for unexpected good to sprout in" (1944, page 76). "I love the vulgar and the simple as dearly as the noble, and nothing moves my heart ... so much as 'ennoblement' (from the Ugly Duckling to Frodo)" (1956, page 232), he added. That ennoblement does not require fighting; it requires personal and spiritual devotion in no way attached to class or family history or success in battle.

In letter 155 Tolkien summarizes his view of evil as he expresses it in *The Lord of the Rings*, but also, I think, as he experienced it more generally and which many of his readers will share: "The supremely bad motive is (for this tale, since it is specially about it) domination of other 'free' wills" (200). Sauron uses his powers "to bulldoze both people and things" and "to terrify and subjugate" (200). This point has eminent personal, religious, social, and political implications, and it appears often in the letters as it is foundational to the fiction. I'm not a great fan of biographical criticism: it can limit readings and mislead readers. But many of us must admit that unsavory notions (however trivial) of an author's life or personality can inflect our readings negatively—who can forget the influence, brief but explosive, just a short generation ago of revelations about the lives or habits of theorists Paul de Mann and Michel Foucault? If we take up the task of criticism, we owe text and author fair opportunity, as free as possible from harmful assumptions or stereotypes or prejudgments, whether that author seems a fixture among some powerful elite or beneath our literary dignity. The text is not the person, and a writer may not live up to all the best of his or her own ideas, let alone all the best of those in times after his or her own life. The way to personal liberation for readers and writers comes from compassionate confrontation and open-minded appraisal, affective and intellectual commodities that, despite Tolkien's efforts and ours and our enormous need for them, may have no greater currency now than they have ever had.

Afterword
Mechanized Landscape and Spiritual Landscape— In Retrospect

"[A]ll of this stuff is mainly concerned with Fall, Mortality, and the Machine. With Fall inevitably ... [w]ith Mortality, especially as it affects art and the creative (or as I should say, sub-creative desire ... an so to the Machine or Magic ... the use of external plans or devices (apparatus) instead of development of the inherent inner powers or talents"—Tolkien, *Letters* 145

Regardless of one's critical prejudices with respect to fantasy, Tolkien used, as I hope I have already shown in this book, a complex landscape of ideas that meld traditions from ancient to Modern (and almost postmodern). Ring tales are nearly as old as tales in general, as are stories of magical (or broken) weapons, oppressive invaders, friendship, and quest—though Tolkien has of course the unusual wrinkle of the quest to destroy a dangerous talisman rather than to acquire a useful one. But Tolkien treats in his fiction many of the troublesome issues of the twentieth century particularly powerfully. He had, for instance, a deep distrust of mechanization: it ruined the landscape he loved, more than decimated his generation in war, and continued to grow and spread through the greenwood he loved. He hadn't a simplistic notion of technology, but had instead a love of nature and growing things that pervades his fiction. He created an intellectual landscape, a landscape with a living intellect: Ents, Tom Bombadil, and Goldberry, even dwarves, for instance, rise directly from the landscape, their thought, knowledge, and memories as old and varied as the land from which they come. While the Forest can encompass dangers, even evils—especially for someone

Afterword. Mechanized Landscape and Spiritual Landscape

who enters with ill intent—destruction of the forest means destruction of life: when Lothlórien declines, the elves depart Middle-earth, and with them goes beauty, knowledge, wisdom, and powers to see beyond the range of human skill and intellect. Tolkien's landscape in some cases romanticizes, but it never sentimentalizes: vast and varied, beautiful and perilous, it extends the range of experience and choice for all sentient beings. And yet it can, without sentimentalizing, ennoble, as it does with Sam: "The ennoblement of the ignoble I find especially moving," Tolkien wrote in a letter of 1955 (*Letters* 220). We can make the most of it, admiring, appreciating, enjoying, and marveling, or we can destroy it and ourselves—taking most other creatures along with us.

Tolkien's landscape has, for fantasy, an astonishing clarity. Even his early work shows, as Rosebury observes, a "gift for admitting the reader to a transparent view of landscape" (83) that comes from sound and idea as well as color, shape, and topography. It has a deep and fully realized history, a creation, remakings, and reshapings, and it houses traumatic and inspiring events and above all a truth to itself, a sense of reality within its own boundaries. It has, as Shippey especially has argued (*Author*), an *applicability* that makes it more complete and fulfilling than allegory because it allows for all readers, not only those for whom a specific allegory has meaning and presence, space to interpret.

In a note that appears in the *Letters* Tolkien wrote that *The Lord of the Rings* "is not about JRRT at all, and is at no point an attempt to allegorize his experience of life" (239). Tolkien got most autobiographical and most allegorical in "Leaf by Niggle." The painting of a landscape metamorphoses into entering a spiritual landscape. The "niggler" may miss the big picture, leaving only a leaf of his or her work behind, but such a person does not meet dismissal from spiritual experience or reward: like Gollum (or Frodo, or Isildur, or Sauron), though, one must give up the niggling, the self-obsession, to find that new and better landscape. Tolkien knew that he niggled with his Middle-earth, drafting and re-drafting and re-drafting, but he maintained sight of its result: of telling complex stories with compelling characters in such a way as to raise ideas and encourage spiritual consciousness.

Tolkien's intellectual landscape begins with the great questions of the Christian faith, but most of his stories occur in a time long before Christianity gives answers for how to deal with them. His creatures must find them in the discovery of their own morality and ethics, in their compassion, heroism, kindness, humility, and self-sacrifice—and in their desire to preserve what they find and make that they can call good. He found narrative answers to philosophical and religious questions and his own aesthetic answers to literary questions; he found meaning and goodness in an age that began to question the possibility of both, and he found ways to hope (even in cases where he himself probably lacked it) in an age that, despite its technology and increasing wealth, found more and more reasons to despair. Like William Blake, with whose interest in world creation he had quite a good deal in common (as well as their mutual Christianity, love of England, and love of art-making), he encouraged others to create for themselves: the act of sub-creation continues the creative act of God and represents humans at our best, our most godly, most inspired, most alive. Middle-earth isn't an exclusive place: we all live there, however unrecognizable it has become, and from it we too can gather the inspiration to make art, music, and literature, to exhibit the divine spark that moves in us if we have only the piety to pay attention.

While quite a number of commentators have considered Tolkien's work in a specifically Christian context, I find Matthew Dickerson's *Following Gandalf* among the most helpful with how Tolkien deals with ideas as *Christian* ideas. Dickerson clearly relates several of Tolkien's themes that we may label as Christian, as coming naturally out of Tolkien's Christian beliefs. I'll list them here.

1. "Freedom to choose is fundamental to what it means to be a self" (86): on Amon Hen Frodo "almost forgets himself," caught in Sauron's power and the power of the Ring. Yet we must remember both the "reality of human free will and the moral responsibility that goes with it," the "doom of choice" (17): we must recognize the responsibility that goes with freedom and the fact that choice can sometimes prove both terrifying and nonetheless necessary. We may find ourselves in a situation where no *right* choice exists: Aragorn and Gandalf trying to decide the means to get past the Misty Mountains where no good path exists, and Aragorn must decide after the breaking of the fellowship whether to follow Frodo and Sam or to try to rescue Merry and Pippin from the orcs—neither choice is clear and simple. Life requires choices, whether it makes them plain or not, and goodness comes from trying to make good

choices. "Freedom," Dickerson observes, "I held the higher gift than safety!" (107). Middle-earth does not permit us to remain neutral (Kocher, *Master* 67), must like the circumstances of the First and Second World Wars. Good versus evil partly implies tensions of "beauty against ruthless ugliness, tyranny against kingship, moderated freedom with consent against compulsion that has long ago lost any object save mere power" (*Letters* 178–79): rule isn't by itself bad, but can become ugly and evil by misdirection from its duties to its own personal desires.

2. The greatest battle we face takes place not on the battlefield, but in the mind or soul, the "battle against despair" (Dickerson 28). Sam, Frodo, and Théoden win it; Denethor and Saruman lose it. Finally freedom, Dickerson notes, "is held the higher gift than safety" (107): one must overcome the internal malaise even to engage the external quest, which aims at last at freedom for everyone. Despair means asking the death of freedom inside oneself. To defeat despair, one must also overcome fear, the chief weapon of the Enemy (Kocher, *Master* 73); Tolkien used but adjusted the medieval "Germanic theory of courage" to fits the problems of the end of the Third Age of Middle-earth.

3. "Even in a society that glorifies war" (the Rohirrim), Tolkien "uses the hobbits ... to de-glorify it" (Dickerson 33): the hobbits tell us plainly that war is hell. They neither have nor acquire any interest in it. Sam's moment of self-glorification in the idea of leadership into battle comes only momentarily as he wears and falls under the spell of the ring, until his better "hobbit-sense" asserts itself and brings him back to the task at hand. In a 1944 letter Tolkien wrote that "humans being what they are ... the only cure ... is not to have wars" (*Letters* 78). He added in 1945, commenting on The Bomb, that "[s]uch explosives in men's hands, while their moral and intellectual status is declining, is about as useful as giving out firearms to all inmates of a gaol and then saying that you hope 'this will ensure peace'" (116).

4. The key to "heroic" goodness comes in finding the strength to resist evil (Dickerson 36): Théoden must choose either to fight with Gondor or in passivity to serve Sauron by failing to fight evil when it stands at the brink of gaining overwhelming power. That choice requires courage, which the king has, but also strength of character, of which Wormtongue had stripped him. His regaining it comes partly with Gandalf's help, but

also in the subsequent choices he makes that come from his own resurgent strength. We must also, though, as Shippey notes, avoid the "mistake just to blame everything on evil forces 'out there,' the habit of xenophobes and popular journalists," though just as big a "mistake to luxuriate in self-analysis" like the "cosseted upper-class writers of the 'modernist' movement" (*Author* 142). We may find evil within or without, and we must resist it wherever we find it, and not in fantasy alone.

5. The hobbits must "scour" the Shire themselves: when they near the Shire at the end of *The Return of the King*, Gandalf leaves them to "settle its affairs" themselves (Dickerson 56). Gandalf came to Middle-earth not to fix everything himself, but to inspire others to do their own fixing, to understand their responsibilities and grow to have the strength and wisdom to meet them.

6. Moral victory outstrips military victory (67). Boromir fails the "Ring test" that Gandalf, Aragorn, and Faramir pass, but he then defends Merry and Pippin with his life. Following the battle for Gondor, Gandalf and Aragorn lead a force too small to win to battle before the gates of Mordor; they do so not for military glory, or even with any hope of surviving it, but to distract Sauron during the last stage of the quest to destroy the Ring—moral right constitutes true victory.

7. We must remain vigilant in our own compassion and kindness, no matter how hard the situation, and we must remain willing to forgive. While we may find the greatest tragedy of *The Lord of the Rings* in Frodo's final inability to let go of the Ring, Tolkien found it in Sam's sharp words as Gollum kneels beside the sleeping Frodo, stretching his hand gently toward him: Gollum comes "within a hair of repentance—but for one rough word from Sam" (*Letters* 110, qtd. in Dickerson 157). Blaming Sam may be too harsh—he has just awakened himself in a difficult situation—but Tolkien's thought reinforces the need for unflagging compassion (Christian or otherwise), however difficult to generate we find it. Forgiveness follows hard upon (Dickerson 163): forgiving Gollum proves easier once he has gone with the Ring to the Fire, but we must do so before, as Frodo does. Forgiving the hobbits who have collaborated with Saruman may prove easier after the scouring of the Shire, but we must do so before hand, as Frodo insists. In Tolkien's world as in Christian ideals, mercy trumps justice.

Afterword. Mechanized Landscape and Spiritual Landscape

8. In the use of without sentimentalizing the *ubi sunt*,[1] the sense of appreciation for things and times lost, though with a "profound sense of sorrow and loss" (212), we find a theme both Anglo-Saxon and Christian that Tolkien pursued in much of his work. Medieval literature and philosophy fairly bleeds *memento mori, sic transit gloria mundi, lif is læne*, and Tolkien carries that idea persistently in *The Lord of the Rings*, *The Silmarillion*, and "Leaf by Niggle" particularly. The things of the world pass; we must not cling to them: Tolkien makes that theme as modern as it is ancient.

9. Tolkien's work does reinforce notions of Christian worth,

> in the Christian understanding of objective morality and moral responsibility; in the Christian importance of hope; in ideas of human worth, nobility, and purpose having their source in a divine Creator; in Christian notions of stewardship; in the understanding of human creativity as also having its source in a Creator; in Christian notions of salvation; in acknowledgment of the reality of the spiritual plane ... and especially in the ever present hand of Authority at work within his creation [Dickerson 219].

Dickerson along with most Christian readers—and many others as well—would point out that Tolkien, unlike many twentieth-century writers, does not shy away from moral imperatives: characters may or may not adhere to them, but his fictional world allows for them and points to them pretty clearly. For some critics that kind of thinking leads to overly simply conclusions, but much of the century's thought has involved the search for what we can still consider morally true and ethically binding. Not everyone will agree with Tolkien's choices, but they make sense for someone concerned about freedom and about future generations and committed to Christian notions of Salvation. And the characters don't so much follow a given code of morality as discover it through their experiences: morality doesn't enslave them, but unfolds for them and becomes true and significant as they practice it.

To that list we may add a few more points, drawn here from Paul Kocher's *Master of Middle-earth: The Fiction of J. R. R. Tolkien*, the first echoing my previous point:

10. Virtually without exception," Kocher asserts, "the elves, men, hobbits, and their allies of the West come to believe in a moral dynamism in the universe to which each of them freely contributes" (34): the idea reinforces tolerance, mutual appreciation, and learning, not moral rel-

ativity. Morality, too, comes from free choice (44), not compulsion. Sauron's problem, and the suffering he causes others, comes from his "whole appetite ... for command of other wills" (59)—a point we would do well to remember in our own time.

11. "Gollum's private torment," Kocher aptly suggests, "stems from the fact that the Ring's conquest of his will is incomplete, leaving intact sufficient impulses toward good to breed an unending inner conflict" (63). The assertion may overstate the case, but the point has grave importance for all of Tolkien's work: the struggle for good brings pain, especially where the impulse to evil is strong. Gollum acts more, I think, out of self-preservation and to indulge his obsession than out of any really good impulses. But when the potential for good impulses emerges, the potential for his suffering—as well as, for a change, actual pleasure—magnifies. Gollum seems actually to experience some joy in Frodo's presence, resulting in the internal struggle between Gollum and Sméagol. But do we really have any doubt about how Gollum will turn at last? He has gone too far down into self-obsession and into all identification of the Ring with himself—"my precious"—to return to good. Gandalf retains hope for him, as does Frodo, partly because one must hope, regardless of the likely result: freedom comes from belief in the will to act and change, not in the idea of fated or wholly determined character. Finding the good may be not just hard, but painful: one must want to search and must do so with persistence. The Ring means loss of self, even at last for Sauron; resisting it means retaining self, the ability to express compassion as well as to choose to act in varying ways for varying circumstance. Sauron comes to define himself as power and control, a self-limitation that eliminates the possibility of love, compassion, or joy. How much joy could Sauron have experienced had he succeeded?

12. "Nothing is evil in the beginning. Even Sauron was not so," Kocher quotes (76), reinforcing not only the need for moral choices and steadfast courage, but also the need for compassion. The powers of the West must give even Sauron (as the members of the Fellowship give Gollum) every chance, even to the very last, to choose other than oppression and cruelty. Each creature bears an obligation to see the good, or at least the potential for it, in every other. How would an orc mother feel about her children? Such thinking can lead to undying friendship between an Elf

Afterword. Mechanized Landscape and Spiritual Landscape

and a Dwarf, so different by nature and taste, because, as in the Fellowship, we must establish a "community of mutual trust" (93) really to have freedom both in our minds and in the world.

13. In "Tolkien's world as in ours," Kocher notes, one need not love his or her burden, but one must endure it, carry it, and dispatch its responsibilities (134). Christian faith does not always prove easy, nor does parenting nor teaching nor keeping a relationship nor going to work from one day to the next. Yet the world requires of us that we find a place and practice its disciplines if we wish to become fully ourselves and to contribute to our world. As does Aragorn, we must trace the steps to maturity, no matter how long they take and how difficult they prove. He must willingly offer his life to defend Frodo, Merry, and Pippin, he must win the battle of the palantír against Sauron, he must avoid entering Minas Tirith to claim his kingship too soon, he must be willing to cede command of the army before the gates of the Enemy to Gandalf, and he must wait until he achieves his kingship to win the Arwen in marriage (149–51). And he must accept at last the passing of Gandalf and the Elves, of so many friends, from the world. His path runs long and circuitous; ours may, too.

And from Marjorie Burns' *Perilous Realms* (which, though it focuses on the influence of Norse and Cymric worlds on Tolkien, has quite a good deal to say about his Christian thought), we may add these further themes.

14. Tolkien's fictional world often exhibits a tension inherent in the act of "possessing and consuming." Many of the scenes that show characters' enjoyment involve eating or acquiring items of value and importance that they take pleasure in having and using. Yet we see stark contrast with those characters who possess to consume *with pain*: Sauron, Shelob, Orcs, even Gollum (165). Such characters as Beorn, Tom Bombadil and Goldberry, and elves don't eat meat at all, and Elf food proves (*viz. lembas*) particularly nourishing to the spirit as well as the body—we may even metaphorically connect Frodo and Sam's consumption of *lembas,* on their journey, Burns notes, to acts of Communion (165). The idea here focuses on necessary consumption as an act of sustenance and community rather than violent consumption as an act of selfishness, greed, and horror.

15. Acts of goodness in Tolkien's world typically involve sacrifice, whereas acts of evil stem from "narcissism, ambition, and greed" (157). Frodo proceeds on his quest "burdened like Christ with the object of his own torture" (166), and he and Sam understand they have little hope of returning. Gandalf sacrifices himself in the battle with the Balrog, Aragorn offers his life to assist and defend the hobbits (as the Rangers have done on a regular basis for a very long time), and Galadriel "relinquish[es] her position in Lothlórien and Middle-earth" by assisting in the destruction of the One Ring, with which will fall the power of the Three the Elves keep and use (168). They point to but of course don't fully recapitulate the sacrifice of Christ: [t]he Resurrection is the eucatastrophe of the story of the Incarnation" wrote Tolkien in "On Faery-Stories" (*Tolkien Reader* 72), and the sentiment reappears in a 1944 letter "the Resurrection was the greatest 'eucatastrophe' possible in the greatest Fairy Story" (*Letters* 100): he did not see the Crucifixion story as fairy tale, but did see it as the Type of sacrifice from which we must learn. "The worship of Ilúvatar is the central element of the *Akallabêth*" in The Silmarillion, Dickerson notes (222), and the worship of God, through our lives and work, the center of the Christian life. Tolkien once observed that he found true joy only in the Eucharist; our human stories, even the best of them, could for him serve only as distant if enjoyable objective correlative. Because of our "quick satiety with good" (qtd. in M. Burns 177), we must as individuals remain vigilant in our own conduct and thoughts: the "real battle is between the soul and its adversaries" (also qtd. in Burns 178). In a letter to his son Michael, Tolkien discoursed on love, romance, marriage, and family, encouraging his son that the greatest love on earth is of the "Blessed Sacrament," that there one may find all the great heroic virtues and a taste of true glory such as one may find fulfilled only in the Afterlife.

No surprise for an orphan, a war veteran, and a Catholic medievalist who watched first hand the mechanization of his society, Tolkien commits to the physical aspects of spirituality. His work builds on traditional comforts of food and place and gods and friends, and it shows how through the adventure of life, good and bad, they all pass away—for some elect who have sacrificed and endured a haven awaits, followed by "a far green land under a swift sunrise" (*RotK* 384). Tolkien once said in an interview that *The Lord of the Rings* is about death: it explores how we approach death and the tension we experience with what lies beyond, but it also explores life, how we live it when death seems to wait at every corner and in every shadow. His Christian answer doesn't eliminate the heroic response of his fiction; it merely adds something that the vast old world, fictional or not, hadn't yet available, all the more poignant for his readers.

16. Goodness often requires humility and deference (M. Burns 43). We do well to treat others with humble respect, either because of class or achievements or abilities. Social humility teaches spiritual humility, a necessary Christian value. The curious thing in Tolkien's work is that the object and subject of deference may occasionally shift. After Bilbo manages by handing over the Arkenstone to bring peace to the troubled allies, he gains a great deal of respect and admiration from all concerned. The crowned Aragorn shows deference to the four hobbits and asks that all of his kingdom do the same. So the small too shall come to be great— the idea may have come straight from the Beatitudes.[2]

While this final list of themes particularly inhabits Christian thought, they are not confined to it: they span human experience, as Tolkien's pre–Christian Middle-earth shows. As Walter Hartt asserts, "Tolkien inclined to … [the idea that] art is subcreation when it is good art, regardless of whether or not it is thematically Christian" (23). Verlyn Flieger adds that Tolkien's Christianity is "tougher and darker than Lewis's, less mystical and occult than Williams's, and far less hopeful than either man's faith…. [It] is measured against experience and constantly put to the test" (*Splintered Light* xviii). That point holds true in principle even the pre–Christian world of Middle-earth. Interestingly, those who fail spiritually in Tolkien's work are often those with specific religious knowledge: Morgoth, Sauron, Saruman, even Denethor. Gandalf succeeds because he holds on to his faith: faith in the Creator, in the Valar, in his mission in Middle-earth, in himself, and in others. He believes in Aragorn and in Frodo, and his belief helps them succeed; he believes as long as he can in Saruman and Gollum, and they doom themselves by their own self-obsessions. As Gollum is his own "precious," so Saruman judges himself more precious than the those he comes to Middle-earth to serve, the same error of Morgoth and Sauron before him, the same error of Adam and Eve as they follow Satan in *Paradise*

Lost. But those flaws span religious, cultural, and geographic differences, and they apply throughout time.

While much of the twentieth century saw the flagging of religion, for a great many persons of Tolkien's time and ours it did not: religion remains a powerful force in daily life, in the major events and choices in a person's life, and in local, national, and international politics. Our impasses come not from the failure of religion, but from our failures in its practice, our forgetting its sentiments, our dismissal of tolerance. In Middle-earth humans, elves, and dwarves have different courses toward and in an after-life, but when they wish, they can work together for the good they can find in the world. They bring different skills, crafts, perspectives, cultures together, and they succeed when they learn to praise and welcome their differences—a message that culturally we learn only once again to forget.

Discussing the work of Joseph Pearce, Drout and Wynne note how the polarizing of Tolkien's readership (the lovers and the haters) may come partly from how Tolkien's "Catholic religious sensibility" included a "rejection of the ironic, atheistic, modernist orthodoxy of the [intellectual] establishment," and Christian readers found and find someone who "spoke to their concerns" (114). While the political Right has approved of Tolkien's Christian orthodoxy and his encouragement of some "traditional" notions of morality and duty, it may shy away from his movement away from consumerism and toward the nascent environmentalism,[3] and while the Left has often rejected that traditional morality, it has approved of his love of the Greenwood, the simple life, and of the general notion of the equality of creatures. I would assert finally that Tolkien succeeds as fiction writer—and even, I dare say, as a thinker—because he treats creatures, ideas, and landscapes with respect, because he cares about and believes in the idea of *good*, because he couches his ideas in stories that resonate with all sorts of readers from all sorts of background, and because the landscape of his ideas draws us as compellingly as does the physical landscape of wood, mountain, and valley. And though he obviously wrote no works that we would formally term *philosophy* and took relatively few leaps into formal criticism,[4] his work explores and expresses a good deal greater range of ideas than the criticism has typically recognized. Obeying the hierarchy (116) may prove good or it may prove bad, but if and when we do it, we

Afterword. Mechanized Landscape and Spiritual Landscape

should do it out of humble respect and belief, not out of thoughtless fear.[5] We appreciate the tenacious persistence of the underdog to do something he doesn't want to do but believes deep down to be right, and we want to believe that, in a pinch, we could do the same. No one wants to identify with Saruman or Sauron, though no doubt some readers, being honest with themselves, could, but everyone feels comfortable identifying with Frodo or Sam, Merry or Pippin, or even Éowyn, Faramir, or Galadriel. They lead us to the ideas that Tolkien expressed most consistently and most powerfully: we must meet and pass our texts of moral and ethical behavior; we must learn generosity, humility, service, and even to enjoy and appreciate the simple pleasures of living if we want to survive. We hope if not believe we can make good moral and ethical choices and that we have within us a spark of something heroic, something worthy of admiration, worthy, as Sam would say, of a song.

Chapter Notes

Introduction

1. The readings and discussions among the Inklings had, of course, an enormous influence on the unfolding of Tolkien's own intellectual landscape, as must have the intellectual life as Oxford as one of the world's great (and oldest) educational institutions.

2. Because *race* has remained such a powerful issue through the twentieth century and into the twenty-first, readers, perhaps especially American readers, can seldom avoid it, even if Tolkien had relatively little to say about it beyond (in his letters) a distaste for racial prejudices.

3. Not the least of these areas is fan fiction, which I haven't explored, but which deserves at least book-length scholarly study of its own.

4. See also Margaret Hiley's *The Loss of Silence: Aspects of Modernism in the Works of C. S. Lewis, J. R. R. Tolkien, and Charles Williams*. Hiley considers the typically modern use of and allusion to myth, fantasy stories as means of dealing with the problems of history, and the necessary yet fraught use of language—its mix of power and inexactness.

5. In Chance and Siewers see especially Verlyn Flieger's and Gergely Nagy's essays on Tolkien's implications for how we understand postmodernism, Andrew Lynch's on the tensions between modern notions of the horror of war and Victorian moralizations of warfare in *The Lord of the Rings*, Rebekah Long's on Tolkien's comments on Tolkien's careful representation of violence versus how commentators may misuse his stories for their own purposes, and Brian McFadden's challenge to some contemporary commentaries that claim to find racism in Tolkien's fiction. All the essays in the volume usefully address aspects of Tolkien and nineteenth- and twentieth-century thought. While I wouldn't go so far as to call Tolkien postmodern, the seeds of the postmodern grew already in the modern, and both form significant parts of the twentieth century's intellectual landscape.

6. See also her essay in Chance and Siewers' collection *Tolkien's Modern Middle Ages*.

7. Birzer cites these numbers, that from "the beginning of recorded history to 1900, governments murdered an estimated 113 million of their own citizens. Between 1901 and 1987, governments killed nearly 170 million of their own citizens" (113). While I can't vouch for the figures, they give a sense of the twentieth century's particular tyrannical brutality.

8. I have always thought that his fiction serves in part as a series of objective correlatives, to borrow T. S. Eliot's term, for his experiences of loss as a child and in the War. Autobiography could not have had the same power, nor could realistic fiction, either of which may fall too easily into sentimentality, inaccuracy, or cliché, or simply plod.

9. I believe Joseph Conrad's and T. S. Eliot's most famous images have more than any others guided twentieth-century imagistics: they foreground the external and internal human "landscapes."

10. For a discussion on the value of story and how Tolkien's ideas fit in the philosophical tradition, see Peter Kreeft's *The Philosophy of Tolkien* (2005).

11. Stream-of-consciousness writing is more fantasy than realism: it can't really follow thought/perception, but instead creates a representation of a mental-emotional world inside a subject's head, an enclosed alternative experience.

12. Paul Kocher observes that in *The Lord of the Rings* the "irony of evil is consummated by its doing the good which good could not do" (43): Gollum unwittingly saves Middle-earth by biting the Ring from Frodo's finger. Irony need not imply sarcasm or any negative tone whatever: it may apply just as well to positive turns of action and thought.

13. Flieger warns in *Green Suns* that Tolkien "turns out to be not quite as green as everybody would like him to be" (235).

14. While Tolkien adhered to traditional Catholic theology and practice, he seems to have had little to say (at least in print) about the state of English or British philosophy. I suspect he would have had some sympathy for R. G. Collingwood, particularly in Collingwood's doubts about the limited capability of science to see "truth" in its focus on sometimes dangerous utility and with F. H. Bradley in his idealism and his critique of hedonism, his idea that the central aspect of religion lies in its practice, in his ideas of good and evil, and in his interest in the complex meaning of words. And while he wouldn't have found appeal in Bertrand's Russell's liberal views on sexual freedom and political activism, he shared his anti–Hitler anti–Stalin views and would probably have shared his sentiments against the Vietnam War and for nuclear disarmament.

15. While Tolkien may have resisted elements of Modernism (e.g., the flavor of its irony, techniques such as stream of consciousness, the influence of Freudian psychology), he remains fully modern in his experimentation with narrative and style, potent use of allusions and analogues, and awareness of if not direct use of contemporary movements toward political oppression. So while he may at time have resisted Modernism, he didn't (and couldn't) evade participating in and contributing to the modern.

16. Any charge that Tolkien encouraged love of war devolves to Peter Jackson's film version, which exploit technology for the video-game audience, rather than applying to anything Tolkien wrote. Readers who have seen the films first often find surprise at how little violence the books actually include, and while certain characters or even cultures in *The Lord of the Rings* may take joy in battle, Gandalf does not, the Hobbits do not, and the Elves do not—even Aragorn does not. They recognize fighting as a part of their world that they would, but can't always, avoid and that brings sorrow and suffering rather than pleasure and achievement.

17. See, for instance, the essays in *Tolkien in the New Century: Essays in Honor of Tom Shippey*, edited by John W. Houghton, Janet Brennan Croft, Nancy Martsch, John D. Rateliff, and Robin Anne Reid (Jefferson, NC: McFarland, 2014).

Chapter 1

1. I write this chapter just after having read an online review of *Author of the Century*. I will not cite it or name the writer, but must say that the person had clearly not read the book, having failed to recognize that Shippey was not calling Tolkien either *the* or *an* author of the century; he was responding to British polls that had named Tolkien so and was aiming to explain why they had done so. That point has importance here because I am making a similar claim: Tolkien is very much an author of the twentieth century.

2. Both Gawain's character and Frodo's require the four Cardinal (Catholic) virtues: fortitude, prudence, justice, and temperance. Gawain fails in justice only toward himself, and Frodo succeeds in his quest because mercy wins out over justice with respect to Gollum.

3. See, for instance, Richard West's essay "The Interlace Structure of *The Lord of the Rings*" in *A Tolkien Compass*, ed. Lobdell.

4. For attentive and complete studies of *The Hobbit* with drafts and notes and ex-

plication see especially John Rateliff's *The History of the Hobbit* (Boston: Houghton Mifflin, 2007) and Douglas Anderson's *The Annotated Hobbit*, rev. and expanded ed. (Boston: Houghton Mifflin, 2002). While *The Hobbit* perhaps includes a less complicated plot and a lesser concentration of ideas than do *The Lord of the Rings* and *The Silmarillion*, probably because of its original intended audience, it hardly lacks important and stimulating themes: the world will probably whisk us into adventure whether we want it or not, we must take care of our friends and colleagues, great acts of generosity and self-sacrifice can occasionally overcome acts of greed and violence, when must remain composed and prudent even in times of great stress—just for example.

5. In addition to architectural influence on civic and university buildings, Tolkien would have had not too far away St. Michael's Cathedral in Coventry (destroyed in 1940), plus others in Chester, Gloucester, and Lichfield, plus any others he would have encountered during travels. Oxford's has more Romanesque features, but some hints of Gothic as well.

6. Albert Einstein's relativity may have had enough intellectual currency to influence Tolkien's thinking casually. Tolkien may have blamed physicists for the creation of the atomic bomb, and he certainly wouldn't have held with any moral relativism that come from misapplication of Einstein's ideas, but the understanding that how we perceive something physically changes based on our relationship in space/time to it may have helped Tolkien envision such complications as how a creature wearing the Ring perceives differently and how palantíri allow (imperfect) communication. In *The Fellowship of the Ring* Legolas says that "time does not tarry ever … but change and growth is not in all things and places alike. for the Elves the world moves, and it moves both very swift and very slow … because they themselves change little, and all else fleets by" (379). In *The Two Towers* Gandalf recounts how, following his battle with the Balrog, "I lay staring upward, while the stars wheeled over, and each day was as long as a life-age of the earth. Faint to my ears came the gathered rumour of all lands" (491). The characters recognize time and experience as relative to their nature and position.

7. As I compile my revisions for this volume, the third of the three of Jackson's *The Hobbit* films has just appeared. The first strays quite a bit—or perhaps most significantly adds quite a bit—to Tolkien's narrative, most flamboyantly in the characters of Radagast and Azog. Jackson also changes Bilbo's character and the themes that derive from it, making him much more heroic: the cinematic Bilbo wants to do what he can to bring the dwarves home from their diaspora and help them restore their kingdom. The second takes very much its own course, with additional characters and changes and even more stress on special effects.

8. In Appendix F following *The Return of the King*, Tolkien explains that the divergence of language among the various peoples is greater than the books themselves show.

9. Tolkien characterizes the hobbits throughout by their good nature and high spirits, their joy in simple pleasures. Notably, even Gollum doesn't entirely lack the same impulse: see the fish song at the beginning of "The Passage of the Marshes" in *The Two Towers*. And in *The Hobbit* goblins can speak quite formally.

10. If I find a stylistic flaw in Tolkien's prose, it comes in the overuse of the word *suddenly* to signal the reader to feel surprise—an understandable verbal tic. I noticed it particularly on my most recent rereading, probably because I was paying special attention to stylistic facets.

Chapter 2

1. An interesting parallel appears in Bede's *History of the English Church and People* in a tale from the reign of the Northumbrian king Edwin in the year 627. As Edwin's council debate whether or not to accept Christianity, one of the king's

Notes—Chapter 2

chief advisors observes that life is like the swift flight of a sparrow through a mead-hall on a winter evening: the bird flies from darkness to darkness, with but a brief instant in the light. The advisor urges that if the new faith sheds light upon that darkness, they should accept it. Much of the art of our own time seems to respond to anxiety about what lies in the darkness outside our mead-hall.

2. This turn begins perhaps with Dark Romanticism as a response to the classically rational but stodgy and materialistic Age of Enlightenment, though Christopher Marlowe (Conrad's name-source for his Marlow?) had already taken such a turn in *Doctor Faustus*, following his age's covert urge to magic, demonology, and alchemy. The fulcrum for the modern period must balance upon Freud, then tumble over with World War I.

3. Writers on aesthetics, medieval or modern, have noted the primacy of light as a symbol of both beauty and goodness. As Gilles Deleuze observes in *The Fold: Leibnitz and the Baroque* (trans. Tom Conley, Minneapolis: University of Minnesota Press, 1993), in the Baroque period Awe can consider light and shadows as 1 and 0, as the two levels of the world separated by a thin line of waters: the Happy and the Damned" (31), but what Deleuze says of Baroque holds fully true for the Middle Ages as well. In *Art and Beauty in the Middle Ages* (trans. Hugh Bredin, New Haven: Yale University Press, 1986) Umberto Eco stresses the centrality of light to medieval aesthetic perceptions, citing such commentators as the neo–Platonist Robert Grosseteste ("He defined light as the greatest and best of all proportions ... made it the image for a universe shaped by a unique flux of light-giving energy, at once the source of beauty and of being," 48–49) and St. Bonaventure (quoting Bonaventure, "by their greater or lesser participation in light, bodies acquire the truth and dignity of their being," 50).

4. The magic cauldron or cup or well, likely an ancestor of Grail stories, pervades early medieval tales about acquiring wisdom, from Irish Finn to Welsh Gwion Bach to Norse Oðin.

5. "God as light" or the quest for the light or the battle between light and darkness pervades Christian thought from early on and through the Middle Ages, perhaps beginning with the influence of Manicheism in the Third and Fourth Centuries and of the Mithraism that spanned the Roman Empire. Augustine felt and perhaps never escaped the influence of Mani, though he reconstitutes the older metaphors as Christian ideas: the image of *illumination*, as perceived physically or spiritually, undergirds not just the *Confessions*, *The City of God*, and the *Soliloquies*, but nearly all of his work. For similar stress upon illumination, and with emphasis upon stages of progressive illumination as one moves toward God, see St. Bonaventure's *Itinerarium Mentis in Deum* (*The Mind's Road to God*); for the idea of light as present with God even preceding its "genesis" in Creation, see Hugh of St. Victor's *De Tribus Deibus* (*The Three Days of Invisible Light*).

6. Am I worthy? Typically the Grail quest begins rather than ends with that question.

7. As green recedes, gold emerges as the dominant color, particularized in Mordred's armor. The use of color symbolism adds ambiguity in *Excalibur*. In the Christian tradition green represents hope, gold the refinement of the soul—unless it be perverted to greed, through the secular application of gold synecdochally as wealth. In Hildegard of Bingen's medical works, green represents *viriditas*: growth, health, healing. In *Excalibur* green represents the power of nature for good or evil use, and gold suggests disease or corruption.

8. Aragorn's darkened, weather-beaten countenance contributes to the hobbits fear of him when they first meet, but the qualities of his character eventually win them over—character rather than color determines the quality of the creature.

9. In *The Return of the King* Pippin, awaiting war in Minas Tirith, says, "This is no longer a bickering at the fords.... This is a great war long-planned, and we are but

one piece in it, whatever pride may say. Things move in the far East beyond the Inland Sea ... and north in Mirkwood ... and south in Harad. And now all realms shall be put to the test, to stand or fall" (43); Middle-earth faces World War, and Tolkien brings to it the soldier's sense of smallness in the face of vast destruction.

Chapter 3

1. Debbie Sly has observed in both *The Silmarillion* and *Paradise Lost* "a creative struggle between religious orthodoxy and aesthetic imperatives," yet both works enhance what they do with light by what they do with darkness: "aesthetic experience at the higher, Elven, level *requires* the existence of darkness," from the "coexistence" and interplay of light and dark; as Tolkien posited the necessity of a fall to story, so evil must have some sort of presence for an aesthetic experience to have power and value (118).

Chapter 4

1. The Shepherd essays as cited here appear in the volume detailed in the Bibliography, "The Prophetic Cædmon," 1–10, "Scriptural Poetry," 11–46, and "*Beowulf*: An Epic Fairy Tale," 47–58.
2. Richard J. Finn has approached this topic in an online essay, "Arthur & Aragorn: Arthurian Influence in *The Lord of the Rings*," where he writes, "Aragorn becomes the completed version of Arthur" (8). He notes commonalities of Aragorn as Arthur, Gandalf as Merlin, Narsil as Excalibur, Avallónë/Eressëa as Avalon. Verlyn Flieger in "J. R. R. Tolkien and the Matter of Britain" compares Frodo to Arthur: in the critical moment he is wounded by his nemesis (as Arthur by Mordred); Frodo's departure for Valinor parallels Arthur's to Avalon; Sam's protest at Frodo's leaving echoes Bedivere's of Arthur; Frodo's drawing Sting from the wooden beam at Rivendell parallels' Arthur's drawing the sword from the stone—Tolkien was "re-visioning Arthur even while en-visioning his own myth," Flieger aptly adds (50).
3. The *J. R. R. Tolkien Encyclopedia* explains this point as Tolkien's mythology "sought to replace the myth of Arthur with a myth of greater depth, history and authentic connection to the ancient English land and language" (34).

Chapter 5

1. Please see, though, Derek Walcott's *Omeros*.
2. Aragorn's doubt and confusion after the breakup of the Fellowship of the Ring makes an interesting counterexample that adds both to the tension of the narrative and the complexity of his character. However, his doubts may be existential, but they are not spiritual.
3. The famous Cottingley Fairy photographs of 1917 had considerable (and embarrassing) public influence, but Victorian interest in fairy stories and fairy paintings had already caught the general imagination. See for instance Carole Silver's book *Strange and Secret Peoples: Faeries and Victorian Consciousness* (1999).
4. Tolkien may also have felt the influence of such French or Anglo-French examples as the thirteenth-century *Huon of Bordeaux* and of Marie de France's "Lanval" and its Middle English version *Sir Launfal*. The elves or fairies in those texts, as in such Welsh examples as "Pwyll, Prince of Dyfed" from *The Mabinogi*, look much if not just like humans and face similar problems, though usually in a parallel Otherworld.
5. See especially chapters 3 and 4, "Fluttering Spirits with Antennae: Victorian and Edwardian Fancies" and "The Fairies, Faith and Folklore," of Dmitra Fimi's *Tolkien, Race, and Cultural History* (London: Palgrave Macmillan, 2009). Fimi aptly finds how "interwoven and interconnected" strands of Tolkien's Christian faith, his mythology for England, and his philological interests blend in the development of Tolkien's elves and fairy-tale elements and what importance images of fairies had in Victorian and Edwardian art (40). She adds

the significant use of fairy-lore in the Irish tradition and its modern revival (51). In terms of the twentieth-century context, her book also includes significant discussions of race and Nazism (Chapter 9) and of early English material culture (Chapter 10), which has some interesting implications given the exponential growth (along with, perhaps, a cheapening) of material culture in the twentieth century.

6. We may also call the Silmarils or the Ring examples of obsessive-compulsive disorder. The creature caught by them can think of little else. Frodo will still finger the jewel that hangs around his neck long after the destruction of the Ring, and Fëanor's obsession with possession of the Silmarils destroys many lives and represents a failure to look past physical objects to a spiritual life that could render them, if not powerless, at least not enslaving.

7. Many stories of the glories and failures of elves parallel those of humans; even figures foreshadow and recur. In "Of the Coming of the Elves" in *The Silmarillion* the Quendi fear and tell stories of the "dark Rider," who is actually the Vala Oromë: a positive figure who yet prefigures the Black Riders of *LotR*. Nauglamir, the Necklace of the dwarves, recalls the Silmarils, the Ring, and the Arkenstone....

8. William Senior has suggested that the most "pervasive and unifying component of atmosphere and mood" in Tolkien's work is "the sustained and grieved sense of loss" (173); that loss comes not only from our sense of morality, but also from the living beauty and potential for beauty that passes from Middle-earth with the departure of the elves, the loss of Númenor, and the failing of the ents.

9. See also Marjorie Burns' *Perilous Realms*.

10. Tom Shippey observes in *Roots and Branches* that orcs "recognize the idea of goodness, appreciate humour, value loyalty, trust, group cohesion and the ideal of a higher cause than themselves, and condemn failings from these ideals in others," so one may observe that "orcish behavior is also perfectly clearly human behavior" (248). Not wholly Other, orcish behavior creates horror partly because it remains within our capabilities. Ringwraiths present a different problem, seemingly immune to enduring physical harm except by magical weapons (or temporary harm by water, particularly that driven by elf-magic); they represent spirit—though spirit in another's control—with only limited physical body. See Shippey 255. The Barrow-wight, a "ghost or animated corpse," apparently seeks to "relive an earlier triumph" by adding hobbits to its list of victims (261); the horror comes from the partial reanimation of a lingering spirit with unsated bloodlust.

11. For some interesting related but more expansive essays on the idea of the body see Christopher Vaccaro's collection *The Body in Tolkien's Legendarium: Essays on Middle-earth Corporeality* (McFarland, 2013). For Instance, Anna Smol's "Frodo's Body: Liminality and the Experience of War" connects the crumbling abjection of Frodo's body/Self with World War I dead soldiers' bodies. Verlyn Flieger's "The Body in Question: The Unhealed Wounds of Frodo Baggins" addresses psychological and metaphoric implications of physical metamorphosis. Yvette Kisor's "Incorporeality and Transformation in *The Lord of the Rings*" suggests a scale of transformation from the Ringwraiths to Gandalf (invisibility to translucency). Jolanta Komarnicka in "the Ugly Elf: Orc Bodies, Perversion, and Redemption in *The Silmarillion* and The Lord of the Rings" deals with the idea of bodies at once familiar and monstrous using definitions of perversion and evil from Augustine, Plato, and Boethius. Robin Reid in "Light (noun, 1) or Light (adjective, 14b)? Female Bodies and Femininities in *The Lord of the Rings*" considers female characters' levels of physical and mental agency. And James Williamson's "Emblematic Bodies: Tolkien and the Depiction of Female Presence" notes the linguistic merging of female bodies with nature and the physical world.

12. The manuscript suffered damage

and perhaps erasure on that folio, so determining the exact nature of the *Beowulf* dragon is probably impossible.

13. Dante explores this idea in Canto XXXIII of *Inferno*, that the soul of a traitor can descend to Hell before the body dies, and a demon may inhabit that body for the rest of its natural life.

Chapter 6

1. Tolkien notes, for instance, in a letter from 1953 that he first discovered "literary pleasure" in Homer (*Letters* 172).

2. See the footnote to "Gondor and the Heirs of Anárion" in Appendix A to *The Return of the King*. The same source does identify Sauron, after the destruction of Númenor, as "black and hideous" thereafter, but the comment applies not to a people or a person, but to a semi-divine figure of great power. The use of dark as opposed to light not in any racial sense, but as a way to distinguish creatures who rebelled against God rather than remained faithful to Him so pervades medieval and Renaissance sources that one can hardly feel surprised that Tolkien borrowed it in this fictional instance that parallels stories of the Fall of Satan and his comrades.

3. For this point see both Kilby (47) and Carpenter (85–86, 100ff.).

4. In his book on *The Silmarillion* Paul Kocher has argued that the Eddic Creation story "did not attract Tolkien" for its "complex and all too physical account," and the "Norse conception of its ending in the Twilight of the Gods (Ragnarök) was quite uncongenial to Tolkien and won no place in *The Silmarillion*"—it prevents free will (5). We must assert the same problem if we read the Apocalypse of St. John in a now culturally common way, as an expression of events God has "destined" for the world. I would assert that Tolkien borrows from both eschatological texts not their specific attitudes, but the idea that we move ourselves from Age to Age either by the progress that results from benevolently sharing "culture among neighboring races," as the Elves do at their best (Kocher, *Master* 57), or through pride and greed by extending militarism to the point of global destruction, as do Elves and humans at their worst. Apocalyptics have personal and social levels and implications as well as cosmological ones—see my argument in *Beasts of Time*. Verlyn Flieger's discussion of catastrophe, dyscatastrophe, and eucatastrophe is useful here, as is her idea "Elves, going toward darkness, are to set men's feet on the path to the light" (*Splintered Light* 131)—the next generation does well to learn from both the failures and successes of those preceding.

5. One should, of course, not neglect *The Hobbit*'s contribution to the enormous growth of children's literature in the twentieth century—literature aimed at young readers has made the fortune of some notable authors and publishers.

Chapter 7

1. Readers of Finnish may want to see Harri Hietikko's *Management by Sauron*, published by Atena in 2010—thanks to an anonymous reader for pointing it out.

2. As Flieger puts it in *Green Suns and Faërie*, "In Tolkien's Middle-earth ... Frodo's body ... pays the highest price and gets the least reward" (291).

Chapter 8

1. One day my sister, a wonderful high school English teacher, sent me a brief e-mail note: "I want to live in Middle-earth!" She had been teaching *The Lord of the Rings* and had once again got thoroughly caught up in it with students reading or studying it for the first time. The fact that teachers and readers of nearly all ages readily enter and enjoy Tolkien's world demonstrates not only the imaginative power of Middle-earth, but also the twentieth-century (and now twenty-first) need for a renewal of the Greenworld.

2. Paul Ricoeur, "'Anatomy of Criticism' or the Order of Paradigms," *Center and Labyrinth: Essays in Honor of Northrop Frye*

Notes—Chapter 8

(Toronto: University of Toronto Press, 1983), 8.

3. Ricoeur, "'Anatomy of Criticism' or the Order of Paradigms," 10.

4. Paul Ricoeur, "Narrative and Hermeneutics," in *Essays on Aesthetics: Perspectives on the Work of Monroe C. Beardsley*, ed. John Fisher (Philadelphia: Temple University Press, 1983), 149.

5. See for this discussion particularly Tom Shippey, "Tolkien as a Post-War Writer," in *Scholarship and Fantasy: Proceedings of The Tolkien Phenomenon*, ed. K. J. Battarbee (Turku, Finland, 1993), 217–36, and more recently *J. R. R. Tolkien: Author of the Century* (Boston: Houghton Mifflin, 2000).

6. While some students find *The Silmarillion* daunting, some come quite to love it. I've had instances of students saying it was their favorite reading in the whole course.

7. Tom Shippey, *The Road to Middle-Earth* (Boston: Houghton Mifflin, 1983), 220. See also Doug Anderson's *Tales Before Tolkien*.

8. Northrop Frye, *Anatomy of Criticism: Four Essays* (Princeton: Princeton University Press, 1957), 349.

9. Tolkien so loved languages that he augmented school instruction with study on his own. In *Tolkien: A Biography* (New York: Ballantine, 1977) Humphrey Carpenter records that in a school debate Tolkien once broke into fluent Gothic (54).

10. See also Anderson's *Tales Before Tolkien*.

11. *Road*, 220.

12. Shippey, "Tolkien as a Post-War Writer," 223 and 228.

13. Generally, but see especially 69, 68, 6.

14. Tolkien mentions Eliot only twice in his letters, in both cases briefly. In letter 261 he writes of C. S. Lewis, "That his [Lewis's] literary opinions were ever dictated by envy (as in the case of T. S. Eliot) is a grotesque calumny. After all it is possible to dislike Eliot with some intensity even if one has no aspirations to poetic laurels oneself." In letter 266, after noting the demise of his former tutor, C. T. Onions, he mentions Eliot's death and adds a note of distaste with respect to John Masefield's verse on Eliot published in *The Times*. See Humphrey Carpenter's edition (with Christopher Tolkien) of *The Letters of J. R. R. Tolkien* (Boston: Houghton Mifflin, 1981), 350 and 353. These passages suggest that Tolkien had no great admiration for Eliot or his work—yet both contribute essentially to the intellectual landscape, and their concerns overlap.

15. Flieger calls Tolkien's Christianity "tougher and darker than Lewis's, less mystical and occult than Williams's, and far less hopeful than either man's faith" (*Splintered Light: Logos and Language in Tolkien's World* [Grand Rapids: Eerdmans, 1983], xviii). Matthew Dickerson (*Following Gandalf: Epic Battles and Moral Victory in The Lord of the Rings* [Grand Rapids, Brazos Press, 2003]) suggests that a reader can hardly come away from *The Lord of the Rings* without "a profound sense of sorrow and loss" (212), and that while Christianity isn't a surface element of the story, it has been absorbed into the text through something similar to the "objective morality and moral responsibility" (219) that *The Lord of the Rings* implies. See more about this idea in the Afterword. Shippey observes that the book is also and perhaps mainly about concepts of evil (*Author of the Century*, see Chapter III). I recommend the first two books for students interested in specifically Christian questions and the third for those interested why the book continues to exhibit the moral and emotional power that it does.

16. Part of the appeal of Middle-earth comes of course from its enormous complexity, from Tolkien's effort to create a fully realized world. As Jonathan Evans has pointed out, Tolkien's "capacity for decentering the anthropological perspective" allows for some stunning effects both narrative and emotional ("The Anthropology of Arda," in *Tolkien the Medievalist*, ed. Jane Chance [London: Routledge, 2003], 197). Gergely Nagy argues the significance of the "impression of depth" of the world that Tolkien creates by "mythopoeic" means,

by creating a nexus of tales that allows him or his readers to "assign equal importance to *all texts* in the corpus and their interrelations" ("The Great Chain of Reading: (Inter-)textual Relations and the Technique of Mythopoiesis in the Turin Story," also in Chance's volume, 239 and 253). That is, allusions with stories behind them and stories behind *them* fan out into a world with its own complete history far beyond even the vast landscape we see. Complexity gives the world a greater capability to suggest "reality."

17. Both *Mabinogi* and *Kalevala* deal also with generational succession, a constant motif in myth, which carries over particularly into *The Silmarillion*.

18. For the most helpful collection of Tolkien's scholarly work see J. R. R. Tolkien, *The Monsters and the Critics and Other Essays* (London: HarperCollins, 2006), which includes not only the famous *Beowulf* essay, but also "On Translating *Beowulf*," "*Sir Gawain and the Green Knight*," "On Fairy-Stories," "English and Welsh," "A Secret Vice," and "Valedictory Address."

19. One group did, though, get to go to the cinema together to see the first of Jackson's *The Hobbit* films.

20. *Nibelungenlied* makes a reasonable substitution for *Volsungasaga*, if one prefers it, as does *The Prose Edda* of Snorri Sturluson, both readily available in readable translations. One also does well to have on hand a copy of Douglas Anderson's excellent *Tales Before Tolkien: The Roots of Modern Fantasy*, for its extensive selection.

21. Though Lewis wrote of Tolkien just after they'd met, "No harm in him: only needs a smack or so" (Carpenter, *Inklings* 23).

Afterword

1. John R. Holmes suggests the use of the Anglo-Saxon word *dustsceawung* for such instances in Tolkien.

2. By attending to this long list of Christian themes I intend not to alienate non–Christian readers, but to enumerate the extent to which Christian thought and experience permeated Tolkien's work as it did his personal experience. Christianity is also an essential part of the twentieth-century intellectual landscape; though in some countries the number of nominal Christians declined, Christianity has so embedded in Western life that one could hardly go a day without feeling some influence of it.

3. Tolkien once wrote, I suspect facetiously, that if "ragnarök would burn all the slums and gas-works, and shabby garages, and long arc-lit suburbs, it cd. for me burn all the works of art—and Id go back to trees" (*Letters* 96).

4. He once wrote, "I am *not* a critic. I do not want to be one. I am capable on occasion (after long pondering) of 'criticism,' but I am not naturally a critical man.... I am usually only trying to express 'liking' not universally valid criticism" (*Letters* 126)—an odd but honest assertion for a professional academic.

5. Tolkien wrote in a 1943 letter to his son Christopher that his "political opinions lean more and more to Anarchy (philosophically understood, meaning abolition of control not whiskered men with bombs)—or to 'unconstitutional' Monarchy" (*Letters* 63).

Bibliography

Anderson, Douglas. *The Annotated Hobbit*. Boston: Houghton Mifflin, 2002.

_____. *Tales Before Tolkien*. New York: Ballantine, 2003.

Arnold, Martin. "Hvat er troll nema þat? The Cultural History of the Troll." *The Shadow Walkers: Jacob Grimm's Mythology of the Monstrous*. Ed. Tom Shippey. Tempe: Arizona Center for Medieval and Renaissance Studies/Brepols, 2005. 111–55.

Auerbach, Erich. *Mimesis: The Representation of Reality in Western Literature*. Trans. Willard Trask. Princeton: Princeton University Press, 1953.

Bal, Mieke. *Narratology: Introduction to the Theory of Narrative*, 2d ed. Toronto: University of Toronto Press, 1997.

Beagle, Peter S. Introductory Note. *The Hobbit: Or, There and Back Again*, by J. R. R. Tolkien. New York: Ballantine, 1973.

Bede. *The History of the English Church and People*. Trans. Michael Frassetto. New York: Barnes & Noble, 2005.

Beowulf, with the Finnesburg Fragment. Ed. C. L. Wrenn, rev. W. F. Bolton. London: Harrap, 1973.

Birzer, Bradley J. *J. R. R. Tolkien's Sanctifying Myth: Understanding Middle-earth*. Wilmington, DE: ISI Books, 2003.

Blake, William. *Milton*. 1804–08. Boulder: Shambhala, 1978.

Boorman, John, Dir. *Excalibur*. Orion, 1981.

Bovey, Alixe. *Monsters and Grotesques in Medieval Manuscripts*. Toronto: University of Toronto Press, 2002.

Brewer, Derek S. "*The Lord of the Rings* as Romance." In *J. R. R. Tolkien, Scholar and Storyteller: Essays in Memoriam*. Ed. Mary Salu and Robert T. Farrell. Ithaca: Cornell University Press, 1979. 249–64.

Burns, James MacGregor. *Leadership*. 1978. New York: Harper, 2010.

Burns, Marjorie. *Perilous Realms: Celtic and Norse in Tolkien's Middle-earth*. Toronto: University of Toronto Press, 2005.

Cahill, Audrey. *T. S. Eliot and the Human Predicament*. Cape Town: University of Natal, 1967.

Campbell, Joseph, with Bill Moyers. *The Power of Myth*. 1988. New York: Anchor, 1991.

Carpenter, Humphrey. *The Inklings: C. S. Lewis, J. R. R. Tolkien, Charles Williams, and Their Friends*. London: Allen and Unwin, 1978.

_____. *Tolkien: A Biography*. New York: Ballantine, 1977.

Chance, Jane. *Tolkien's Art: A Mythology for England*. Lexington: University of Kentucky Press, 2001.

_____, ed. *Tolkien the Medievalist*. London: Routledge, 2003.

Chance, Jane, and Alfred K. Siewers, eds. *Tolkien's Modern Middle Ages*. New York: Palgrave Macmillan, 2005.

Churchill, Winston S. *The World Crisis*. New York: Charles Scribner's Sons, 1931.

Clark, George, and Daniel Timmons,

eds. *Tolkien and His Literary Resonances*. Westport, CT: Praeger, 2000.

Cruttwell, C. R. M. F. *A History of the Great War, 1914–1918*, 2d ed. Oxford: Clarendon, 1934.

Curry, Patrick. *Defending Middle-earth: Tolkien, Myth and Modernity*. 1997. Boston: Houghton Mifflin, 2004.

Deleuze, Gilles. *The Fold: Leibnitz and the Baroque*. Trans. Tom Conley. Minneapolis: University of Minnesota Press, 1993.

Dickerson, Matthew. *Following Gandalf: Epic Battles and Moral Victory in The Lord of the Rings*. Grand Rapids: Brazos Press, 2003.

Dobbie, Elliott van Kirk, ed. *The Anglo-Saxon Minor Poems. Anglo-Saxon Poetic Records* 6. New York: Columbia University Press; London: Routledge and Kegan Paul, 1942.

Drout, Michael D. C. "Tolkien's Prose Style and Its Literary and Rhetorical Effects." *Tolkien Studies* 1 (2004): 137–63.

Drout, Michael, and Hilary Wynne. "Review Essay: Tom Shippey's J. R. R. Tolkien: Author of the Century and a Look Back at Tolkien Criticism Since 1982." *Envoi* 9.2 (Fall 2000): 101–67.

Duriez, Colin. *The J.R.R. Tolkien Handbook*. Grand Rapids: Baker, 1992.

Eco, Umberto. *Art and Beauty in the Middle Ages*. Trans. Hugh Bredin. New Haven: Yale University Press, 1986.

Eliot, T. S. *The Complete Poems and Plays 1909–1950*. New York: Harcourt, Brace, & World, 1958.

Ellis, Hilda R. "Fostering by Giants in Old Norse Saga Literature." *Medium Ævum* 10 (1941): 70–85.

Evans, Jonathan. "The Anthropology of Arda." In Chance, *Tolkien the Medievalist*, 194–224.

Everdell, William R. *The First Moderns: Profiles in the Origins of Twentieth-century Thought*. Chicago: University of Chicago Press, 1997.

Field, Syd. *Screenplay: The Foundations of Screenwriting*. New York: Delta, 1979.

Fimi, Dmitra. *Tolkien, Race and Cultural History*. London: Palgrave Macmillan, 2009.

Finn, Richard J. "Arthur & Aragorn: Arthurian Influence in *The Lord of the Rings*." www.scribd.com/doc/19165420/Arthur-and-Aragorn-Arthurian-Influence-in-LOTR.

Fisher, Jason, ed. *Tolkien and the Study of His Sources*. Jefferson, NC: McFarland, 2011.

Flieger, Verlyn. "The Body in Question: The Unhealed Wounds of Frodo Baggins." In Vaccaro, *The Body in Tolkien's Legendarium*, 12–19.

_____. *Green Suns and Faërie: Essays on J. R. R. Tolkien*. Kent, OH: Kent State University Press, 2012.

_____. *Interrupted Music: The Making of Tolkien's Mythology*. Kent, OH: Kent State University Press, 2005.

_____. "J. R. R. Tolkien and the Matter of Britain." *Mythlore* 87 (Summer/Fall 2000): 47–59.

_____. "A Postmodern Medievalist?" In Chance and Siewers, *Tolkien's Modern Middle Ages* 17–28.

_____. *A Question of Time: J. R. R. Tolkien's Road to Faërie*. Kent, OH: Kent State University Press, 1997.

_____. *Splintered Light: Logos and Language in Tolkien's World*. Grand Rapids: Eerdmans, 1983.

Focillon, Henri. *The Art of the West in the Middle Ages. Volume Two: Gothic Art*. Trans. Donald King. Greenwich, CT: Phaidon, 1963.

"From Book to Script." *The Lord of the Rings: The Fellowship of the Ring: Extended Edition*. Disc 3. New Line Cinema, 2001.

Frye, Northrop. *Anatomy of Criticism: Four Essays*. Princeton: Princeton University Press, 1957.

Gardner, John W. *On Leadership*. New York: Free Press, 1990.

Bibliography

Garth, John. *Tolkien and the Great War*. Boston: Houghton Mifflin, 2005.

Green, Martin. *The Children of the Sun: A Narrative of "Decadence" in England after 1918*. Mount Jackson, VA: Axios Press, 1976.

Greenleaf, Robert K. *Servant Leadership*. New York: Paulist Press, 1977.

Grimm, Jacob. *Teutonic Mythology*. Vol. 2. 1883–88. Mineola, NY: Dover, 2004.

Hartt, Walter F. "Godly Influences: The Theology of J. R. R. Tolkien and C. S. Lewis." *Studies in the Literary Imagination* 14.2 (Fall 1981): 21–29.

Hiley, Margaret. *The Loss and the Silence: Aspects of Modernism in the Works of C. S. Lewis, J. R. R. Tolkien, and Charles Williams*. Zollikofen: Walking Tree Publishers, 2011.

Holmes, John R. "Tolkien, Dustsceawung, and the Gnomic Tense: Is Timelessness Medieval or Victorian?" In Chance and Siewers, *Tolkien's Modern Middle Ages* 43–58.

Houghton, John W., Janet Brennan Croft, Nancy Martsch, John D. Rateliff, and Robin Anne Reid, eds. *Tolkien in the New Century: Essays in Honor of Tom Shippey*. Jefferson, NC: McFarland, 2014.

Jackson, Rosemary. *Fantasy: The Literature of Subversion*. London: Methuen, 1981.

J. R. R. Tolkien Encyclopedia: Scholarship and Critical Assessment. Ed. Michael D. C. Drout. New York: Routledge, 2006.

Kilby, Clyde S. *Tolkien & The Silmarillion*. Wheaton, IL: Harold Shaw, 1976.

Kirk, Elizabeth. "'I Would Have Rather Written in Elvish': Language, Fiction and *The Lord of the Rings*." *Novel: A Forum on Fiction* 5 (1971): 5–18.

Kirk, Russell. *Eliot and His Age: T. S. Eliot's Moral Imagination in the Twentieth Century*. New York: Random House, 1971.

Kisor, Yvette. "Incorporeality and Transformation in *The Lord of the Rings*." In Vaccaro, *The Body in Tolkien's Legendarium* 20–38.

Kocher, Paul H. *Master of Middle-earth: The Fiction of J. R. R. Tolkien*. New York: Ballantine, 1972.

———. *A Reader's Guide to* The Silmarillion. Boston: Houghton Mifflin, 1980.

Komarnicka, Jolanta N. "The Ugly Elf: Orc Bodies, Perversion, and Redemption in *The Silmarillion* and *The Lord of the Rings*." In Vaccaro, *The Body in Tolkien's Legendarium* 83–97.

Krapp, George Philip, and Elliott van Kirk Dobbie, eds. *The Exeter Book*. ASPR 3. New York: Columbia University Press; London: Routledge and Kegan Paul, 1936.

Kreeft, Peter J. *The Philosophy of Tolkien: The Worldview Behind* The Lord of the Rings. San Francisco: Ignatius Press, 2005.

Long, Rebekah. "Fantastic Medievalism and the Great War in J. R. R. Tolkien's *The Lord of the Rings*." In Chance and Siewers, *Tolkien's Modern Middle Ages* 123–37.

Lynch, Andrew. Archaism, Nostalgia, and Tennysonian War in *The Lord of the Rings*." In Chance and Siewers, *Tolkien's Modern Middle Ages* 77–92.

McFadden, Brian. "Fear of Difference, Fear of Death: The *Sigelwara*, Tolkien's Swertings, and Racial Difference." In Chance and Siewers, *Tolkien's Modern Middle Ages* 155–69.

Merriman, John. *History of Modern Europe*. Vol. 2. New York: Norton, 2009.

Miller, James E., Jr. *T. S. Eliot's Personal Waste Land: Exorcism of the Demons*. University Park: Penn State University Press, 1977.

Mustard, Helen M., and Charles E. Passage, trans. Introduction. *Parzifal*. Wolfram von Eschenbach. New York: Vintage, 1961. vii–lv.

Nagy, Gergely. "The Great Chain of Reading: (Inter-)textual Relations and Technique of Mythopoiesis in the

Túrin Story." In Chance, *Tolkien the Medievalist*, 239–58.

_____. "The Medievalist('s) Fiction: Textuality and Historicity as Aspects of Tolkien's Medievalist Cultural Theory in a Postmodernist Context." In Chance and Siewers, *Tolkien's Modern Middle Ages* 29–41. Bicholson, Lewis E., ed. *An Anthology of Beowulf Criticism*. Notre Dame: University of Notre Dame Press, 1963.

North, Michael. *Reading 1922: A Return to the Scene of the Modern*. New York: Oxford University Press, 1999.

Otty, Nick. "The Structuralist's Guide to Middle-earth." In *J. R. R. Tolkien: This Far Land*. Ed. Robert Giddings. London: Vision Press; Totowa, NJ: Barnes & Noble, 1983. 154–78.

Rabkin, Eric S. *The Fantastic in Literature*. Princeton: Princeton University Press, 1976.

Rateliff, John. *The History of* The Hobbit. Boston: Houghton Mifflin, 2007.

Reid, Robin Anne. "Light (noun, 1) or Light (adjective, 14b)? Female Bodies and Femininities in *The Lord of the Rings*." In Vaccaro, *The Body in Tolkien's Legendarium* 98–118.

_____. "Mythology and History: A Stylistic Analysis of *The Lord of the Rings*." *Style* 43.4 (2009): 517–38.

Ricoeur, Paul. "'Anatomy of Criticism' or the Order of Paradigms." *Centre and Labyrinth: Essays in Honour of Northrop Frye*. Ed. E. Eleanor Cook, et al. Toronto: University of Toronto Press, 1983. 1–13.

_____. "Narrative Hermeneutics." *Essays on Aesthetics: Perspectives on the Work of Monroe C. Beardsley*. Ed. John Fisher. Philadelphia: Temple University Press, 1983. 149–60.

Rosebury, Brian. *Tolkien: A Critical Assessment*. New York: St. Martin's, 1992.

Said, Edward. *Orientalism*. New York: Vintage, 1979.

Scholes, Robert, James Phelan, and Robert Kellogg. *The Nature of Narrative*, 40th anniv. ed. New York: Oxford University Press, 2006.

Senior, W. A. "Loss Eternal in J. R. R. Tolkien's Middle-earth." *J. R. R. Tolkien and His Literary Resonances*. Ed. George Clark and Daniel Timmons. Westport, CT: Greenwood Press, 2000. 173–82.

Shepherd, Geoffrey. *Poets and Prophets: Essays on Medieval Studies*. Ed. T. A. Shippey and John Pickles. Cambridge: D. S. Brewer, 1990.

Shippey, Tom. *J. R. R. Tolkien: Author of the Century*. Boston: Houghton Mifflin, 2000.

_____. *The Road to Middle-Earth*. Boston: Houghton Mifflin, 1983.

_____. *Roots and Branches: Selected Papers on Tolkien by Tom Shippey*. Zurich: Walking Tree Publishers, 2007.

_____. "Tolkien as Post-War Writer." *Scholarship & Fantasy: Proceedings of the Tolkien Phenomenon. Anglicana Turkuensia 12*. Ed. K. J. Battarbee. Turky, Finland, 1993. 217–36.

Silver, Carole. *Strange and Secret Peoples: Faeries and Victorian Consciousness*. New York: Oxford University Press, 1999.

Sly, Debbie. "Weaving Nets of Gloom: 'Darkness Profound' in Tolkien and Milton." *J. R. R. Tolkien and His Literary Resonances: Views of Middle-earth*. Ed. George Clark and Daniel Timmons. Westport, CT: Greenwood Press, 2000. 109–19.

Smol, Anna. "Frodo's Body: Liminality and the Experience of War." In Vaccaro, *The Body in Tolkien's Legendarium* 9–62.

Swoboda, Karl Maria. "Preface." *Idealism and Naturalism in Gothic Art*. Max Dvořák. Notre Dame: University of Notre Dame Press, 1967. xix–xxx.

Thompson, Kristin. *Storytelling in the New Hollywood: Understanding Classical Narrative Technique*. Cambridge: Harvard University Press, 1999.

Todorov, Tzvetan. *The Fantastic: A Structural Approach to a Literary Genre*.

Trans. Richard Howard. Ithaca: Cornell University Press, 1975.

Tolkien, J.R.R. "Chaucer as a Philologist: 'The Reeve's Tale.'" Morgantown: University of West Virginia Press, 2013. Web. Jan. 21, 2014.

_____. *Farmer Giles of Ham*. *The Tolkien Reader*. New York: Ballantine, 1966.

_____. *The Fellowship of the Ring*. 1954. Boston: Houghton Mifflin, 1994.

_____. "Leaf by Niggle." *The Tolkien Reader*. New York: Ballantine, 1966. 100–120.

_____. *The Letters of J.R.R. Tolkien*. Ed. Humphrey Carpenter and Christopher Tolkien. Boston: Houghton Mifflin, 2000.

_____. *"The Monsters and the Critics" and Other Essays*. Ed. Christopher Tolkien. London: HarperCollins, 2006.

_____. "On Fairy-Stories." *The Tolkien Reader*. New York: Ballantine, 1966. 33–99.

_____. *The Return of the King*. 1955. Boston: Houghton Mifflin, 1994.

_____. *The Silmarillion*, 2d ed. 1977. Ed. Christopher Tolkien. New York: Ballantine, 2002.

_____. *Tree and Leaf*. Boston: Houghton Mifflin, 1965.

_____. *The Two Towers*. 1954. Boston: Houghton Mifflin, 1994.

Tripp, Raymond. *More About the Fight with the Dragon: Beowulf 2208B-3182: Commentary, Edition, Translation*. Lanham, MD: University Press of America, 1983.

Vaccaro, Christopher, ed. *The Body in Tolkien's Legendarium: Essays on Middle-earth Corporeality*. Jefferson, NC: McFarland, 2013.

Walcott, Derek. *Omeros*. New York: The Noonday Press (Farrar, Straus, & Giroux), 1990.

Walker, Steve. *The Power of Tolkien's Prose: Middle-earth's Magical Style*. New York: Palgrave Macmillan, 2009.

West, Richard. "The Interlace Structure of *The Lord of the Rings*." *A Tolkien Compass*, 2d ed. Ed. Jared Lobdell. LaSalle, IL: Open Court, 2003. 75–92.

Williamson, James T. "Emblematic Bodies: Tolkien and the Depiction of Female Presence." In Vaccaro, *The Body in Tolkien's Legandarium* 134–56.

Index

Age of Reason 7
Aglæca 126, 131, 132, 138
"Akallabêth" 72, 91, 162, 163, 179, 208
Ancrene Riwle 31, 106, 185
Anderson, Douglas 5, 185, 215, 220, 221, 222
Andúril 72, 114, 119–121
Aragorn 39, 42, 47, 48, 52, 54, 56, 57, 63, 64, 79, 82, 97, 105, 106–113, 119–122, 132, 134, 150, 163, 164, 168, 171–174, 196, 202, 207–209, 214, 216, 217, 223
Aristotle 40
Arnold, Martin 141, 222
Arnold, Matthew 94, 133
art 9–11, 15, 19, 22, 28, 29, 34, 40, 43, 54, 60, 67, 108, 189, 200, 202, 209, 216, 217, 221, 223, 225
Arthur, King 34, 36–38, 44–45, 48, 67–80, 97, 106–118, 185, 223
Arwen 39, 42, 110, 113, 136, 172, 178, 196, 207, 217–218
"Ash Wednesday" 87, 88, 96
Auden, W.H. 18, 19, 91
Auerbach, Erich 97–100, 222
Augustine, St. 98, 99, 139, 216, 218
autobiography 20, 70, 201, 213

Balrog 42, 82, 136, 141–142, 172, 174, 208, 215
Barfield, Owen 4
Baroque 48, 216, 223
Barrow wights 42, 51, 120, 121, 190, 218
The Battle of Maldon 25, 46, 97, 99–106, 185
Battle of the Somme 157, 164
Beagle, Peter 127, 181–182, 222

Bede 215, 222
Belle Epoque 107
Beowulf 12, 24–26, 28–41, 45, 86, 95, 99–104, 106, 114–115, 124–132, 137–138, 140, 144, 172–173, 177, 185–186, 188–189, 191, 217, 219, 221–222, 225–226
"*Beowulf*: The Monsters and the Critics" 28, 33, 101, 221, 226
Beren 161, 163, 196
Bible 31, 87, 97, 98, 155, 185
Bilbo Baggins 33, 37, 38, 45, 51, 52, 59, 66, 67, 104, 105, 121, 129–131, 142, 144, 150, 154, 161, 177, 209, 215
Birzer, Bradley 4, 213, 222
Blake, William 90, 121, 202, 222
Bloomsbury Group 15, 18, 19
Bombadil, Tom 42, 45, 47, 49–51, 53, 90, 121, 132, 154, 170, 190, 196, 200, 207
Bonaventure, St. 216
Boromir 33, 42, 47, 63, 64, 111, 120–122, 132, 138, 150, 187, 204
Bovey, Alixe 139, 222
Bradley, F.H. 214
Brewer, Derek 47, 48, 222, 225
British Empire 11, 148, 151
Burns, James MacGregor 168, 171, 172, 222
Burns, Marjorie 92, 164, 192, 193, 207–209, 218, 222
Byrhtnoð 100–106

Cædmon 99–100, 217
Campbell, Joseph 35, 48, 83, 94, 109, 222
Caradhras 22
Carmina Burana 76

Index

Carpenter, Humphrey 5, 21, 127, 188, 219, 221–222, 226
Carson, Rachel 18
Cassirer, Ernst 4
cathedrals 43, 54–57, 215
Catholicism 19, 26, 54, 94, 185, 196–198
Chance, Jane 4–5, 213, 220–225
Chanson de Roland 99
Chaos theory 41, 48, 107
Chaucer, Geoffrey 27–28, 31, 226
chiaroscuro 22, 43, 56, 67, 71, 80
Children of the Sun 15, 18–19, 224
Christianity 71, 84, 88, 94–96, 108, 118, 126, 138, 194, 201–202, 209, 215, 220–221
Chrysophylax 137, 145
Churchill, Winston 156–159, 222
Clark, George 5, 222, 225
Cloud of Unknowing 68
Cold War 53–54, 86, 92
Collingwood, R.G. 214
Conrad, Joseph 34, 67–68, 70–71, 84, 144, 213, 216
consolation 29, 41, 47, 55, 92, 133–134, 177
Contemptus mundi 105
cosmopoiesis 20, 190
Cottingley (fairy photographs) 136, 217
Council of Elrond 60, 63–64, 121, 177
courage 6, 8, 12, 21, 33, 37–39, 75, 79, 81–82, 85–86, 94–95, 100–101, 103–104, 107, 110–111, 113, 115, 120, 122, 125–127, 129, 130–131, 135–136, 149, 151, 154, 157, 160, 172, 177, 187–189, 190–191, 193, 203, 206
courtoisie 36, 37
Cruttwell, C.R.M.F. 156, 223
Curry, Patrick 5, 16–17, 223

D'Ardenne, Simone 31
Deleuze, Gilles 216, 223
Denethor 33, 60, 85, 134, 172, 203, 209
Dickerson, Matthew 202–205, 208, 220, 223
dragon 33, 40, 45, 52, 70, 74, 94, 104, 114–115, 125–127, 129–130, 132–133, 135, 137, 139–141, 144–146, 189, 191, 219, 226

Drout, Michael 6, 24, 60–61, 210, 223–224
Dvořák, Max 54, 225
dwarves 52, 59, 81, 130, 133, 136, 145, 154, 158, 162, 170, 174, 178, 180, 200, 207, 210, 215, 218

Eärendil 83, 163
Eddas 12, 25, 106, 185
education 14, 148, 158, 172, 190, 213
Einstein, Albert 9, 215
Eliot, T.S. 19, 22, 41, 62, 67–71, 84–90, 92–96, 187, 213, 220, 222–224
Ellis, Hilda 141, 223
Elrond 52, 60, 63–64, 119–121, 163, 170, 172, 187
Elves 25, 40, 44, 53, 59, 62, 64, 79, 81–82, 90, 108, 126, 128, 130, 132, 134–137, 140–142, 153–155, 158, 162, 170, 173, 174, 178–180, 190, 201, 205, 207–208, 210, 214–215, 217–219
"English and Welsh" 29, 221
Enuma Elish 159
environment (natural) 14–15, 17, 18, 20, 49, 53, 60, 84
Éowyn 60, 110, 122–123, 150, 196–197, 211
epic 3, 13, 22, 71, 86, 99, 101, 113–114, 124–127, 132–133, 143, 148–149, 173, 175, 190, 217, 220, 223
Eschaton 178–179
eucatastrophe 29, 35, 52, 56, 93, 108, 112, 134, 208, 219
Everdell, William 7–8, 223
evil 2, 13, 20, 22, 25, 33, 36, 39, 43, 45–46, 51–54, 58, 74–75, 79–81, 83, 85, 86, 89–92, 95, 106, 108, 120, 125, 127–131, 136, 139, 141–143, 148–151, 153–155, 166, 170, 175–176, 178–180, 182, 184, 186–187, 192, 196, 198–200, 203–204, 206, 208, 214, 216–218, 220
Excalibur 68–69, 71–81, 109, 216–217, 222

Faërie 5, 22, 29, 45, 63, 108, 128, 131–135, 191, 217, 219, 223, 225
The Faerie Queene 45
Fafnir 115, 137, 140, 144
fantastic 13, 102, 107–109, 125, 128, 138, 148, 159, 167, 184, 224–225

228

Index

fantasy literature 1, 3, 5, 9–10, 13, 15–16, 19–20, 29, 59, 61–62, 105, 124–128, 132–134, 147, 186, 188, 190, 192, 200–201, 204, 213–214, 220–221, 224–225
Faramir 47, 82, 105, 113, 122, 132, 150, 204, 211
Farmer Giles of Ham 62, 132, 138, 145, 226
fascism 5, 14, 193
Fëanor 136, 162, 218
The Fellowship of the Ring 41, 64–65, 92, 120, 215, 223, 226
Field, Syd 57, 223
Fimi, Dmitra 217, 223
Finn, Richard 217, 223
Fisher, Jason 5, 223
Fleming, Ian 18–19
Flieger, Verlyn 4–6, 56, 90, 132, 134, 209, 213–214, 217–220, 223
Focillon, Henri 54, 223
Forster, E.M. 19
fractals 43, 48, 51, 57–58
Freud, Sigmund 9, 67–68, 214, 216
Frodo Baggins 21, 33–40, 42, 44, 47–49, 51–52, 56, 59–60, 63–64, 67, 79–80, 82–83, 85–86, 90, 111–113, 120–123, 129–131, 136, 142–143, 154, 169, 173, 177–178, 187, 193, 199, 201–204, 206–209, 211, 214, 217–219, 223, 225
Frye, Northrop 183, 185, 219–220, 223, 225

Galadriel 39, 65, 82, 138, 170, 172, 178, 196–197, 208, 211
Galahad 44, 56, 76, 78, 110–112, 115–117
Gandalf 33, 42, 56, 64, 66, 79, 82–83, 90, 105, 112, 122, 130–132, 134, 137–138, 140, 168, 170–174, 177, 187, 202–204, 206–208, 214–215, 217–218, 223
Gardner, John W. 167–168, 172, 223
Garth, John 5, 224
Gawain 12, 24–26, 28–29, 31, 33–38, 45–46, 73, 106, 109, 111–113, 117, 177–178, 185–186, 188–191, 214, 221
Geoffrey of Monmouth 106
Gilgamesh 70, 125
Gisla Saga Surssonar 114
Glámr 140
Goldberry 42, 49, 190, 196, 200, 207

Golding, William 13, 17, 20
Gollum 34, 36, 40, 45, 49, 66, 81–83, 112, 120, 122, 130, 143, 187, 201, 204, 206–207, 209, 214–215
Gondor 42, 48, 56, 63–64, 89, 172–173, 203–204, 219
good 2, 9, 12, 22, 33, 40, 43–45, 53–54, 56, 67, 74–75, 78–83, 86, 90–93, 95, 100, 108–109, 112, 113, 120, 125–130, 136, 138, 142, 153, 156, 166, 170, 174–180, 184, 187–188, 192, 196–199, 202–203, 206, 208–211, 214–216, 218
Gordan, E.V. 31
Gothic 41, 43, 54–57, 185, 215, 220, 223, 225
Green, Martin 18, 224
Greene, Graham 18–19, 87, 90, 96
Greenleaf, Robert 168–169, 174, 224
Greenworld 84, 182, 219
Grettir 140
Grimm Brothers 13, 25–26, 94, 141, 185, 222, 224
Grosseteste, Robert 216
Grundtvig, Nikolai 13, 25–26, 185
Gwenevere 73–74, 77–78

Halliday, M.A.K. 60
Harry Potter 16, 21
The Heart of Darkness 8, 15, 68, 70, 144
Hesiod 158
Hildegard of Bingen 216
Hiley, Margaret 213, 224
The Hobbit 14, 40, 41–43, 49–50, 66, 85, 89, 105, 124, 133, 136, 138, 141, 144–145, 148, 161, 189, 214–215, 219, 221–222, 225
hobbits 18, 34, 36–37, 39, 45, 50–53, 58–59, 64, 81, 86, 107, 111, 120–121, 123, 125–133, 137, 143, 150, 153–154, 158, 170–174, 176, 178, 187, 190, 203–204, 208–209, 214–216, 218
The Homecoming of Beorhtnoth, Beorhthelm's Son 31, 97, 104
Horace 57, 176
Hugh of St. Victor 216

The Iliad 44
Ilúvatar 62, 91, 139, 142, 161–162, 179, 180, 208

Index

Indiana Jones 23
Inklings 2, 21, 84, 185, 213, 221–222
intertextuality 85
Isildur 81–82, 118–119, 121, 179, 201

Jackson, Peter 1, 25, 33, 41–44, 57–58, 90, 95, 147, 214–215
Joyce, James 16, 84

Kalevala 13, 25, 94, 185, 188–191, 221
Kalevipoeg 13
Kellogg, Robert 83, 225
Kilby, Clyde 219, 224
Kirk, Elizabeth 60–61, 224
Kirk, Russell 87, 224
Kocher, Paul 105, 176, 203, 205–207, 214, 219, 224
Kreeft, Peter 213, 224

Lancelot 38, 44, 46, 69, 73–75, 78, 117
"Leaf by Niggle" 33, 39, 135, 189, 201, 205, 226
Lewis, C.S. 13, 20, 29, 85, 192, 194, 197, 209, 213, 220–222, 224
liminality 17, 41, 56, 144, 150, 191, 218, 225
linearity 41–44, 46, 48–50, 53, 56–57
lof and dom 130
Lönnrot, Elias 13, 190
The Lord of the Rings 6, 13–14, 16–17, 25, 30, 33, 35, 41, 43–44, 49, 60, 62, 63, 65–66, 76, 78, 81, 85–86, 88–90, 95, 101, 111, 114, 116, 119, 124, 126–127, 132–133, 136, 138, 141–143, 147–150, 164, 167–169, 176, 178, 181, 184, 187–189, 193, 199, 201, 204–205, 208, 213–215, 217–220, 222–226
Lothlórien 50, 52, 82, 134, 187, 201, 208
Lúthien 136, 161, 163, 196

Mabinogi 46, 159, 185, 188–191, 217, 221
MacDonald, George 135, 185, 192
Maiar 142, 161
Malory, Thomas 71, 76–78, 106–107, 110, 114, 116
manicheism 216
Marianism 36, 194
Marie de France 135, 217
Marlowe, Christopher 216

McFadden, Brian 213, 224
Melkor 91, 136, 161–162, 179–180
Merlin 69, 71–74, 76–77, 217
Merriman, John 10, 224
Merton, Thomas 70, 197
Minas Tirith 63, 80, 90, 110, 207, 216
Les Miserables 50
Moby-Dick 50
modernism 7–8, 17, 58, 85, 93–94, 134, 213–214, 224
monomyth 48
Mordor 42–43, 48, 56, 80–83, 89, 96, 101, 112, 121, 173, 177, 187, 204
Mordred 74–75, 77–78, 107, 109, 216–217
Morgoth 81, 91, 138–139, 142, 145, 161–163, 170, 180, 209
Moria 52, 60, 81, 134, 190, 222
Morris, William 10, 185, 192
Le Morte Darthur 48, 76, 116–118
Muir, John 17
Mythopoiesis 181, 190, 220–221, 224

Nagy, Gergely 213, 220, 224
narrative 7–8, 10, 19, 24, 26, 29, 39, 41–52, 59, 66–68, 78, 83–85, 92, 94–95, 97, 103, 105, 114, 117–119, 127, 134, 142, 153, 155, 161, 168, 184, 191, 202, 214–215, 217, 220, 222, 224–225
Narsil 72, 114, 118–120, 217
Nibelungenlied 221
Norse (language and literature) 12, 26, 94, 106, 118, 138–141, 143, 146, 155, 159–160, 185, 190–191, 207, 216, 219, 222, 223
Númenor 72, 91, 109, 149, 154, 163, 171, 173–174, 179, 218

Oðin 115–116, 139–140, 144, 158, 191, 216
The Odyssey 14, 44, 97
Old Man Willow 42, 45, 51, 92, 132, 190
Olympic Games 10
"On Fairy-Stories" 29, 47, 128, 133, 134, 221, 226
orcs 18, 52, 53, 59, 65, 66, 82, 122, 127, 132, 136, 137, 140, 141, 148, 150, 153, 154, 162, 202, 206, 207, 218
Orwell, George 13, 18–20, 96

Index

Othering 147–155
Otherworld 46, 70, 135, 159, 191, 216

Parsifal 78
Parzival 114, 117–118
Pearce, Joseph 5, 210
Percival 69, 74–77
philology 4, 23–26, 30–31, 59, 93–94, 124, 184, 191
Piers Plowman 68
Plato, 98, 216, 218
postmodernism 4, 8, 9, 200, 213, 223, 225
Prufrock, J. Alfred 88

Quest of the Holy Grail 44, 46, 68, 69, 71, 76, 78, 110, 116

Rabkin, Eric 127, 225
race 64–65, 81, 131, 134, 139, 141, 144, 150, 153–155, 158, 162, 213, 217, 218, 219, 223
Ragnarök 104, 158, 219, 221
Rateliff, John 214–215, 224, 225
realism 7, 9, 10, 13, 19, 62, 68, 97–98, 128, 186, 191, 214
Reid, Robin 60, 214, 218, 224, 225
Renaissance 7, 10, 45, 86, 126, 190, 219
The Return of the King 34, 42–43, 46, 63, 76, 85, 89, 90, 96, 101, 120, 122, 154, 171, 173, 204, 208, 215, 216, 219, 226
Ricoeur, Paul 183–184, 219, 220, 225
Ring, the One 18, 34, 36–45, 56, 58, 63, 67, 80–83, 86, 107, 110–113, 120–123, 129–131, 136, 142–143, 154, 169, 172, 174, 177–179, 184, 187, 190, 202–208, 214, 215, 217, 218
Ringwraiths 38, 47, 53, 121, 142, 178, 187, 218
Rivendell 57, 50, 52, 120–121, 163, 177, 187, 217
Rococo 48
Rohirrim 42, 60, 122, 203
romance 13, 24, 29, 36, 47–48, 53, 58, 111, 113, 117, 124, 133, 135, 163, 182, 185, 222
Romanesque 54, 215
Roosevelt, Theodore 17

Rosebury, Brian 4, 61–62, 147, 210, 225
Russell, Bertrand 214

Said, Edward 148, 151–153, 225
Sam Gamgee 38–39, 42, 47–49, 53, 56, 60, 63–64, 79, 82–83, 86, 89, 111, 120, 122, 131, 143, 150, 154, 173, 176, 187, 193, 196, 201–204, 207, 208, 211, 217
Sapir, Edward 4
Saruman 18, 33, 42, 43, 45, 54, 66, 81, 109, 122–123, 137, 140, 170–171, 174, 187, 203, 204, 209, 211
Sauron 17, 34, 38, 40, 43, 45, 53, 80–83, 89, 91, 107, 109, 112–113, 118–121, 130, 136–138, 141–144, 149, 154, 162–163, 169–175, 178, 187, 199, 201–204, 206–207, 209, 211, 219
Saving Private Ryan 68, 71, 76
Saxo Grammaticus 185
Scholes, Robert 83, 225
"A Secret Vice" 30, 221
Senior, William 218, 225
Shakespeare, William 26, 27, 31, 50, 131
Shelob 57, 82, 122, 196, 207
Shepherd, Geoffrey 99–102, 217, 225
Shippey, Tom 1, 4–6, 13–16, 20, 24–28, 32–33, 36, 47, 49, 59, 85–86, 91–95, 104–105, 128, 148–149, 160–161, 164, 184–187, 201, 204, 214, 218, 220, 222, 223, 224, 225
Shire 18, 34, 38–39, 43, 45, 51–52, 57–58, 79, 80, 86, 112, 123, 138, 150, 173–174, 177, 187, 204
Siddhartha, Gotama 87
Sigmundr 115–116, 140
Sigurðr 115, 144
The Silmarillion 14, 25, 33, 40, 43, 62, 78, 84, 87, 89–92, 116, 118–119, 124, 126, 132–133, 136, 138, 142–145, 148, 153, 155–165, 170, 178–180, 184, 189, 205, 208, 215, 217, 218, 219, 220, 221, 224, 225, 226
Silver, Carol 217, 225
Sir Gawain and the Green Knight 12, 24–26, 28–29, 31, 33–38, 45–46, 73, 106, 109, 111–113, 117–118, 185–186, 188–191, 214, 221
Sir Orfeo 132–133, 135, 185
Smaug 83, 137, 144–145

Index

Smith of Wooten Major 63, 132, 134
Snorri Sturluson 26, 94, 158, 185, 191, 221
Spenser, Edmund 45–46, 70, 133
stream of consciousness 214
style 4, 9–10, 13, 18, 46, 59–66, 91, 93, 95, 98–100, 150, 214, 223, 225, 226
subcreation 127–128, 179, 182, 209
surrealism 9
Swoboda, Karl Maria 54, 225

Ted Sandyman 138, 176
Théoden 60, 110, 122, 134, 172, 203
theology 12, 15, 141, 164, 197, 216, 220, 221, 226
Thompson, Kristin 57, 225
Thoreau, Henry David 17
Timmons, Daniel 5, 222
Todorov, Tzvetan 125, 225
Tolkien, Christopher 28, 32, 42, 197, 216, 220, 221, 226
trawþe 45, 11, 113
Treebeard 17, 47, 56, 65, 92, 132, 137
Túrin 119, 136, 221, 225
The Two Towers 18, 42, 46, 65–66, 96, 122, 154, 215, 226
tyranny 4–5, 72, 131, 170, 172, 179, 203

ubi sunt 205
Uther Pendragon 72, 117

Vaccaro, Christopher 218, 226
Valar 81, 91, 161–163, 172–174, 179, 209, 218
Valinor 80, 162, 163, 217

Victorian (influence) 8, 18, 126, 132, 135, 213, 217, 224, 225
Volsungasaga 114–117, 137, 139–140, 144, 185–188, 191, 221
Vonnegut, Kurt 13

Wagner, Richard 25, 27, 78
Walcott, Derek 217, 226
Walker, Steve 61, 226
waste land 8, 15, 17, 67, 89, 92, 94–96, 113, 128, 155, 187
The Waste Land 22, 68–71, 84–90, 96, 224
Waterstone's (bookstore poll) 16
Waugh, Evelyn 18–19
West, Richard 214, 226
White, Michael 5
White, T.H. 13, 20, 106
Whorf, Benjamin 4
Williams, Charles 21, 192, 209, 213, 220, 222
Wilson, Woodrow 17, 156
Woolf, Virginia 16, 19, 84
World War I 5, 8, 11, 20, 30, 39, 71, 83, 84–93, 95, 105–107, 110, 113, 123, 147–148, 155–156, 159, 164, 175, 176, 184, 186, 189, 196–197, 203, 216, 217, 218
World War II 8, 12, 18, 20, 39, 91–93, 104–105, 107, 110, 113, 123, 147–148, 175, 184, 193, 197, 203, 217
Wormtongue 54, 66, 122–123, 137, 174, 203
Wulfstan 100, 103
Wynne, Hilary 6, 24, 60, 210, 223
Wyrd 125, 129, 131, 177

www.ingramcontent.com/pod-product-compliance
Ingram Content Group UK Ltd.
Pitfield, Milton Keynes, MK11 3LW, UK
UKHW041944140426
5217IPUK00014B/646